KT-454-631

Green Political Thought
Third Edition

Andrew Dobson

London and New York

First edition first published 1990
by HarperCollins Academic
Reprinted 1991
Reprinted 1992, 1994
by Routledge

Second edition published 1995
by Routledge
Third edition published 2000
Reprinted 2001
11 New Fetter Lane, London EC4P 4EE
Simultaneously published in the USA and Canada
by Routledge
29 West 35th Street, New York, NY 10001

Routledge is an imprint of the Taylor & Francis Group

This edition typeset in Goudy by Taylor & Francis Books Ltd
Printed and bound in Great Britain by TJ International Ltd,
Padstow, Cornwall

British Library Cataloguing in Publication Data
A catalogue record for this book is available from the British Library

Library of Congress Cataloging in Publication Data
Dobson, Andrew
Green Political Thought / Andrew Dobson – 3rd ed.
Includes bibliographical references and index.
1. Green movement I. Title.
JA75.8.D63 2000
320.5–dc21   99–053151

ISBN 0–415–22203–6 (hbk)
ISBN 0–415–22204–4 (pbk)

For Concha Pérez Moreno

Contents

Preface to the third edition ix
Preface to the second edition xi
Acknowledgements xiii

Introduction 1

1 Thinking about ecologism 13
Sustainable societies *16*
Reasons to care for the environment *18*
Crisis and its political-strategic consequences *20*
Universality and social change *21*
Lessons from nature *21*
Left and right: communism and capitalism *26*
Historical specificity *31*
Conclusion *34*

2 Philosophical foundations 36
Ethics: a code of conduct *40*
Ethics: a state of being *46*
Anthropocentrism *51*

3 The sustainable society 62
Limits to growth *62*

Possible positions 70
More problems with growth 74
Questioning consumption 77
Energy 87
Trade and travel 89
Work 91
Bioregionalism 99
Agriculture 101
Diversity 102
Decentralization and its limits 103

4 Strategies for green change   112
Democracy and authoritarianism 114
Action through and around the legislature 124
Lifestyle 130
Communities 136
Direct action 142
Class 145
Conclusion 162

5 Ecologism and other ideologies   163
Liberalism 164
Conservatism 172
Socialism 179
Feminism 189
Conclusion 200

Conclusion   201

Bibliography   215
Index   226

Preface to the third edition

In the preface to the second edition of this book I noted the explosion of material on its central theme – ecologism – that surrounded publication of the first. This rush has shown no signs of abating – indeed, it has become even faster and more furious. The standard of this material is very high, and to the chapter-length analyses of ecologism referred to in the preface to the second edition, we must now add some outstanding longer reflections: for example, Goodin, 1992; Hayward, 1995, 1998; Dryzek, 1997; Smith, 1998; and J. Barry, 1999. These books form part of what we might call the 'second wave' of theorizing about environmental politics. The first wave was devoted to explaining and analysing the political-ideological aspects of environmental politics, and the first edition of this book was very much a part of that wave. Second-wave work, on the other hand, has focused more on political theory than on political ideology, and has taken the form of a critical exploration of the relationship between environmental politics and enduring themes and concepts in political theory such as democracy, justice and citizenship. Something of the influence of this second wave can be found in the third edition of *Green Political Thought* where I have added a section to Chapter 4 entitled 'Democracy and authoritarianism' and made references in Chapter 5 to the prickly relationship between social justice and environmental objectives. Chapter 5, indeed, has been changed rather radically. I have responded to the interest students have shown in the relationship between ecologism and other ideologies, and to some outstanding comparative studies by scholars working in that area, by expanding the coverage to include not only socialism and feminism, but liberalism and conservatism too. I have taken the opportunity this presented to cement the central theme of the book: that ecologism is a political ideology in its own right, distinct and different from the others with which it competes at the dawn of the twenty-first century. The sympathetic and not-so-sympathetic reactions to the development of ecologism which I identified and discussed in the Conclusion to the second edition have continued unabated. There is now a strong belief that the objectives of ecologism can be achieved without it, as it were. I think this is wrong, and I have updated the Conclusion once again to try to explain why. I am happy to report that the community of scholars working on environmental politics is strong, vibrant and still growing, and it continues to be an intellectual and social pleasure to work with them. It is particularly gratifying to see scholars from outside the 'green field' beginning to grapple with the intellectual challenges that environmental political theory has uncovered. I am, as ever, grateful to all those who have participated in this coruscating conversation for their influence on what I have written here. I am also grateful to my editor at Routledge, Mark Kavanagh, for inviting me to throw my hat in the ring once again. Finally, thanks to the building contractors at Keele University who unwittingly provided the material for Miho Suganami's cover photograph.

Andrew Dobson
Keele University
August 1999

Preface to the second edition

It was only some time after the publication of the first edition of this book that I realized what I had been trying to do in it. The arrival of the owl of Minerva was prompted by many generous readings of *Green Political Thought* made by colleagues throughout the world, the collective weight of which made me see that securing a place for ecologism in the list of modern political ideologies was my prime intention first time round. Introductory textbooks on political ideologies have abounded for some time, but only recently has ecologism found its way into them. In 1989 I knew of no textbook of this sort that included a chapter on ecological political thought, but now there are several (for example: Ball and Dagger, 1991; Leach, 1991; Heywood, 1992; Macridis, 1992; Vincent, 1992; Dobson, 1993a; Kenny, 1994). The dawning realization of what I was up to has – I hope – sharpened the focus of the second edition, and I try (particularly in the Introduction) to embed my view of ecologism more firmly both in the theory of political ideology and in the context of popular overviews such as those mentioned above. This focus has also enabled me to hone further the distinction between environmentalism and ecologism: a distinction which is now part and parcel of environmental-political debate.

An overwhelming amount of literature on environmental politics has appeared in the past five years, and keeping track of it is a time-consuming task. I have been pleasantly surprised to find that this often very sophisticated work has resulted in modulation of my earlier views rather than outright reconstruction (although how could I bear to say anything else?). I have, though, brought my remarks and examples up to date, and responded to challenges where they have been made.

The basic shape of the book has therefore remained the same. Attentive readers will spot that the material in Chapter 1 has been thrashed around somewhat due to the critical attention given it by a number of commentators. I hope to have made some of the arguments in Chapter 2 clearer than they were in the first edition, and I have a more catholic (yet simultaneously more principled) view of the shape of the sustainable society (Chapter 3) than I had in 1989. I have updated Chapter 4 and added a short section on direct action; and the sections on socialism in Chapter 5 have (I hope) benefited from contact with what is one of the largest growth areas in the literature – that which deals with ecosocialism. Ecofeminism seems to me to have bifurcated more obviously in recent years than it had by 1989, and I try to reflect this in my reworking of ecofeminist themes in Chapter 5. Finally, there has been a recent and significant swing towards the view that while environmentalism and ecologism might be conceptually distinct, they converge at all the points that really matter if the objective is protecting the environment. This debate provides the focus for the book's conclusion.

It is trite (but true) to say that this second edition of *Green Political Thought* would not have been possible without all the people who read (or otherwise absorbed bits of) the first edition, and told me what was wrong with it. It is invidious to mention just a few of them, but I shall do so anyway: Wouter Achterberg, Adrian Atkinson, John Barry, Ted Benton, Janet Biehl, Murray Bookchin, Anna Bramwell, Alan Carter, Brian Doherty, John Dryzek, Robyn Eckersley, Judy Evans, Bob Goodin, Peter Hay, Tim Hayward, Mike Kenny, Keekok Lee, Paul Lucardie, Mary Mellor, David Pepper, Dick Richardson, Mike Saward, Jan van der Straaten, Andrew Vincent, Albert Weale, Caroline Wintersgill, Marcel Wissenburg and Stephen Young.

Casting my eye over this list I realize that only one of these people was known to me personally in 1989. Perhaps the best thing to have come out of *Green Political Thought* is my good fortune at having come into contact with some outstanding scholars, a number of whom have turned into friends. One on the list, Caroline Wintersgill, is not an academic, but my editor at Routledge. I owe Caroline a debt for having cajoled me into the formative experience of preparing this second edition, and for having been the most longsuffering sounding board regarding what I should do with it. I hope that the result is worthy both of her persistence and of the attempts of my colleagues to illuminate my own intellectual darkness.

Andrew Dobson
Keele University, 1995

Acknowledgements

This book began life as a Workers' Educational Association course on green politics in Oxford in 1987, and the learning process which I began there has continued in the presence of two successive groups of students studying post-industrial politics at Keele University. I owe a debt of gratitude to all those who attended these courses for their enthusiasm and for their commitment to the difficult business of coaxing some coherence out of my confusion.

I have benefited enormously from conversations with David Hay, Anna Bramwell, David Pepper, Jon Carpenter, Jean Lambert, Tim Andrewes and Andrew Simms, while Tim O'Riordan and Warwick Fox have given me valuable guidance in correspondence. Similarly, various anonymous publishers' referees pointed out weak spots as the project unfolded and I have done my best to act on their wise advice. In this context my editor, Gordon Smith, has been a very gratifying source of good sense and timely encouragement throughout. Thanks are also due to my brother, Mike Dobson, who not only supplied a stream of scientific articles on the state of the environment, but whose work for the Rio Mazan project in a cloud forest in Ecuador provided me with a salutary visit to the front line. At the same time I could not have done without the invaluable secretarial assistance which Pauline Weston and Ruth Battye have unhesitatingly lent me.

But my deepest debt of gratitude is owed to my colleague Margaret Canovan, for responding to frequent requests for help with a forbearance and a readiness far beyond that which I could reasonably have expected. She was quick to spot mistakes and generous with suggestions, and I have benefited greatly from her interventions. Needless to say, no one but myself can accept responsibility for any shortcomings which may remain.

Andrew Dobson
Keele University
October 1989

Introduction

Global warming. Deforestation. Acid rain. Species loss. Ozone depletion. Pesticide poisoning. Genetically modified food. These are the issues that invigorated political life in the late twentieth century and will continue to do so in the twenty-first. This is an extraordinary circumstance and it has happened extraordinarily quickly. Even thirty years ago, the development of a political movement around these issues would have been unimaginable. Knowledge of some of them – pesticide poisoning, for example – was restricted to a few scientists and even fewer social commentators, and there was no knowledge at all of others, such as global warming. Now it would be hard to find anyone in the 'developed' world who has never heard of these environmental problems, and probably even harder to find anyone in the 'developing' world who would not accept that environmental decay was either a cause or a symptom of their social, political and economic difficulties. Upon this realization, in both the North and the South, a vibrant environmental movement has been built – a movement which now has an influential presence both in civil society and in the more formal political world of parliamentary politics.

This movement has given rise to a veritable academic industry designed to analyse it, and this analysis takes many forms. There are books and articles devoted to green political parties, to environmental policy-making, to the sociology of the environmental movement, and to international environmental treaty-making. There are also books devoted to discussing and analysing the political and social ideas that lie behind the environmental movement, and this is one of those books. My principal objective is to describe and assess that set of ideas regarding the environment which can properly be regarded as an ideology – the ideology of ecologism. This is a book about 'ecologism', then, in the same sense as you might read a book about liberalism, socialism, conservatism or fascism.

Near the beginning of the first edition of this book, I rather casually suggested that 'just as there are many socialisms and many liberalisms, so there are many ecologisms' (Dobson, 1990, p. 11) – and then proceeded to ignore the promiscuous advice implicit in the remark by describing only one of them. I defended this strategy on the grounds that it was (and still is) important to distinguish *ecologism* from its more visible cousin *environmentalism*. This book is about the former, not the latter. The intention was to clarify the academic debate surrounding environmental politics and to put down a marker in it. I believed (and still do) that environmentalism and ecologism are so different as to make their confusion a serious intellectual mistake – partly in the context of thinking about ecologism as a political ideology and partly in the context of an accurate representation of the radical green challenge to the political, economic and social consensus that dominates contemporary life. In respect of what is to come, the following can be taken as a rough and ready distinction between environmentalism and ecologism:

> *environmentalism* argues for a managerial approach to environmental problems, secure in the belief that they can be solved without fundamental changes in present values or patterns of production and consumption,

and

> *ecologism* holds that a sustainable and fulfilling existence presupposes radical changes in our relationship with the non-human natural world, and in our mode of social and political life.

So the Queen of England does not suddenly become a political ecologist by having her fleet of limousines converted to lead-free petrol.

I want to argue that environmentalism and ecologism need to be kept apart because they differ not only in degree but also in kind. In other words, they need to be kept apart for the same reasons that liberalism and socialism, or conservatism and nationalism, need to be kept apart. This may seem controversial because the standard view is that environmentalism and ecologism belong to the same family, with the former simply being a less radical manifestation of concern for the environment than the latter. It is less radical, of course, and this is not without importance, but I wish to establish that the nature of the difference takes us beyond the question of radicalism into territory of a more fundamental kind – the kind of territory, indeed, that obliges us to distinguish liberalism and socialism as families and not simply, or only, as offspring of the same parents.

In the first place, environmentalism is not an ideology at all. Most commentators ascribe the same three basic features to ideologies in the sense in which I am talking about them: they must provide an analytical description of society – a 'map' composed of reference points enabling its users to find their way around the political world. Second, they must prescribe a particular form of society employing beliefs about the human condition that sustain and reproduce views about the nature of the prescribed society. Finally, they must provide a programme for political action, or show how to get from the society we presently inhabit to the one prescribed by the ideology in question.

As far as the first characteristic is concerned, and in the context of keeping ecologism and environmentalism apart, it is important to stress that whatever problem is being confronted by any given ideology, it will be analysed in terms of some fundamental and (as it were) necessary feature of the human condition, and not in terms of contingent features of particular social practices. In our context, ecologism will suggest that acid rain is not simply a result of not fixing enough carbon dioxide scrubbers to coal-fired power-station chimneys, but rather that it is symptomatic of a misreading of the possibilities (or more properly here, constraints) inherent in membership of an interrelated biotic and abiotic community. My point is that while ideologies will disagree over analysis and prescriptions, they will always couch them in terms of fundamental 'truths' about the human condition. On this score, ecologism counts as political ideology while environmentalism most certainly does not.

A similar remark can be made in respect of the second point raised above: that of political prescription. The prescriptions made by political ideologies will not only be issue-based, but will be founded on some notion of the human condition and its associated limitations and possibilities. Moreover, this will translate into some principled vision of the Good Life and will contrast strongly with prescriptions that amount to no more than a set of technical adjustments which derive their legitimacy from the exercise of instrumental rationality. In other words, the legitimacy of ideological prescriptions will be rooted in the kinds of observations to be found in works of political theory; they will not be thought through with the same rigour, but they will be there. Again, ecologism qualifies as a political ideology in these terms, but environmentalism does not.

The importance of these remarks about the source of legitimacy of ideologies' descriptions and prescriptions should not be underestimated, for they help both to distinguish between 'first-order' sets of description and prescription (like ecologism and liberalism) and 'second-order' sets (like environmentalism and democracy), as well as constituting the markers that separate ideologies from one another. In their *Politics and Ideology*, James Donald and Stuart Hall state that 'In this collection, the term ideology is used to indicate the frameworks of thought which are used in society to explain, figure out, make sense of or give meaning to the social and political world' (1986, p. xi). In my assessment, the markers that serve to separate these frameworks are those different views of the nature of the human condition in which the legitimacy of ideologies' descriptions and prescriptions are rooted.

In principle, the warning I gave at the beginning of this book's first edition is more than justified by our experience of describing political ideologies. After all, we spend much time putting adjectives in front of ideologies in order to demonstrate the distinctions that exist within them: *social* liberalism, *democratic* socialism, *communist* anarchism, and so on. Each of these offspring can be distinguished from other members of its family in such a marked way that we are entitled to refer to liberalisms, socialisms and anarchisms. Indeed, so strong is our sense of demarcation that we feel *obliged* to refer to them in the plural, and we will regard anyone who omits to do so as being insufficiently sophisticated.

This is all right and proper – as long as we remember that we are not dealing with some ideological soup, and that as well as being sensitive to differences *within* ideologies we must also retain a sense of the differences *between* them. However plural the meanings we can construct from the historical experience of any given ideology and however close some of these meanings in the margins of ideologies might appear to bring them, we still want to keep them apart, and we find ways of doing so. How?

We begin, in Roger Eatwell's words, by describing and assessing the 'intrinsic structure' of ideologies – their 'key tenets, myths, contradictions, tensions, even [their] morality and truth' (Eatwell and Wright, 1993, p. 1). This implies that each ideology has key tenets, myths and so on that distinguish it from other ideologies, and part of my task will be to outline what these are for ecologism – tenets that distinguish it from other ideologies and (I argue) from environmentalism, too. I am unashamedly involved, then, in producing an 'ideal type', and I say this early on so as to head off criticism that the ideology I describe is not that outlined in the latest manifesto of the Swedish Green Party (for example). Ecologism as presented here should 'not be confused with specific movements, parties or regimes which may bear [its] name' (Eatwell and Wright, 1993, p. 10). The corollary of this is that one would not necessarily expect any single real-life political ecologist to subscribe in equal measure to all of the tenets and beliefs discussed in this book. This is to avoid the otherwise mistaken impression that 'the great majority of those who would consider themselves political ecologists in real life will not see their beliefs reflected in this description [of ecologism]' (Riechmann, 1997, p. 10; my translation). For what it is worth, I would be happy to accept Riechmann's real-world twin condition of a belief in the 'limits to growth and a questioning of strong anthropocentrism' (ibid.; my translation) for qualification for political-ecological membership. This is more than sufficient to mark off political ecologists in the real world from socialists, liberals, conservatives and so on.

My position on definitional tenets seems to fly in the face of warnings in all contemporary political ideologies textbooks against the

> misguided belief that ideologies have a definitive essential core of principles and values ... Each ideology may possess a characteristic set of ideas and beliefs, but these ideas are constantly being revised and defined. In reality all political concepts are 'elastic'; they have no self-evident or unchallengeable meaning.
>
> (Heywood, 1992, p. 8)

Robert Eccleshall makes a similar point: 'political concepts do not travel through history with a fixed, inherent meaning. They are, rather, essentially contested concepts which embody various, often incompatible meanings' (Eccleshall *et al.*, 1994, p. 30). Fortunately for me there is no contradiction between believing that ideologies 'have a definitive essential core of principles and values' and recognizing that these principles and values are 'constantly being revised and defined'. I can believe that liberalism has liberty as a core value and that its meaning is contested; I can believe that equality is a core value of socialism and that its meaning is contested; and I can believe that ecocentrism is a core value of ecologism and that its meaning is contested.

Our distinguishing of ideologies one from another rests not only on identifying distinctive tenets, but also on saying something about the relationship between them. Most understandings of ideology refer to the way in which ideologies systematize their key beliefs. This is often loosely put: 'An ideology is a fairly coherent ... set of ideas' (Ball and Dagger, 1991, p. 8), 'Here, the concept of ideology will be taken to mean any more or less coherent system of beliefs or views on politics and society' (Leach, 1991, p. 10) and 'A political ideology is a relatively coherent set of empirical and normative beliefs and thought' (Eatwell and Wright, 1993, p. 9). These are cagey remarks, and it is striking how rarely the 'fairlys', and 'relativelys' and 'more or lesses' are spelled out, even in spaces given over to discussing the nature of ideology *per se*. Malcolm Hamilton, for instance, in his survey of eighty-five sources for defining the notion of ideology, comes up with twenty-seven possible definitional components, six of which he retains together with a combination of a further two. His own amalgam goes like this:

> An ideology is a system of collectively held normative and reputedly factual ideas and beliefs and attitudes advocating a particular pattern of social relationships and arrangements, and/or aimed at justifying a particular pattern of conduct, which its proponents seek to promote, realise, pursue or maintain.
>
> (Hamilton, 1987, p. 37)

Focusing on what he means by a 'system' of ideas, Hamilton writes: 'The ideas may be loosely structured, ambiguous and even contradictory as long as they are in some way, and to some minimal degree, interrelated' (Hamilton, 1987, p. 22). Up to a point this is acceptable, but the limits of looseness, ambiguity and contradiction are reached when they threaten the distinctiveness of ideology, built up by describing its central tenets and contrasting them with those of other ideologies. The relationship between an ideology's ideas should not be so loose that the comfortable and non-contradictory importation of ideas from other, distinct, ideologies is possible. Indeed, if the importation *is* comfortable and non-contradictory then we are not talking about a distinct ideology at all. The central tenets should hang together in such a way as to contribute to distinctiveness, and I hope to show that ecologism's tenets can be shown to do this.

All this points up the need to keep ideologies apart as well as respecting the differences to be found within them. I mentioned above that we typically signal differences within ideologies by placing adjectives in front of the ideology in question: *social* liberalism, *democratic* socialism, *communist* anarchism, and so on. Some adjectives work better than others (in the sense that the resulting hybrid is viable), while some seem not to work at all: we'd be hard pressed, for example, to imagine or describe a liberal fascist. The thing worthy of note here is that the hybrids we are happiest with are those that do not mix ideologies. Put differently, the adjective used to distinguish positions within ideologies is unlikely, itself, to derive from an ideology. Again, as Ball and Dagger observe, 'almost all political ideologies claim to be democratic, a claim they could hardly make if democracy were an ideology itself' (Ball and Dagger, 1991, p. 11). Even when the adjective does appear to derive from an ideology (as in communist anarchism, above), on closer inspection it usually turns out that the adjective refers to a common, rather than a political-ideological, usage of the word. In fact, *communal* anarchism is less likely to sow confusion than *communist* anarchism, and this is a result of the latter term sending off uncomfortable hybrid signals.

These remarks comprise more circumstantial evidence of the stubbornly resistant need to keep ideologies apart. More important in the present context, they allow us further purchase on the nature of, and relationship between, ecologism and environmentalism. For *environmentalism* is a word that could quite happily be pressed into adjectival service by virtually any ideology we care to name without producing any of the contradictions observable in hybrids such as liberal fascist. This fact alone should make us wary of thinking of environmentalism as a political ideology in its own right.

But my second and more controversial claim is that the ideology least susceptible to being hybridized by environmentalism is, curiously, ecologism itself. Environmentalism is so easily accommodated by other ideologies and ecologism is so different from those ideologies that we need to be very careful before allowing environmentalism to be a strand within ecologism. A belief in ecocentrism (for example) serves to distinguish ecologism from the other political ideologies, and as environmentalism does not subscribe to it either, it can only hybridize ecologism at the cost of radically altering it.

Perhaps I could make the same point anecdotally. A piece I once wrote on ecologism was quite rightly considered to be unbalanced in that I had not devoted enough space to talking about the ideology's history. As the piece was already the right length, the inclusion of more historical material meant cutting down on some other part of the chapter. Revealingly, it was suggested that I reduce the length of the section on ecocentrism. This struck me as odd, given the nature of the ideology, for it sounded like advising someone writing about socialism to say less about equality, or recommending that a commentator on liberalism write sparingly about liberty; or suggesting that a chapter on feminism have fewer pages on the public/private distinction.

The recommendation to say less about ecocentrism in an article on ecologism is a symptom of confusing ecologism and environmentalism, and is based on a misunderstanding of both of them. The 'frameworks' to which Donald and Hall refer are simply too different in respect of environmentalism and ecologism to allow us to mix them up without committing a serious intellectual mistake. The differences between the two are of kind rather than degree, and we obscure the nature of the political-environmental debate if we refuse to acknowledge this. Ideologies map the world in different ways and it is the responsibility of the student of ideologies to enunciate their different logics. In short, if we take Robyn Eckersley's description of environmental positions as a starting point: 'resource conservation, human welfare ecology; preservationism, animal liberation and ecocentrism' (Eckersley, 1992, p. 34), then this book is principally about the last of these, where ecocentrism eschews basing its political prescriptions on the exclusive moral considerability of humans (Eckersley, 1992, p. 50).

This connects back to an earlier suggestion: that to misunderstand the nature of green politics is to misconceive its historical significance as a challenge to the political, social and scientific consensus that has dominated the last two or three hundred years of public life. Green politics self-consciously confronts dominant paradigms, and my task here is to ensure that it is not swallowed up by them and the interests they often seem to serve. In this sense it is in a similar position to notions like 'post-industrialism'. Michael Marien is right to suggest that, contrary to general opinion, there is not one but 'two visions of post-industrial society' and, importantly, that one of these is dominant and the other is subordinate. If we allow the subordinate one to disappear we risk intellectual sloppiness and are likely to mistake consensus for disagreement, and the same goes for light-green and dark-green politics – or what I have called environmentalism and ecologism.

Marien writes that there are 'two completely different modes of usage: "Post-industrial society" as a technological, affluent, service society, and "post-industrial society" as a decentralized agrarian economy following in the wake of a failed industrialism' (Marien, 1977, p. 416), and suggests that the former is dominant with respect to the latter. Clearly the second usage constitutes a challenge to the first usage in that it calls itself by the same name while reconstituting its meaning. Using his typology, Marien sensitizes us to the variety of possible interpretations of post-industrial society. This variety would be invisible if we were to pay attention to the dominant interpretation: that of an affluent, service economy.

Analogously, I have suggested that dominant and subordinate understandings of green politics have emerged from discussion of the topic as well as its political practice. The point is to remain open to the existence of these understandings rather than to let the bright light of the dominant one obscure the subordinate one behind.

But, of course, it is not simply a question of analogy. It just happens that Marien's dominant version of post-industrialism – a technological, affluent, service society – is a fair description of the twenty-first century political aspiration to which most people would probably subscribe, if asked. We are certainly encouraged at every turn to aspire to it, at any rate. Now the content of post-industrialism in this dominant sense can work powerful magic on all with which it comes into contact – it moulds challenges to it in its own image and so draws their sting. This is, I think, precisely what has happened to environmental politics as it has emerged from the wings on to the main stage. There is now a perfectly respectable claim to be made that green politics can be a part of a technological, affluent, service society – a part, in other words, of Marien's dominant version of what post-industrial society both is and might be like. This is the green politics of carbon dioxide scrubbers on industrial chimneys, CFC-free aerosols and car exhausts fitted with catalytic converters.

In this guise, green politics presents no sort of a challenge at all to the twenty-first century consensus over the desirability of affluent, techno-logical, service societies. But my understanding of the historical significance of radical green politics is that it constitutes precisely such a challenge, and that we shall lose sight of that significance if we conceive of it only in its reformist mode: a mode that reinforces affluence and technology rather than calling them into question. Radical green politics is far more a friend of the subordinate interpretation of post-industrialism – a decentralized economy following in the wake of a failed industrialism – than of its dominant counterpart. Jonathon Porritt and Nicholas Winner assert that,

> the most radical [green aim] seeks nothing less than a nonviolent revolution to overthrow our whole polluting, plundering and materi-alistic industrial society and, in its place, to create a new economic and social order which will allow human beings to live in harmony with the planet. In those terms, the Green Movement lays claim to being the most radical and important political and cultural force since the birth of socialism.
>
> (Porritt and Winner, 1988, p. 9)

It is in these terms that I see green politics in this book; first, so as to keep a fuller picture of the movement in mind than is presently the case; second, to understand better the challenge that it presents to the dominant consensus; and third, to establish ecologism as a political ideology in its own right. This last is important because, as I argued in more detail above, I believe Barbara Goodwin (among others) to be wrong in calling ecologism a 'cross-cutting ideology' which 'falls into other existing ideological categories' (Goodwin, 1987, p. vii).

In a sense Porritt and Winner do the movement a disfavour by liken-ing the profundity of its challenge to that of early socialism. Much of socialism's intellectual work, at least, had already been done by the time it came on the scene. Liberal theorists had long since laid the ground for calls of liberty and equality, and socialism's job was to pick up and reconstitute the pieces created by liberalism's apparent failure to turn theory into practice. In this sense, the radical wing of the green movement is in a position more akin to that of the early liberals than that of the early socialists – it is self-consciously seeking to call into question an entire world-view rather than tinker with one that already exists. For the sake of convenience, but at the risk of blind blundering on territory where specialists themselves quite properly fear to tread, the world-view that modern political ecologists challenge is the one that grew out of the (early) Enlightenment. Norman Hampson has suggested a number of characteristics salient to the Enlightenment world-view: 'a period when the culture of the educated man was thought to take in the whole of educated knowledge' (Hampson, 1979, p. 11); 'that man was to a great extent the master of his own destiny' (ibid., p. 35); that 'God was a mathematician whose calculations, although infinite in their subtle complexity, were accessible to man's intelligence' (ibid., pp. 37–8); and that 'universal reason' was held to be preferable to 'local habit', principally because it helps to drive out superstition (ibid., p. 152).

All these characteristics are examined in detail by Adrian Atkinson (1991), and their general tenor is the exaltation of human beings and their particular faculties (e.g. reason) – the placing of the human being in a pre-eminent position with respect to the rest of not only terrestrial phenomena, but the universe at large. If Isaac Newton humbly saw himself as a boy playing on the sea shore, finding only the odd shiny pebble while the 'great ocean of truth' lay before him, this was surely more because he hadn't the time to set sail than because he thought he lacked the equipment to do so. This belief in the centrality of 'man' was encapsulated in the principle of *bienfaisance*, or benevolence, according to which the world was the best of all possible worlds for human beings. Hampson quotes Pluche as writing that 'It is for him [Man] that the sun rises; it is for him that the stars shine', and goes on to observe that 'Almost everything could be pressed into service, from the density of water, which Fenelon considered exactly calculated to facilitate navigation, to the shape of the water-melon, which makes it easy to slice' (Hampson, 1979, p. 81). In these respects the Enlightenment attitude was that the world had been made for human beings and that, in principle, nothing in it could be kept secret from them.

In a tortuous way this attitude has remained dominant ever since in the cultures and societies that have most obviously incubated the modern green movement. They inform, too, Marien's dominant interpretation of what post-industrial society both is and ought to be: Baconian science has helped produce its technology and its material affluence, and the Promethean project to which the Enlightenment gave birth in its modern form is substantially intact. Now the historical significance of radical green politics as I see it is that it constitutes a challenge to this project and to the norms and practices that sustain it. This ecocentric politics explicitly seeks to decentre the human being, to question mechanistic science and its technological consequences, to refuse to believe that the world was made for human beings – and it does this because it has been led to wonder whether dominant post-industrialism's project of material affluence is either desirable or sustainable. All this will be missed if we choose to restrict our understanding of green politics to its dominant guise: an environmentalism that seeks a cleaner service economy sustained by cleaner technology and producing cleaner affluence.

These thoughts on the Enlightenment help to identify ecologism's present historical significance, but there is danger here, too. The analytic temptation is to see the ideology as a recreation of the Romantic reaction that the Enlightenment and then early forms of industrialization themselves brought about. So we cast ecologism in terms of passion opposing reason, of the joys of a bucolic life and of mystery as against transparency. And of course it is true that many manifestations of the green movement argue for a repopulation of the countryside and for the reawakening of a sense of awe in the face of natural phenomena.

At the same time, however, modern green politics turns out to be based on a self-consciously hard-headed assessment of the unsustainability of present political and economic practices – it is remarkable, indeed, to see the extent to which the success of modern political ecology has been mediated and sustained by scientific research. This could hardly be said of the Romantic reaction to the Enlightenment. Similarly, ecologism's political Utopia is (by and large) informed by interpretations of the principle of equality – a principle that was minted and put into circulation during the Enlightenment, and certainly not popular with the Romantics. Again, as far as Romanticism is concerned, green politics has little time for individualism or for geniuses, and one suspects (although this will be disputed by members of the movement) that the nonconformity so beloved of Romantics would be a pretty scarce commodity in green communities. Finally, if we hold the green movement to believe that one can only recognize the value of the natural world through intuition (as we are likely to do if we see it merely as a resurgence of Romanticism), then we are blind to the enormous range and influence of rationalist attempts to account for such value, and which are of great importance to the movement's intellectual archaeology (Chapter 2).

So while (in terms of its present historical significance) radical green politics ought to be characterized as a challenge to the contemporary consensus over norms and practices that has its most immediate sources in the early Enlightenment, it would be a mistake to think it pays no mind whatever to those norms and practices. And this would be an especially big mistake if we were to jump to the conclusion that modern green politics is only a form of reincarnated Romanticism. To guard against this, we should say that its challenge most generally takes the form of an attempt to shift the terms of the burden of persuasion from those who would question the dominant post-industrial embodiment (an affluent, technological, service society) of politics and society, on to those who would defend it. In doing so greens may sometimes speak, even if often *sotto voce*, in the Enlightenment idiom. Indeed, in the context of an extended enquiry into the relationship between ecology and enlighten-ment, Tim Hayward writes that, 'the ecological challenge, precisely to the extent that it is a critical challenge, can be seen as a renewal of the enlightenment project itself' (Hayward, 1995, p. 39).

Finally, a remark needs to be made about the use of the word 'ideology' here. The study of ideology is immensely more complex than the standard 'functional' definition of the word would have us believe. At a more profound level than this, ideology 'asks about the bases and validity of our most fundamental ideas' (McLellan, 1986, p. 1) and as such involves us in critical thought about the most hidden presuppositions of present social and political life – even more hidden than those that political ecologists claim to have uncovered. Drawing on Marx, this conception of ideology urges us to take nothing for granted and suggests that words used in any given description of the world are opaque rather than translucent, and demand deciphering.

However, it seems that there is still something useful to be said about socialism, liberalism and conservatism from within the functional idiom, if only in the sense that we can indeed sensibly view political ideologies as providing 'the concepts, categories, images and ideas by means of which people make sense of their social and political world, form projects, come to a certain consciousness of their place in that world and act in it' (Donald and Hall, 1986, p. x). It is this functional understanding of ideology that informs the content of the present book. I aim to set out the ideas with which radical greens describe the political and social world, prescribe action within it, and seek to motivate us to such action. This is an uncontroversial perspective in the context of describing political ideologies, but the understanding of 'ideology' that it presupposes is far from uncontroversial in the wider context of the study of ideology itself. In this wider context, both ecologism and the present book about it would have to be subjected to interrogation.

1   Thinking about ecologism

The British environmentalist Jonathon Porritt once wrote that 'Having written the last two general election manifestos for the Ecology Party, I would be hard put even now to say what our ideology is' (Porritt, 1984a, p. 9). In this chapter I want to establish some of the ground rules for this ideology. In the Introduction I began to establish three points: first, that ecologism is not the same as environmentalism; second, that environmentalism is not a political ideology; and third, that while environmentalism is sufficiently non-specific for it to be hybridized with most ideologies, it is at its most uncomfortable with ecologism.

I should say at the outset that these points set my views at odds with most of those who have written recently on political ecology as ideology. The more common position is that both environmentalism and ecologism need to be considered when green ideology is at issue, with writers typically offering a 'spectrum' of green ideology with all the necessary attendant features such as 'wings' and 'centres'. Elsewhere I have referred to these two approaches to green ideology as 'maximalist' and 'minimalist' (Dobson, 1993a). Maximalist commentators define ecologism tightly: 'people and ideas will have to pass stringent tests before they can be properly called political-ecological', while minimalists 'cast their net wider so that the definition of ecologism is subject to fewer and/or less stringent conditions' (Dobson, 1993a, p. 220). It will be clear that I take a maximalist position, partly because of the ground rules that I consider any description of any ideology must follow, which are betrayed by including environmentalism as a wing within a description of green ideology: partly because the submerging of ecologism in environmentalism is in danger of skewing the intellectual and political landscape, and partly because of how little the minimalist position actually ends up saying.

At the risk of being boringly repetitive, I want to emphasize that the maximalist approach is at its most appropriate when the issue of green politics *as ideology* is at stake. If the rubric is green political thinking in general then minimalism is fine, and a number of commentators have made productive use of the long-frontiered spectrum that then becomes available (see, for example, Young, 1992). I myself felt somewhat liberated at being asked on one occasion to write on 'environmentalism' rather than 'ecologism' (Dobson, 1994a) – yet there are disadvantages, and vagueness is one of them.

Andrew Vincent has written the most articulate and robust accounts from the minimalist position that I have come across (Vincent, 1992 and 1993), but even he concludes with some rather limp-looking 'broad themes' in (what he calls) green ideology:

> most [political ecologists] assert the systematic interdependence of species and the environment ... [and] there is a tendency to be minimally sceptical about the supreme position of human beings on the planet. Furthermore there is a general anxiety about what industrial civilisation is actually doing to the planet.
>
> (Vincent, 1993, p. 270)

Vincent's fourth theme – that there is 'a much less damaging and more positive attitude to nature' than in other ideologies – is only uncontestably true of (what I call) ecologism rather than of environmentalism, so it should not really be in his 'broad theme' list at all. The second and third points are rather watered down by the words 'tendency', 'minimally' and 'general', and the first three points (with the possible exception of the second) are so general as to be acceptable to a large number of people in modern industrial societies today – certainly a larger number than would style themselves political ecologists.

But it is only right to outline two advantages of the minimalist position, both of which are passed up in the present approach. The first is that it reflects clearly the rather eclectic nature of the green movement itself. Many of the people and organizations whom we would want to include in the green movement are environmentalist rather than political-ecologist, and defining ecologism as strictly as I want to can obscure this very important truth about green politics. (On the other hand, of course, overstressing the environmentalist credentials of the movement can hide ecologism from view.)

The second advantage is that the minimalist approach allows us to see that the movement has a history – a fact which is less obvious from the maximalist point of view because it tends to date the existence of ecologism from the 1960s or even the 1970s. Minimalists will typically look to the nineteenth century for the beginnings of ecologism, and my opposition to this view is based on the observation that while some of the ideas we now associate with ecologism were flagged over a hundred years ago, this is a far cry from saying that ecologism itself existed over a hundred years ago. Jesus Christ's cleaving to a measure of social equality did not make him a socialist, and nor does it mean that socialism existed in the first century AD. These, then, are the general issues at stake in thinking about ecologism, and they will resurface as detail in what remains of this chapter.

The need for the rethink of values proposed in the radical green agenda is derived from the belief that there are natural limits to economic and population growth. It is important to stress the word 'natural' because green ideologues argue that economic growth is prevented not for social reasons – such as restrictive relations of production – but because the Earth itself has a limited carrying capacity (for population), productive capacity (for resources of all types) and absorbent capacity (pollution). 'The earth is finite,' write the authors of *Beyond the Limits*, sequel to the seminal *The Limits to Growth* report, and '[G]rowth of anything physical, including the human population and its cars and buildings and smoke-stacks, cannot continue forever' (Meadows *et al.*, 1992, p. 7). This ought to make it clear that from a green perspective continuous growth cannot be achieved by overcoming what might appear to be temporary limits – such as those imposed by a lack of technological sophistication; continuous and unlimited growth is *prima facie* impossible. This theme will be pursued in Chapter 3.

At this point ecologism throws into relief a factor – the Earth itself – that has been present in all modern political ideologies but has remained invisible, either because of its very ubiquity or because these ideologies' schema for description and prescription have kept it hidden. Ecologism makes the Earth as physical object the very foundation-stone of its intellectual edifice, arguing that its finitude is the basic reason why infinite population and economic growth are impossible and why, consequently, profound changes in our social and political behaviour need to take place. The enduring image of this finitude is a familiar picture taken by the cameras of Apollo 8 in 1968 showing a blue-white Earth suspended in space above the moon's horizon. Twenty years earlier the astronomer Fred Hoyle had written that 'Once a photograph of the Earth, taken from the outside, is available ... a new idea as powerful as any other in history will be let loose' (in Myers, 1985, p. 21). He may have been right. The green movement has adopted this image and the sense of beauty and fragility that it represents to generate concern for the Earth, arguing that everyday life in industrial society has separated us from it: 'Those who live amid concrete, plastic, and computers can easily forget how fundamentally our well-being is linked to the land' (Myers,

1985, p. 22). We are urged to recognize what is and has always been the case: that all wealth (of all types) ultimately derives from the planet.

Sustainable societies

The centrality of the limits to growth thesis and the conclusions drawn from it lead political ecologists to suggest that radical changes in our social habits and practices are required. The kind of society that would incorporate these changes is often referred to by greens as the 'sustainable society', and the fact that we are able to identify aspects of a green society distinguishable from the preferred pictures of other ideologies is one of the reasons why ecologism can be seen as a political ideology in its own right.

I shall sketch what I understand the sustainable society to look like in Chapter 3, but one or two points about it should be borne in mind from the outset. Political ecologists will stress two points with regard to the sustainable society: one, that consumption of material goods by individuals in 'advanced industrial countries' should be reduced; and two (linked to the first), that human needs are not best satisfied by continual economic growth as we understand it today. Jonathon Porritt writes: 'If you want one simple contrast between green and conventional politics, it is our belief that quantitative demand must be reduced, not expanded' (Porritt, 1984a, p. 136). Greens argue that if there are limits to growth then there are limits to consumption as well. The green movement is therefore faced with the difficulty of simultaneously calling into question a major aspiration of most people – maximizing consumption of material objects – and making its position attractive.

There are two aspects to its strategy. On the one hand it argues that continued consumption at increasing levels is impossible because of the finite productive limits imposed by the Earth. So it is argued that our aspiration to consume will be curtailed whether we like it or not: 'In common parlance that's known as having your cake and eating it, and it can't be done,' announces Porritt (Porritt, 1984a, p. 118). It is very important to see that greens argue that recycling or the use of renewable energy sources will not, alone, solve the problems posed by a finite Earth – we shall still not be able to produce or consume at an ever-increasing rate. Such techniques might be a part of the strategy for a sustainable society, but they do not materially affect the absolute limits to production and consumption in a finite system:

> The fiction of combining present levels of consumption with 'limitless recycling' is more characteristic of the technocratic vision than of an ecological one. Recycling itself uses resources, expands

energy, creates thermal pollution; on the bottom line, it's just an industrial activity like all the others. Recycling is both useful and necessary – but it is an illusion to imagine that it provides any basic answers.

(Porritt, 1984a, p. 183)

This observation is the analogue of the distinction made earlier between environmentalism and ecologism. To paraphrase Porritt, the recycling of waste is an essential part of being green but it is not the same thing as being radically green. Being radically green involves subscribing to different sets of values. As indicated by Porritt above, greens are generally suspicious of purely technological solutions to environmental problems – the 'technological fix' – and the relatively cautious endorsement of recycling is just one instance of this. As long ago as the highly influential *The Limits to Growth* thesis, it was suggested that 'We cannot expect technological solutions alone to get us out of this vicious circle' (Meadows *et al.*, 1974, p. 192) and this has since become a central dogma of green politics.

The second strategy employed by green ideologues to make palatable their recommendation for reduced consumption is to argue for the benefits of a less materialistic society. In the first place, they make an (unoriginal) distinction between needs and wants, suggesting that many of the items we consume and that we consider to be needs are in fact wants that have been 'converted' into needs at the behest of powerful persuasive forces. In this sense they will suggest that little would be lost by possessing fewer objects. The distinction between needs and wants is highly controversial and will be considered in more detail in Chapter 3.

Second, some deep-greens argue that the sustainable society that would replace the present consumer society would provide for wider and more profound forms of fulfilment than that provided by the consumption of material objects. This can profitably be seen as part of the green contention that the sustainable society would be a spiritually fulfilling place in which to live. Indeed, aspects of the radical green programme can hardly be understood without reference to the spiritual dimension on which (and in which) it likes to dwell. Greens invest the natural world with spiritual content and are ambivalent about what they see as mechanistic science's robbery of such content. They demand reverence for the Earth and a rediscovery of our links with it: 'It seems to me so obvious that without some huge groundswell of spiritual concern the transition to a more sustainable way of life remains utterly improbable' (Porritt, 1984a, p. 210). In this way the advertisement for frugal living and the exhortation to connect with the Earth combine to produce the spiritual asceticism that is a part of political ecology.

A controversial theme in green politics which is associated with the issue of reducing consumption is that of the need to bring down population levels. As Fritjof Capra explains: 'To slow down the rapid depletion of our natural resources, we need not only to abandon the idea of continuing economic growth, but to control the worldwide increase in population' (Capra, 1983, p. 227). Despite heavy criticism, particularly from the left – Mike Simons has described Paul Ehrlich's proposals as 'an invitation to genocide' (Simons, 1988, p. 13) – greens have stuck to their belief that long-term global sustainability will involve reductions in population, principally on the grounds that fewer people will consume fewer objects: 'the only long-term way to reduce consumption is to stabilize and then reduce the number of consumers. The best resources policies are doomed to failure if not linked to population policy' (Irvine and Ponton, 1988, p. 29). The issue of population will be critically assessed in Chapter 3.

Reasons to care for the environment

In an obvious way, care for the environment is one of ecologism's informing (although not exhaustive) principles. Many different reasons can be given for why we should be more careful with the environment, and I want to suggest that ecologism advances a specific mix of them. In this sense, the nature of the arguments advanced for care for the environment comes to be a part of ecologism's definition.

In our context such arguments can be summarized under two headings: those that suggest that human beings ought to care for the environment because it is in our interest to do so, and those that suggest that the environment has an intrinsic value in the sense that its value is not exhausted by its being a means to human ends – and even if it cannot be made a means to human ends it still has value.

Most of the time we encounter arguments of the first sort: for example, that tropical rainforests should be preserved because they provide oxygen, or raw materials for medicines, or because they prevent landslides. These, though, are not radical green reasons. The ecological perspective is neatly captured in *The Green Alternative* in response to the question, 'Isn't concern for nature and the environment actually concern for ourselves?':

> Many people see themselves as enlightened when they argue that the nonhuman world ought to be preserved: (i) as a stockpile of genetic diversity for agricultural, medical and other purposes; (ii) as material

for scientific study, for instance of our evolutionary origins; (iii) for recreation and (iv) for the opportunities it provides for aesthetic pleasure and spiritual inspiration. However, although enlightened, these reasons are all related to the instrumental value of the nonhuman world to humans. What is missing is any sense of a more impartial, biocentric – or biosphere-centred – view in which the nonhuman world is considered to be of intrinsic value.

(Bunyard and Morgan-Grenville, 1987, p. 284)

Lurking behind this statement are complex issues which will be discussed in detail in Chapter 2, but in this context of thinking about ecologism we need to make a distinction between the 'public' and the 'private' ecologist.

The private ecologist, in conversation with like-minded people, will most likely place the intrinsic value position ahead of the human-instrumental argument in terms of priority, suggesting that the latter is less worthy, less profoundly ecological, than the former. The public ecologist, however, keen to recruit, will almost certainly appeal first to the enlightened self-interest thesis and only move on to talk about intrinsic value once the first argument is firmly in place.

So the political ideology of ecologism clearly wants to subscribe to a particular set of reasons for care for the environment but is confronted by a culture that appears to engender a crisis of confidence, and that forces it to produce another set – which it would like to see as subordinate – in public. This, then, is another characteristic of ecologism: that its public face is in danger of hiding what it 'really' is; and yet what it 'really' is is its public face.

Something similar might be said of the spirituality that sometimes surfaces in the writings of ecologists. Its advocates argue that radical green politics is itself a spiritual experience in that it is founded on a recognition of the 'oneness' of creation and a subsequent 'reverence for one's own life, the life of others and the Earth itself' (Porritt, 1984a, p. 111). Moreover, it is suggested that political change will involve such a recognition and that only green politics has the possibility of re-creating the spiritual dimension of life that the grubby materialism of the industrial age has torn asunder. This kind of talk, though, is hardly a vote-winner, and so although 'spirituality' might be conspicuous in the ecologist's private conversation it does not get the public airing this would seem to warrant.

Crisis and its political-strategic consequences

No presentation of ecologism would be complete without the appropriate (usually heavy) dosage of warnings of doom and gloom. Political ecologists invariably claim that dire consequences will result if their warnings are not heeded and their prescriptions not followed. *Beyond the Limits* provides a typical example:

> Human use of many essential resources and generation of many kinds of pollutants have already surpassed rates that are physically sustainable. Without significant reductions in material and energy flows, there will be in the coming decades an uncontrolled decline in per capita food output, energy use, and industrial production.
>
> (Meadows *et al.*, 1992, pp. xv–xvi)

The radical green's consistent use of an apocalyptic tone is unique in the context of modern political ideologies, and it might be argued that the movement has relied too heavily on these sorts of projections as a means of galvanizing people to action. The consequences of this have been twofold. First, there is the unfounded accusation by the movement's critics that it is informed by an overwhelming sense of pessimism as to the prospects of the planet and the human race along with it. The accusation is unfounded because the movement's pessimism relates only to the likely life expectancy of current social and political practice. Greens are generally unerringly optimistic with respect to our chances of dealing with the crisis they believe they have uncovered – they merely argue that a major change of direction is required. As *Beyond the Limits* concludes:

> [T]his decline is not inevitable. To avoid it two changes are necessary. The first is a comprehensive revision of policies and practices that perpetuate growth in material consumption and in population. The second is a rapid, drastic increase in the efficiency with which materials and energy are used.
>
> (Meadows *et al.*, 1992, p. xvi)

The second and perhaps more serious consequence of the movement's reliance on gloomy prognostications is that its ideologues appear to have felt themselves absolved from serious thinking about realizing the change they propose. This, indeed, is another feature of the ideology that ought to be noted: the tension between the radical nature of the social and political change that it seeks, and the reliance on traditional liberal-democratic means of bringing it about. It is as though the movement's advocates have felt that the message was so obvious that it only needed to be given for it to be acted upon. The obstacles to radical green change have not been properly identified, and the result is an ideology that lacks an adequate programme for social and political transformation. Further comment on this will be made in Chapter 4.

Universality and social change

A related feature that ought to be mentioned, however, is the potentially universal appeal of the ideology. Up to now it has not been aimed at any particular section of society but is addressed to every single individual on the planet regardless of colour, gender, class, nationality, religious belief, and so on. This is a function of the green movement's argument that environmental degradation and the social dislocation that goes with it are everybody's problem and therefore ought to be everybody's concern: 'we are *all* harmed by the ecological crisis and therefore we *all* have a common interest in uniting together with people of *all* classes and *all* political allegiances to counter this mutually shared threat' (Tatchell in Dodds, 1988, p. 45; emphasis in the original). Ecologism thus has the potential to argue more easily than most modern political ideologies that it is, literally, in everyone's interest to follow its prescriptions.

This is not so obviously true of other modern political ideologies. None of them is able to argue that the penalty for not following its advice is the threat of major environmental and social dislocation for everyone. The potentially universal appeal generated by this observation has undoubtedly been seen by the green movement as a positive characteristic, to be exploited for all it is worth. I shall examine this position in Chapter 4 and ask whether or not this belief is misplaced, and whether it has in fact been counterproductive in the sense of providing another reason for not attending sufficiently rigorously to the issue of social change.

Lessons from nature

The importance of nature to ecologism, already identified, is not exhausted by reasons why we should care for it. Ecologism's thoroughgoing *naturalism* rests on the belief that human beings are natural creatures. On the one hand, this may involve the recognition (already canvassed) that there are natural limits to human aspirations; on the other – and even more controversially – there is often a strong sense in which the natural world is taken as a model for the human world, and many of ecologism's prescriptions for political and social arrangements are derived from a particular view of how nature 'is'. This view – not surprisingly – is an ecological view. 'Professional ecologists,' writes Jonathon Porritt, 'study plant and animal systems in relation to their environment, with particular emphasis on the inter-relations and interdependence between different life forms' (1984a, p. 3). This characterization conveys the benign sense of nature that has been adopted by political ecologists. This is a natural world in which interdependence is given priority over competition and in which equality comes before hierarchy. Nature for ecologism is not 'red in tooth and claw' but pacific, tranquil, lush – and green.

The principal features of the natural world and the political and social conclusions or prescriptions that have been drawn from them are:

diversity	toleration, stability and democracy
interdependence	equality
longevity	tradition
nature as 'female'	a particular conception of feminism

These points will be discussed in greater detail in subsequent chapters, but some introductory remarks are in order here. First, they stand in some tension to one another, and they are radically underspecified. Just what *kind* of equality and democracy can be 'derived' from nature? And is it not the case that democracy and tradition, or tradition and equality, are potentially incompatible? The problems associated with a list of this kind are such, indeed, that Michael Saward has been led to suggest that 'the vagueness and incompatibilities in the table render it next to meaningless' (Saward, 1993a, p. 69). Meaningless in political-theoretical terms, perhaps, but useful from an ideological point of view where persuasion is so important. Rooting one's political prescriptions in a reading of nature is risky because of the lack of determinacy involved, but the symbolic potency acquired by doing so may make the price of vagueness worth paying (or even render it irrelevant). Ideologies seek to persuade, and sometimes this is most effectively done by enlisting the big theme rather than the theoretical detail. This is not, I stress, to say that ecologism's naturalism is unproblematic (far from it), but merely to point out that the demands of ideology and the demands of theory are rather different.

It is, then, an ecological axiom that stability in an ecosystem is a function of diversity in that ecosystem. Thus, the more diverse the flora and fauna (within limits imposed by the ecosystem) the more stable the system will be. Further, stability is seen as a positive feature of an ecosystem because it proves the system to be sustainable; an ecosystem that is subject to fluctuation has not reached the 'climax' stage and is therefore characterized as immature. Socially, this translates into the liberal aspiration of the toleration of peculiarity and generosity with respect to diverse opinions, and these are most certainly characteristics of liberalism that have been adopted by greens (I will say more about the relationship between liberalism and ecologism in Chapter 5). There is a strong sense in ecologism that the 'healthy society' (organic metaphor intended) is one in which a range of opinions is not only tolerated but celebrated, in that this provides for a repository of ideas and forms of behaviour from which to draw when confronted with political or social problems:

> Diversity must also be the codeword for the way we manage ourselves. Not only shall we need to draw from a wide range of cultural and minority options to improve the quality of our lives, but also to draw upon a broad, participatory power base in our political systems to oppose and reverse present trends towards homogeneity, over-centralization, the abuse of power, and an uncaring society.
>
> (Myers, 1985, p. 254)

It will be suggested later (in Chapter 3) that this aspiration stands in tense relation to the potential rigidity of norms and standards in a small-scale sustainable society. To this extent, ecologism encounters a similar problem to that found in the liberal tradition from which it draws: how to have a conception of the Good Society that requires people behaving in a certain way, and yet argue for diverse forms of behaviour.

Nevertheless, it is a green maxim that dissenting voices be allowed to speak, and in this sense ecologism subscribes to the democratic principle of government by consent. Nor is a vague sort of consent considered to be good enough: most greens argue for a radically participatory form of society in which discussion takes place and explicit consent is asked for and given across the widest possible range of political and social issues. All this implies the kind of decentralist politics often associated with the sustainable society, which will be explored in greater detail in Chapter 3.

Some will no doubt object that this is too rosy a view of the green movement's political prescriptions, and that its history is full of suggestions described more accurately as authoritarian than democratic. Anna Bramwell's history of ecology in the twentieth century (1989) certainly provokes such an impression, and it is true that even in the modern movement there was a time when avoiding environmental catastrophe was seen as the chief end, and the means used to achieve it were largely irrelevant: 'It [social design leading to a sustainable society] is a process that can be carried out within present authority structures whether they be democratic or dictatorial. It is not necessary, although it might be preferable, that authority relationships be changed' (Pirages, 1977b, p. 10).

This kind of agnosticism with respect to social organization was (and is) meat and drink to critics of the green movement who accuse it of political irresponsibility and reaction. The problem stems from the fact that, despite green attempts to make democracy *necessarily* a member of a green list of values, the link appears actually to be a *contingent* one, and I shall discuss the relationship between ecologism, democracy and authoritarianism more fully in Chapter 4.

Ecologism's next political 'lesson from nature' is that the view of the natural world as an interlocking system of interdependent objects (both sentient and non-sentient) generates a sense of equality, in that each item is held to be necessary for the viability of every other item. In this view no part of the natural world is independent and therefore no part can lay claim to 'superiority'. Without the humble bacteria that clean our gut wall, for example, human beings would be permanently ill. Likewise, those particular bacteria need our gut in which to live.

The social ecologist Murray Bookchin presents the scientific picture of ecology in the following way:

> If we recognize that every ecosystem can also be viewed as a food web, we can think of it as a circular, interlacing nexus of plant-animal relationships (rather than as a stratified pyramid with man at the apex) that includes such widely varying creatures as microorganisms and large mammals. What ordinarily puzzles anyone who sees food-web diagrams for the first time is the impossibility of discerning a point of entry into the nexus. The web can be entered at any point and leads back to its point of departure without any apparent exit. Aside from the energy provided by sunlight (and dissipated by radiation), the system to all appearances is closed. Each species, be it a form of bacteria or deer, is knitted together in a network of interdependence, however indirect the links may be. A predator in the web is also prey, even if the 'lowliest' of the organisms merely makes it ill or helps to consume it after death.
>
> (Bookchin, 1982, p. 26)

Bookchin continues with a comment on the social implications of this:

> What renders social ecology so important is that it offers no case whatsoever for hierarchy in nature and society; it decisively challenges the very function of hierarchy as a stabilizing or ordering

principle in *both* realms. The association of order as such with hierarchy is ruptured.

(Bookchin, 1982, p. 36)

In this way, the science of ecology works in favour of egalitarianism
through its observations of the interdependence of species.

The kind of assertion made by Bookchin, however, is fraught with
difficulties and I am saying nothing new – although the point bears
repetition – if I suggest that extrapolations from 'nature' to 'society' are
dangerous to make. It may be the case that the science of ecology has
neutered hierarchy as an organizing principle in the 'natural' world (and
this is, in any case, disputable), but that is not to say that we can say the
same of the social world.

I shall return to this issue later, but it ought to be pointed out now how
the radical political ecologist would respond to this criticism. She or he
would agree that the details of the implications of interdependence need
to be worked out, but that the general point is to encourage different ways
of thinking about the 'natural' world. If we accept that a degree of inter-
species equality of value is generated by the fact of our interdependence,
then the onus will be upon those who want to destroy species to justify
their case, rather than upon those who want to preserve them.

The fact of the longevity of the natural world is not, obviously, an
observation specific to ecology, but nevertheless it has important
ramifications for political ecologists. In a sense it is argued for the natural
world that whatever is, is good, provided that it has not been meddled
with by human beings with ideas above their station. Nature speaks with
the wisdom borne of long experience and attendance to 'her' lessons
guarantees the best of all possible outcomes. The contrast between our
puny modern knowledge and the tools it produces and the rich vein of
wisdom generated by forebears with an ear to the ground is clear:

> In modern farming the farm worker is increasingly isolated from the
> soil he is tilling; he sits encased in his tractor cab, either with ear
> muffs to shut out the noise or with radio blaring, and what goes on
> behind the tractor has more to do with the wonders of technology
> than with the wisdom of countless generations of his predecessors.
>
> (Bunyard and Morgan-Grenville, 1987, p. 71)

As with farming, so with politics. Ecologists argue that we should live
with, rather than against, the natural world, and this has significant
repercussions in the context of the kind of community in which they
would have us live. At the same time, the natural world's longevity can

help generate a sense of awe and humility and thus contribute to the move away from anthropocentrism that the green movement considers necessary: 'The ecological approach ... [introduces] an important note of humility and compassion into our understanding of our place on earth' (Eckersley, 1987, p. 10).

Not only, however, is nature held to be our best teacher, but 'she' is also female. This has important consequences for the feminism to which ecologism subscribes, because there is a tendency to map nature's beneficial characteristics on to the 'female personality'. Thus, nature and women come to be tender, nurturing, caring, sensitive to place, and partly defined by the (high) office of giving birth to life. To the extent that much feminist momentum has been geared towards ridding the woman of stereotypical behaviour and character patterns, this ecological vision might seem retrograde. More pertinently, the features of this vision (if we assume women actually possess them to the general exclusion of other characteristics) are precisely those that have consigned women to an inferior status because they are held to be subordinate qualities. It will probably be of little comfort to some feminists that ecologism seeks to turn the tables in this context, arguing that the predominance of 'male' values is part of the reason for the crisis that they have identified, and that nature's 'female' lead is the one to follow. Brian Tokar puts it like this: 'The values of nurturance, cooperation and sharing which are traditionally identified more closely with women than with men need to become the deepest underlying principles of our society' (Tokar, 1994, p. 91). These are important matters for ecologism and for feminism, both because ecologism claims feminism as a guiding star (not least in terms of how to 'do' politics) and because some feminists have balked at the kind of feminism shunted into ecological service. Much more will be made of this debate in Chapter 5.

Left and right: communism and capitalism

In standard political terms and in order to help distinguish ecologism from other political ideologies, it is useful to examine the widespread green claim to 'go beyond' the left–right political spectrum: 'In calling for an ecological, nonviolent, nonexploitative society, the Greens (*die Grünen*) transcend the linear span of left-to-right' (Spretnak and Capra, 1985, p. 3). Jonathon Porritt translates this into a transcendence of capitalism and communism, and remarks that 'the debate between the protagonists of capitalism and communism is about as uplifting as the dialogue between Tweedledum and Tweedledee' (Porritt, 1984a, p. 44). The basis for this claim is that from an ecocentric green perspective the similarities between communism and capitalism can be made to seem greater than their differences:

> Both are dedicated to industrial growth, to the expansion of the means of production, to a materialist ethic as the best means of meeting people's needs, and to unimpeded technological develop-ment. Both rely on increasing centralisation and large-scale bureau-cratic control and co-ordination. From a viewpoint of narrow scientific rationalism, both insist that the planet is there to be con-quered, that big is self-evidently beautiful, and that what cannot be measured is of no importance.
>
> (Porritt, 1984a, p. 44)

The name generally given to this way of life is 'industrialism', which Porritt goes so far as to call a 'super-ideology' within which communism and capitalism are inscribed, and which he describes elsewhere as 'adherence to the belief that human needs can only be met through the *permanent* expansion of the process of production and consumption' (in Goldsmith and Hildyard, 1986, pp. 343–4). This observation is central to green ideology, pointing up both the focus of attack on contemporary politics and society – industrialism – and the claim that ecologism calls into question assumptions with which we have lived for at least two centuries. Ecologists argue that discussion about the respective merits of communism and capitalism is rather like rearranging the deckchairs on the *Titanic*: they point out that industrialism suffers from the contradic-tion of undermining the very context in which it is possible, by unsustainably consuming a finite stock of resources in a world that does not have a limitless capacity to absorb the waste produced by the industrial process.

Although the green movement appears to view 'left and right' and 'capitalism and communism' as synonymous pairs, I want to look at them separately, if only because the terms used to examine them will be different. It ought nevertheless to be said that the green claim in both cases has come in for criticism, especially regarding the second pair, and especially from the left.

In some respects we can talk of the green movement quite happily in terms of left and right because the terms we use to discuss the difference between the two can easily be applied to it. If, for example, we take equality and hierarchy as characteristics held to be praiseworthy within left-wing and right-wing thought respectively, then ecologism is clearly left-wing, arguing as it does for forms of equality among human beings and between human beings and other species. However, to argue that ecologism is unequivocally left-wing is not so easy. For instance, green politics is in principle averse to anything but the most timid engineering of the social and natural world by human beings. Since the French Revolution it has been a theme of left-wing thought that the existence of a concrete natural order of things with which human beings should conform and not tamper is a form of medieval mumbo-jumbo used by the right to secure and ossify privilege. The left has consistently argued that the world is there to be remade in the image of 'man' (usually) in accordance with plans drawn up by 'men' (usually), and in which the only reference to a natural order is to an abstract one outside of time and place.

The radical green aspiration to insert the human being in its 'proper place' in the natural order and to generate a sense of humility in the face of it is clearly 'right-wing' in this context:

> The belief that we are 'apart from' the rest of creation is an intrinsic feature of the dominant world-order, a man-centred or anthropocentric philosophy. Ecologists argue that this ultimately destructive belief must be rooted out and replaced with a life-centred or biocentric philosophy.
>
> (Porritt, 1984a, p. 206)

Ecologists can only perversely be accused of using this idea to preserve wealth and privilege, but the understanding of the place of the human being in a pre-ordained and immensely complex world with which we meddle at our peril is nevertheless a right-wing thought. Joe Weston, writing from a socialist perspective, puts it like this:

> Clearly the green analysis of environmental and social issues is within the broad framework of right-wing ideology and philosophy. The belief in 'natural' limits to human achievement, the denial of class divisions and the Romantic view of 'nature' all have their roots in the conservative and liberal political divisions.
>
> (Weston, 1986, p. 24)

John Gray has picked up some of this and turned it into a virtue, from a conservative point of view. He suggests that there are three 'deep affinities' between green and conservative thinking. The first is that 'both conservativism and Green theory see the life of humans in a multi-generational perspective'; second, '[B]oth conservative and Green thinkers repudiate the shibboleth of liberal individualism, the sovereign subject, the autonomous agent whose choices are the origin of all that has value'; and third, 'both Greens and conservatives consider risk-aversion the path of prudence when new technologies, or new social practices, have consequences that are large and unpredictable' (Gray, 1993b, pp. 136–7). Although Gray does not count a common opposition to 'hubristic humanism' in his list, he might have done (ibid., p. 139). The similarities Gray outlines are well chosen, but there is plenty in the detail that may yet provide for lengthy arguments between political ecologists and conservatives (just what is to replace the shibboleth of the liberal individual? What are the rules for distribution across generations to be?) – and of course there is no mention of ecocentrism (as a fundamental distinguishing characteristic) at all. I shall examine the relationship between ecologism and conservatism in greater detail in Chapter 5. Generally, for now, the difficulty of describing ecologism as either obviously left- or right-wing is a legacy of its ambiguous relationship with the Enlightenment tradition referred to in the Introduction, and is consistent with its self-image of calling into question stock responses to that tradition.

Second, the green claim to transcend capitalism and communism, in the sense that ecologism calls into question an overriding feature common to them both (industrialism), has drawn heavy criticism from the left. There are two reasons for this. In the first place it brings back grim memories of the 'end of ideology' thesis of the 1960s. This thesis has been interpreted by the left as itself ideological in the sense of observing a putative veneer of agreement about the basic goals of society, and so obscuring and delegitimatizing alternative strategies. The 'end of ideology' position was buttressed by the convergence thesis, which argued that communist and capitalist nations were beginning to converge on a similar course of social and political action. The left pointed out that such analyses served to cement existing power relationships – particularly in the capitalist nations – and therefore performed a conservative social function.

For socialists there is no more important political battle to be fought than that between capital and labour; and any politics that claims to transcend this battle is regarded with suspicion. The idea that the interests of capital and labour have somehow converged amounts to a betrayal, from the socialist point of view, of the project to liberate labour from capital. The interests of capital and labour are not the same, yet the green belief that both are inscribed in the super-ideology of industrialism makes it seem as though they are.

At root, proposes Joe Weston, the green movement's mistake is to refuse a class analysis of society – it 'argues that traditional class divisions are at an end' (Weston, 1986, p. 22), and uses the concept 'industrial society … to distinguish contemporary society from orthodox capitalism;

it is not a neutral term' (Weston, 1986, p. 22). It is not neutral in the sense that it removes capitalism from the glare of criticism and thus contributes to its survival and reproduction. Similarly the original 'end of ideology' thesis was accompanied by an analysis of how policies are formulated and social conflicts resolved, collected under the term 'pluralism'. Socialists have always considered this to be a dubious description, principally because the apparently democratic diversity and openness it implies serve to obscure capitalism's hierarchy of wealth and power, based on the domination of labour by capital.

From Weston's point of view it is no accident, therefore, that the green movement's 'industrialism' thesis, kept company by the abandonment of a class analysis of society, also results in a political practice based around the pressure groups of pluralism. In this sense, there is no difference between Daniel Bell and Jonathon Porritt. In the first place, Porritt's attack on industrialism prevents him from seeing that the real problem is capitalism; second, his failure to subscribe to a class analysis of society leads him to the dead-end of pressure-group politics; and third – and probably most serious from a socialist point of view – not only is he not attacking capitalism as he should, but he is contributing to its survival by deflecting criticism from it.

So the left's belief that it is not possible to transcend capitalism while capitalism still exists makes it suspicious of claims to the contrary. David Pepper, for instance, has suggested that we should not see 'environmentalist concerns or arguments' as 'above or unrelated to traditional political concerns, but stemming from, and used very much as agents to advance, the interests of one traditional political side or the other' (Pepper, 1984, p. 187). The general conclusion the left draws is that ecologism serves the interests of the *status quo* by diverting attention from the real battleground for social change: the relationship between capital and labour. We will be in a better position to assess the green claim to transcend this battleground in Chapter 3 when ecologism's analysis and solutions to the crisis it identifies are set out, and I shall make more of ecologism's relationship with socialism in Chapter 5. The main point for now, though, is that it is undoubtedly a central feature of ecologism that it identifies the 'super-ideology' of industrialism as the thesis to be undermined, and it has been relatively easy for green ideologues to point to high levels of environmental degradation in Eastern Europe to make their point that there is little to choose – from this perspective – between capitalism and communism. It makes no appreciable difference who owns the means of production, they say, if the production process itself is based on doing away with the presuppositions of its very existence.

Historical specificity

The issue of the history of ecologism has been the focus of considerable disagreement in recent commentaries. What is generally accepted is that there are three views in contention (Vincent, 1992; Dobson, 1993a). The first attempts to trace ecological sentiments back to the dawn of the human species, at least to the palaeolithic or neolithic period; the second 'dates the ecology movement from the 1960s and 1970s'; and the third 'identifies the roots of ecological ideas in the nineteenth century' (Vincent, 1993, pp. 210–11).

The first position is often associated with the view that many thousands of years ago there existed a golden age of peaceful coexistence with nature which ended – on Max Oelschlaeger's reading – with the onset of the neolithic era (Oelschlaeger, 1991, p. 28), and which we have (in the modern industrial world) failed to recapture to this day. Apart from the insecure nature of the evidence for such claims (disputed with some success in Lewis, 1992, pp. 43–81, for example), the links between what human beings thought tens of thousands of years ago and modern ecology seem too tenuous to tell us much about the nature of a contemporary ideology.

The third view – that ecologism has its roots in the nineteenth century – is probably the most widely accepted (see Vincent, 1992; Heywood, 1992; Macridis, 1992, for example), and is often based on a reading of Anna Bramwell's seminal *Ecology in the 20th Century* (1989). Among the similarities between nineteenth-century thinking (some of it, anyway) and contemporary ecologism, Vincent notes: 'a critical reaction to the European Enlightenment tradition … [E]cologism looks sceptically at the supreme value of reason', a denial of 'the central place of human beings and [the belief] that nature is without value and can simply be manipulated by humans', and finally the impact of Malthus and Darwin made for the integration of a 'strongly materialist and scientific perspective with an immanent and naturalistic understanding of religion and morality' (Vincent, 1992, pp. 211–12).

We might want to quibble over the detail of these claims, but it would be foolish to deny the broad parallels between the combination of scientific rationalism and Romantic arcadianism in both the nineteenth century and today's ecology movement. These (and other) parallels have been reaffirmed by Bramwell in the belief that the import of her earlier work has been largely accepted (Bramwell, 1994, pp. 25–33). Vincent believes that these parallels have been deliberately overlooked because of the reactionary political views associated with such positions in the late nineteenth and early twentieth centuries. Basing his argument largely on Bramwell's work, he suggests that the carriers of ecology in this period were primarily conservatives and nationalists (particularly of a 'folkish' persuasion) and, later, fascists and Nazis – it is by now *de rigueur* to point out that Himmler established an organic farm at Dachau concentration camp, and that both Himmler and Hitler were vegetarians (Bramwell, 1989, pp. 204 and 270, fn. 1). These, argues Vincent, are embarrassing skeletons for today's predominantly left-leaning political ecologists, and so they are confined to the cupboard by the simple expedient of dating ecologism from, say, 1966 or 1973 rather than 1866 or 1873 (the main contenders for when German biologist Ernst Haeckel first used the word 'ecology'; Bramwell, 1989, p. 253, fn. 2).

Quite how much there is in this political reason for making ecologism very contemporary rather than merely modern is hard to determine, but my own contribution to the debate (for what it is worth) is to distinguish the search for the roots of ecologism from a description of the ideology itself. It is undeniable that ideas similar to those entertained by modern greens can be found in late nineteenth- and early twentieth-century industrial and industrializing societies – and although Vincent does not mention the 'energy economists' of France, Britain, the USA, Russia and Germany in the first quarter of the twentieth century, he might have done (Bramwell, 1989, pp. 64–91). This is not, though, the same as saying that ecologism – as ideology – existed at that time, and two modern-day factors have served to bring ecologism fully into focus.

First, the scope of concerns in the modern age is new. Most of the resource, waste and pollution problems that were raised in earlier times had a fundamentally local character. Modern ecologism rests a large part of its case on the belief that environmental degradation has taken on a global dimension – most obviously in cases such as global warming and ozone depletion, but also in view of the potentially global climatic implications of deforestation. Humans have always interacted with their environment, of course, and not always wisely (Ponting, 1991). But greens believe that in the modern age the scale of human activity relative to the biosphere's capacity to absorb and sustain it has increased to the point where long-term human survival and the biosphere's integrity are put in doubt. This view – right or wrong – helps to distinguish ecologism from its more *ad hoc* environmentalist past and present.

Second, political ecologists believe that single-issue approaches to dealing with environmental problems do not address their seriousness at a sufficiently fundamental level. Greens campaign against acid rain, deforestation and ozone depletion, of course, but they do so by arguing that these problems stem from basic political, social and economic relations that encourage unsustainable practices. This systemic analysis leads to systemic prescriptions for change, and the interrelated and wide-ranging nature of the critique is a characteristic of modern ecologism missing from its nineteenth- and early twentieth-century progenitors.

It may be ill advised to try to be precise about dates in this context, but *The Limits to Growth* report of 1972 is hard to beat as a symbol for the birth of ecologism in its fully contemporary guise. As Eckersley has put it: 'the notion that there might be ecological limits to economic growth that could not be overcome by human technological ingenuity and better planning was not seriously entertained until after the much publicized "limits to growth" debate of the early 1970s' (Eckersley, 1992, p. 8). This is how the report expressed its principal conclusion.

> We are convinced that realization of the quantitative restraints of the world environment and of the tragic consequences of an overshoot is essential to the initiation of new forms of thinking that will lead to a fundamental revision of human behaviour and, by implication, of the entire fabric of present day society.
>
> (Meadows *et al.*, 1974, p. 190)

The sense of the radical change proposed by deep-greens is captured in the final phrases of this quotation, and clearly goes beyond the managerial environmentalism that I am keen to separate from ecologism proper.

Recognizing the historical situatedness of the ideology helps us to understand what it is. We are provided with a boundary beyond which (in the past) ecologism could not have existed, and therefore any movement or idea behind that boundary can bear only an informing relation to ecologism as I think we ought to understand it. Rachel Carson's book *Silent Spring* (first published in 1962), then, can only inform ecologism rather than 'be' it because of the absence of an overriding political strategy for dealing with the problems it identifies. My suggestion is that, in 1962, ecologism (and therefore the possibility of being radically green) did not exist, and that Rachel Carson's book and the period in which it was written are best viewed as part of the preconditions for ecologism. Looking at it in this way we shall avoid the mistake made in many commentaries on and anthologies of socialism, say, which talk of the cleric John Ball (who spoke on behalf of the peasants during the rebellion of 1381) as if he were a socialist. The most that can be said of him, living as he did well before the French and Industrial Revolutions that gave birth to socialism proper, was that his sentiments were socialistic. Similarly, the pre-1970 ideas and movements that have an affinity with ecologism are 'green' rather than green.

The final important consequence of historicizing the ideology is that it enables us to emphasize the novelty of its analysis. It has been remarked that, despite its claims to the contrary, the green movement's perspective is merely a reworking of old themes. Thus, for example, its warnings about population growth are substantially contained in the work of Thomas Malthus; its reluctance fully to embrace the mechanistic reason characteristic of the Enlightenment was a recurrent theme in the Romantic movement of the nineteenth century; and even its apocalyptic tone has been prefigured on countless occasions in countless Messianic movements. Such critics generally take these observations to indicate that, as has happened before, the subordinate themes associated with the green movement will eventually be submerged by their dominant and opposed counterparts. This interpretation fails to take full account of the historically specific nature of ecologism. For it is precisely the ideology's point that, while the terms of its analysis are not new in themselves, the fact of them being posited here and now gives those terms a novel resonance. So the critique of mechanistic forms of reason, for instance, cannot be directly mapped back on to similar critiques made in the nineteenth century. The additional factor to be taken into account, argues the green movement, is the potentially terminal state to which slavish usage of this reason has led us. In this way history defines the context within which ecologism operates (and therefore helps define ecologism itself), and provides the ground on which old themes acquire new resonances, coalescing to form a full-blown modern political ideology.

Conclusion

It needs to be stressed time and again that this is a book about ecologism and not about environmentalism. The reason that this needs to be stressed is that most people will understand environmentalism – a managerial approach to the environment within the context of present political and economic practices – to be what green politics is about. I do not think it is – at least in its political-ideological guise. Ecologists and environmentalists are inspired to act by the environmental degradation they observe, but their strategies for remedying it differ wildly. Environmentalists do not necessarily subscribe to the limits to growth thesis, nor do they typically seek to dismantle 'industrialism'. They are unlikely to argue for the intrinsic value of the non-human environment and would balk at any suggestion that we (as a species) require 'metaphysical reconstruction' (Porritt, 1984a, pp. 198–200). Environmentalists will typically believe that technology can solve the problems it creates, and will probably regard any suggestions that only a reduction in material throughout in the production process will provide for sustainability as wilful nonsense. In short, what passes for green politics in the pages of today's newspapers is not the ideology of political ecology, properly understood. This is why the student of green politics needs to do more than scratch the surface of its public image in order to appreciate the full range of the debate that it has opened up.

2 Philosophical foundations

In 1855, Chief Seattle is supposed to have said:

> We know that the white man does not understand our ways. He is a stranger who comes in the night, and takes from the land whatever he needs. The earth is not his friend, but his enemy, and when he's conquered it he moves on. He kidnaps the earth from his children. His appetite will devour the earth and leave behind a desert. If all the beasts were gone, we would die from a great loneliness of the spirit, for whatever happens to the beasts also happens to us. All things are connected. Whatever befalls the Earth, befalls the children of the Earth.
>
> (quoted in Bunyard and Morgan-Grenville, 1987, p. 3)

Although it turns out that this speech was a fake, that has not stopped greens from making liberal use of it and the sentiments it contains. Central to the theoretical canon of green politics is the belief that our social, political and economic problems are substantially caused by our intellectual relationship with the world and the practices that stem from it.

In this regard, what sets ecologism apart from other political ideologies is its focus on the relationship between human beings and the non-human natural world. No other modern political ideology has this concern. Green, or environmental, *philosophy* is largely concerned with expressing what it is about the non-human natural world that political ecologists believe to be ethically important, and how best to defend it intellectually. These defences differ from the pragmatic, 'limits to growth' arguments referred to in Chapter 1 and discussed in detail in Chapter 3. It is not just that the non-human world constitutes a set of resources for human use and that if we run them down we threaten the very basis of human life itself: it is that even if resources were infinite, there might still be good reason not to treat the non-human world in a purely instrumental fashion.

Political ecologists are moved by what Robert Goodin has called a 'green theory of value', which 'links the value of things to some naturally occurring properties of the objects themselves' (Goodin, 1992, p. 24). This theory of value is importantly different from other, more familiar ones associated with other political ideologies:

> It differs from a producer based theory of value in so far as it insists that … value-imparting properties are natural, rather than being somehow artefacts of human activities. And it differs from a consumer-based theory of value in so far as it insists that those value-imparting properties somehow inhere in the objects themselves, rather than in any mental states (actual or hypothetical, now or later) of those who partake of those objects.
>
> (Goodin, 1992, p. 25)

It is, then, the 'natural value' of things, imparted by their 'having been created by natural processes rather than by artificial human ones' (Goodin, 1992, p. 27) that political ecologists are particularly keen to preserve and promote. This is not to say that they are not interested in other types of things with different kinds of value, but what sets ecologism apart from other political ideologies is, precisely, its primordial interest in natural value and its promotion and preservation. This is, as Goodin says, the 'logical primitive' of green moral theory (Goodin, 1992, p. 120).

As a consequence of this, radical greens will have a particular view of what the much-vaunted objective of 'environmental sustainability' is about. Environmental sustainability, and its close cousin, sustainable development, have become all things to all people in the rush for environmental political correctness (but see Dobson, 1998, Chapter 2, and Jacobs, 1999). So used and abused have these terms become that they sometimes seem to have lost all meaning, but political ecologists will give an unequivocal answer when asked what environmental sustainability means for them. Any definition of environmental sustainability must answer the fundamental question, 'What is to be sustained?' and while there are a number of possible responses, political ecologists will answer, 'Natural value'. What they want to see sustained into the future is, to repeat Goodin, the value of things created by natural processes rather than artificial human ones.

Just what these 'things' might be is open to some debate, of course. Individual animals? Species? Only living things? Or non-living things like mountains and rivers too? Environmental philosophy is not only concerned with preserving and promoting natural value, therefore, but also with deciding which possessors of natural value should be preserved and promoted. I shall try and give a flavour of all these debates in what follows, but my principal intention is to focus on the kind of environmental philosophy that I believe underpins the radical ideology of ecologism being examined in this book. Environmental philosophy seeks to judge between various reasons for restraint, and I shall suggest that not all reasons that can be given are radically ecological reasons, and that this leads to a distinction between what has come to be known as 'deep ecology', on the one hand, and the public face of ecologism as a political ideology on the other. I shall explore this shortly.

In green thinking, the general targets of attack are those forms of thought that 'split things up' and study them in isolation, rather than those that 'leave them as they are' and study their interdependence. The best knowledge is held to be acquired not by the isolated examination of the parts of a system but by examining the way in which the parts interact. This act of synthesis, and the language of linkage and reciprocity in which it is expressed, is often handily collected in the term 'holism'. Thus holistic medicine is preferable to interventionist surgery, and ecology – which studies 'wholes' rather than 'parts' – is preferable to biology. Greater recognition of mutual dependence and influence, it is argued, will encourage a sensitivity in our dealings with the 'natural' world that discrete atomism has conspicuously failed to do.

Political ecologists often derive evidence for a holistic description of the universe from developments in physics during the twentieth century. It is no accident that one of the intellectual champions of the green movement, Fritjof Capra, is a teacher and researcher of theoretical physics. His books *The Tao of Physics* (1975) and *The Turning Point* (1983) have had a tremendous impact within the movement, and it is significant that Jonathon Porritt, erstwhile leading spokesperson for green politics in Britain, should write of the latter: 'This is a brilliant book. Give yourself plenty of time for it … It was certainly a turning point for me' (Porritt, 1984a, p. 242). It is the work of thinkers like Capra that gives greens the confidence to claim that their world-view is located at the sharp end of the latest thinking in science in general and physics in particular.

In this context, if twentieth-century physicists Niels Bohr and Werner Heisenberg are popular figures in the green pantheon, then Francis Bacon, René Descartes and Isaac Newton are their complementary opposites. These three, according to the analysis of most green theorists, produced a world-view at variance in virtually all respects with that demanded by ecological survival in the twentieth century. Briefly, Bacon developed methods and goals for science that involved (and involve) the domination and control of nature; Descartes insisted that even the organic world (plants, animals, etc.) was merely an extension of the general mechanical nature of the universe; and Newton held that the workings of this machine-universe could be understood by reducing it to a collection of 'solid, massy, hard, impenetrable, movable particles' (Newton, quoted in Capra, 1983, p. 52).

In contrast, twentieth-century physics' exploration of the subatomic world has led to a very different picture of the nature of the 'physical' universe. The Newtonian atomic description has given way to a universe in which (at the subatomic level at least) there are no solid objects, but rather fields of probability in which 'particles' have a tendency to exist. Nor are these 'particles' held to be definable in themselves: rather, their nature is in their relationship with other parts of the system. As Niels Bohr commented: 'Isolated material particles are abstractions, their properties being definable and observable only through their interaction with other systems' (quoted in Capra, 1983, p. 69). Further, Werner Heisenberg's Uncertainty Principle (fundamental to the practice of quantum physics) shows that the observer – far from being independent of her or his experiment – is inextricably a part of it. Capra draws from this the requisite ecological-theoretical conclusion: 'We can never speak about nature without, at the same time, speaking about ourselves' (Capra, 1983, p. 77). The differences between a seventeenth- and a twentieth-century description of the universe should be clear from this brief survey. The important similarity in our context, however, is that these descriptions have been used to generate, and then buttress, descriptions and prescriptions of how the social world is and ought to be. The 'bootstrap' interpretation of particle physics (that no one 'particle' is more or less 'fundamental' than any other) militates against hierarchy and works in favour of egalitarianism. Similarly, the fact that definitely bounded particles appear not to exist is held to count against atomistic pictures of society. As Capra and Charlene Spretnak have argued:

> Although Western culture has been dominated for several hundred years by a conceptualisation of our own bodies, the body politic, and the natural world as hierarchically arranged aggregates of discrete components, that world-view is giving way to the systems view, which is supported by the most advanced discoveries of modern science and which is deeply ecological.
>
> (Spretnak and Capra, 1985, p. 29)

If twentieth-century physics provides ammunition against hierarchy and discreteness, then so does the science most obviously connected with the green movement – ecology. At the same time, the science of ecology takes up the theme of egalitarianism implicit in the 'bootstrap theory' and adds a crucial ingredient: the apparently equal status of *species*. As I remarked in the previous chapter, the word 'ecology' was first used by the German biologist Ernest Haeckel in 1866 or 1873. The science of ecology has to do, in the words of ecologist Denis Owen, with 'the relationships between plants and animals and the environment in which they live' (Owen, 1980, p. 1). The political implications of this study lie in the observation of the interrelationship and interdependence of these animal and plant systems, and if one were to have to point to a basis for political ecology then this would probably be it.

One further implication of the science of ecology derived from its governing principle of interdependence, and which is central to the political ideology of ecologism, is its anti-anthropocentrism. If there is an identifiable equality of value of species then, as Murray Bookchin suggests, the 'stratified pyramid with man at the apex' (Bookchin, 1982, p. 26) is not a presentable picture of the way things are, although Bookchin's own non-anthropocentric credentials are equivocal, as I shall show. This, within the context of ecologism, is uncontroversial, and the issue of anthropocentrism itself will be dealt with later in the chapter. I now turn, though, to the issue of 'deep ecology'.

Ethics: a code of conduct

The first influential use of the term 'deep ecology' is generally credited to the Norwegian Arne Naess. In September 1972 Naess gave a lecture in Bucharest in which he drew a distinction between what he called the 'shallow' and the 'deep' ecology movements. The distinction had to do with the difference between a shallow concern at 'pollution and resource depletion', for the deleterious effects this might have on human life, and the deep concern – for its own sake – for ecological principles such as complexity, diversity and symbiosis (Naess, 1973, p. 95). I suggest that deep ecology informs radical green politics in a way that will not be obvious to those who make such politics synonymous with environmentalism. Indeed, ecologism's being informed by deep ecology is precisely what (partly) helps distinguish it from environmentalism: environmentalists will be happy with shallow ecological reasons for care for the environment, while deep ecologists, although they will often make shallow ecological remarks, will probably feel uncomfortable as they do so. This is not to say that deep ecology is unproblematic from a political point of view, as I shall show.

The first question to which any ethical theory must have an answer is: to whom or what should it apply? This is tied to a second question: in respect of the possession of what attributes do we admit a subject to membership of the ethical community? One ethical theory might hold, for example, that it should cover human beings (and only human beings), and that this is in virtue of their possession of a rational faculty. In this way, the attribute (possession of a rational faculty) defines the boundaries of the ethical community. Environmental philosophy in general, and deep ecology in particular, can be regarded as a series of answers to these two questions. In this context the influence of the animal rights movement and its intellectual backers has been profound. It is largely true to say that the extension by the animal rights movement and its theorists of the ethical domain from human to (some) animals has until recently been seen by ecophilosophers and deep ecology theorists as the right course to pursue in their aim of producing an ethic for non-sentient nature.

An ethic for animals is by no means the same as an ethic for the environment, but to the extent that it constitutes a foray across the species divide, it is a start. As long ago as the third century BC Epicurus argued that just as humans can experience pleasure and pain, so can animals, and more recently Peter Singer has famously turned this argument into reasons for moral constraint in our behaviour towards animals (Singer, 1975). Tom Regan builds a different bridge across the divide by arguing that humans and some animals can similarly be regarded as 'subjects-of-a-life', and that if this is the reason why we regard humans as morally considerable, it would be inconsistent to deny (some) animals similar moral considerability too (Regan, 1988).

Neither Singer nor Regan get anywhere near an environmental ethic, however. Singer restricts moral considerability to sentient beings, while Regan's extension of the moral community is timid indeed; besides humans it includes no more than 'normal mammalian animals aged one or more' (Regan, 1988, p. 81). However, both theories do raise the spectre of 'speciesism' – discrimination on the grounds of species alone – and ask us whether such discrimination can be rationally justified. Rationalist approaches to a properly *environmental* ethic proceed along similar lines, with ethicists seeking less restrictive attributes for non-human entities than either sentience or a degree of mental complexity. This is not to say that I believe environmental ethicists to have some prejudged view as to what they want to have invested with intrinsic value, despite what Robin Attfield thinks: 'Dobson writes as if the debate among ecophilosophers mainly involves casting around to find some ground or other for upholding this advocacy [of non-instrumental care for the biosphere]' (Attfield, 1990, p. 62). It is merely to say that a change in the attribute that invokes moral considerability inevitably brings with it a shift in the boundaries of ethical concern.

Lawrence Johnson, for example, argues that organisms and collections of organisms (including species and ecosystems) have well-being needs, and therefore an interest in having them met. This 'well-being interest' is the attribute, according to Johnson, which accords moral significance to those entities said to possess it (Johnson, 1991). This is an environmental ethic in two senses: first, it can be argued to apply to the whole environment; and second, it grants moral considerability to 'wholes' (species, ecosystems) as well as to individuals. It therefore covers the ground outlined by Aldo Leopold in his classic statement of the reach of an environmental ethic in *A Sand County Almanac*:

> All ethics so far evolved rest upon a single premise: that the individual is a member of a community of interdependent parts. His instincts prompt him to compete for his place in that community; but his ethics prompt him also to co-operate (perhaps in order that there be a place to compete for).
>
> The land ethic simply enlarges the boundaries of the community to include soils, waters, plants, and animals, or collectively: the land.
>
> (Leopold, 1949, p. 204)

Leopold also provided us with a general rule of thumb for sound environmental action by writing that '[A] thing is right when it tends to preserve the integrity, stability and beauty of the biotic community. It is wrong when it tends otherwise' (Leopold, 1949, pp. 224–5). This has worried subsequent commentators for its apparent implication that *individual* entities can justifiably be sacrificed for the *general* good, thereby bearing out Tom Regan's worries regarding 'environmental fascism' (Regan, 1988, p. 362).

Rationalist seekers after an environmental ethic have responded to this common criticism by advancing the cause of attributes which grant moral considerability to both individuals *and* wholes. Lawrence Johnson's 'well-being interests' are a case in point, as is the attribute of 'autopoiesis' which Robyn Eckersley describes as the 'characteristic of self-reproduction or self-renewal' (Eckersley, 1992, p. 60), building on Fox's observation that '[L]iving systems ... are not merely *self-organizing* systems, they are self-regenerating or *self-renewing* systems' (Fox, 1990, p. 170). Eckersley continues:

> [A]n autopoietic approach to intrinsic value is not vulnerable to the objections that are associated with either extreme atomism or extreme holism. Whereas atomistic approaches attribute intrinsic value only to individual organisms, and whereas an unqualified holistic

approach attributes intrinsic value only to whole ecosystems (or perhaps only the biosphere or ecosphere itself), an autopoietic approach recognizes ... the value not only of individual organisms but also of species, ecosystems, and the ecosphere ('Gaia').

(Eckersley, 1992, p. 61)

Of course, this attribution of moral considerability to wholes as well as parts does not preclude the possibility of clashes between them – in fact, such clashes are inevitable. Attfield has pointed out, while considering the 'Gaian' argument that the biosphere as a whole has moral standing, that 'there can be a conflict between maximising its excellences and maximising the intrinsic value of its components' (Attfield, 1983, p. 159). The difficulties involved in resolving conflicts between the claims of different 'ecological subjects' have proved very awkward, and these problems emerged early on in the history of deep ecology with Naess's 'Principle Two' of deep ecology, described in his seminal 1973 paper. The idea is: 'Biospherical egalitarianism in principle' (Naess, 1973, p. 95). The difficulty with this becomes clear if one focuses on the small-print clause 'in principle', and Naess's own comment upon it: 'The "in principle" clause is inserted because any realistic praxis necessitates some killing, exploitation and suppression' (Naess, 1973, p. 95). This has become a famous phrase in environmental-ethical literature – how much killing, and who or what is to be exploited and suppressed?

The notion of biospherical egalitarianism is evidently problematic. Mary Midgley caustically rejects the principle of an 'equal right to live and blossom' when she says that biospherical egalitarians

> have ... made things extremely hard for themselves lately by talking in a very wholesale, *a priori* French-revolutionary sort of way about all animals being equal, and denouncing 'speciesism' as being an irrational form of discrimination, comparable to racism. This way of thinking is hard to apply convincingly to locusts, hookworms and spirochaetes, and was invented without much attention to them.
>
> (Midgley, 1983a, p. 26)

So how are problems of conflict to be resolved? How is the 'in principle' clause to be filled out?

In general terms, environmental ethicists cope with this in the same way as the rest of us: by constructing a *hierarchy* of valued entities and collections of entities. These hierarchies are usually arrived at on the basis of taking the valued attribute in question and arguing that some entities or collections of entities have more of this attribute than others and therefore weigh more heavily in the moral balance. Lawrence Johnson, it will be remembered, bases moral considerability on the possession of well-being interest. But it becomes clear that not all entities have the same (kind of) well-being interest: 'certainly it seems that humans are capable of a much higher level of well-being than is the smallpox organism' (Johnson, 1991, p. 261).

Indeed, it is striking how often these intrepid philosophical adventurers return, in a pretty traditional way, to home base. Complexity is a favourite datum around which to construct the requisite hierarchies. Warwick Fox has related value to complexity in the following way:

> To the extent that value inheres in complexity of relations, and to the extent that complexity of relations is evidenced in the degree of an organism's central organisation (and therefore for capacity of richness of experience), then organisms are entitled to moral consideration commensurate with their degree of central organisation (or capacity for richness of experience) for the duration of their existence.
>
> (Fox, 1984, p. 199)

He goes on: 'Recognising this, we should be clear that the central intuition of deep ecology does not entail the view that intrinsic value is spread evenly across the membership of the biotic community' (Fox, 1984, p. 199), and that therefore 'these hierarchical conceptions of intrinsic value ... provide a guide to action in situations where values come into genuine conflict' (Fox, 1990, p. 182). In similar vein, another Australian philosopher, Freya Mathews, has written that, '[T]he greater the complexity of a living system ... the greater its power of self-realisation ... [and] the greater the intrinsic value ... it may be said to embody' (Mathews, 1991, p. 123). Now this evidently makes rather a mess of the principle of biospherical egalitarianism: it is, in fact, a principle of biospherical inegalitarianism.

In this way, attempts to solve the difficulties with Naess's principle have ended by undermining the principle itself. This is clear evidence of the intractability of the problem – and it is an absolutely practical problem for the politics of the green movement. Anyone who has drowned slugs in a cup of beer to stop them eating the lettuces may be congratulated on a certain ecological sensibility, but was the action environmentally ethical? As Richard Sylvan has commented: 'The guidelines as regards day-to-day living and action for a follower of deep ecology remain unduly and unfortunately obscure' (Sylvan, 1984b, p. 13).

At the root of all of this is the search for a way of investing value in beings other than human beings such that we cannot legitimately treat them only as means to our ends: 'We need an ethic that recognises the intrinsic value of all aspects of the nonhuman world' (Bunyard and Morgan-Grenville, 1987, p. 284). Thus, it is hoped, an ethical non-anthropocentrism will underpin responsible behaviour towards the non-human natural world.

But what would intrinsic value look like? In a detailed survey, John O'Neill outlines three possibilities. First '[A]n object has intrinsic value if it is an end in itself [as opposed to] a means to some other end'; second, '[I]intrinsic value is used to refer to the value an object has solely in virtue of its "intrinsic properties" ', and third, '[I]ntrinsic value is used as a synonym for "objective value", i.e. the value that an object possesses independently of the valuation of valuers' (O'Neill, 1993, p. 9). O'Neill concludes that holding an environmental ethic involves holding that 'non-human beings have intrinsic value in the first sense', but that holding a *defensible* environmental ethic might involve commitment to intrinsic value in the second or third senses (O'Neill, 1993, pp. 9–10).

As far as the issue of objective value is concerned, several attempts have been made to counter the subjectivist's objection that value is a quality invested in objects by human beings – in other words, objects do not possess value in their own right, rather we confer it upon them. Often, these attempts amount to an appeal to our intuition. For example, Holmes Rolston writes that 'We can be thrilled by a hawk in a windswept sky, by the rings of Saturn, the falls of Yosemite.' He admits that 'All these experiences are mediated by our cultural education', but asserts that they 'have high elements of giveness, of finding something thrown at us, of successful observation' (Rolston, 1983, p. 144). Similarly, he says that 'we have sometimes found values so intensely delivered that we have saved them wild, as in the Yellowstones, the Sierras and the Smokies' (Rolston, 1983, p. 156). It is not the demand on our intuition that offends here, but while Rolston might persuade us to agree about the value of nature's 'spectaculars', it might not stretch as far as other offerings such as the anopheles mosquito and the tsetse fly.

Another favourite gambit of the intrinsic valuers is to ask us to conduct a thought experiment so as to test our susceptibility to their suggestions. The experiment can take many forms but the general idea is always the same. Consider, for example, Robin Attfield's version. Attfield asks us to think of the last surviving human being of a nuclear holocaust confronted by the last surviving elm tree. Attfield's question is: would this human being be doing anything wrong in cutting down the elm tree, knowing that she or he would die before the tree? He reports that 'most people who consider this question conclude that his [sic] act would be wrong' (Attfield, 1983, p. 155), and that this is evidence of a visceral feeling for intrinsic value. His rationalization of this effect is that trees have a 'good of their own' and 'are thus at least serious candidates for moral standing' (Attfield, 1983, p. 145).

It will be clear that cashing out all the complexities of intrinsic value involves detailed argumentation – any more of which would be misplaced here. The point at present is to contrast instrumental with non-instrumental value – and to say that although O'Neill (above) talks only of non-human 'beings', environmental ethicists also talk of the 'states, activities and/or experiences' of objects as potential sites of intrinsic value (e.g. Attfield, 1990, p. 63), and *collections* of entities, likewise.

A number of ecophilosophers now regard the difficulties of extending the work of animal rights theorists and sustaining an 'intrinsic value' position for nature as insurmountable, and have preferred to concentrate on the cultivation of a 'state of being' rather than a 'code of conduct' (Fox, 1986b, p. 4). This approach involves the belief that the development of an ecologically sound ethics is not possible within the current mode of ethical discourse (rights, duties, rational actors, the capacity for pain and suffering, and so on), and that such an ethics can only, and must, emerge from a new world-view. Those who argue from this perspective point out that the current mode of discourse demands that ecologists present reasons why the natural world should *not* be interfered with. What is required, they suggest, is the cultivation of an alternative world-view within which justifications would have to be produced as to why it *should* be interfered with (Fox, 1986a, p. 84). I turn to this now.

Ethics: a state of being

There was a time, then, when deep ecology was associated primarily with the belief that the non-human world could have (and did have) intrinsic value. This appeared to be a radical move within traditional ethical discourse, with far-reaching practical implications for the relationship between human beings and their environment. In ethical terms it was (and is) an attempt to move beyond human-prudential arguments for concern for the biosphere.

But, as I have indicated, a number of deep ecology theorists began to balk at the implications of developing a cast-iron intrinsic value theory. This has led them to propose the necessity for an ethics proceeding from a changed state of consciousness, rather than hoping that it might be developed from within the present dominant one. Some of these latter theorists have argued that deep ecology has always been a 'consciousness first, ethics later' enterprise. I believe this to be wrong, although that hardly matters here. What there has always been is a mixture of the two, but it is only relatively recently that the problems encountered with 'values-in-nature' have led to the explicit separation of a 'state of being' and a 'code of conduct'.

The 'state of being' position begins from the following sort of premise: that an 'ecological consciousness connects the individual to the larger world' (Bunyard and Morgan-Grenville, 1987, p. 282), and it has been developed in its most sophisticated form by Fox (1990). This 'ecological consciousness' serves as a new foundation on which a different (ecological) ethics and new (ecological) forms of behaviour would be built. The idea involves the cultivation of a sense of self that extends beyond the individual understood in terms of its isolated corporal identity. To this is added the notion that the enrichment of self depends upon the widest possible identification with the non-human world. Naess puts this in the following way:

> Self-realisation cannot develop far without sharing joys and sorrows with others, or more fundamentally, without the development of the narrow ego of the small child into the comprehensive structure of a Self that comprises all human beings. The ecological movement – as many earlier philosophical movements – takes a step further and asks for a development such that there is a deep identification of all individuals with life.
>
> (quoted in Fox, 1986a, p. 5)

Ecological consciousness, then, has to do with our identification with the non-human world, and the understanding that our self-realization is presaged upon such identification, and the behaviour that would logically result. It is not hard to see how an environmentally sound attitude emerges from this. Fox writes,

> For example, when asked why he does not plough the ground, the Nez Percé American Indian Smohalla does not reply with a closely reasoned explanation as to why the ground has intrinsic value but rather with a rhetorical question expressive of a deep identification with the earth: 'Shall I take a knife and tear my mother's breast?'
>
> (Fox, 1986a, p. 76)

In other words, the ethics issues 'naturally' from an alternative vision of reality, and this is the reason for the rejection of the primacy of ethics:

I'm not much interested in ethics and morals, [writes Naess] I'm interested in how we experience the world ... If deep ecology is deep it must relate to our fundamental beliefs, not just to ethics. Ethics follows from how we experience the world. If you experience the world so and so then you don't kill.

(quoted in Fox, 1986a, p. 46)

Fox himself observes that his 'transpersonal ecology' sense of self,

has the highly interesting, even startling, consequence that ethics (conceived as being concerned with moral 'oughts') is rendered superfluous! The reason for this is that if one has a wide, expansive, or field-like sense of self then (assuming that one is not self-destructive) one will naturally (i.e. spontaneously) protect the natural (spontaneous) unfolding of the expansive self (the ecosphere, the cosmos) in all its aspects.

(Fox, 1990, p. 217)

Now there are at least three points to be made about this notion of ecological consciousness and its implications. In the first place: how far does it involve a reversion to the original sin of anthropocentrism? It seems clear that the principle of self-realization described above, although it generates concern for the non-human world, generates it for human-prudential reasons. To this extent, the development of an ecological consciousness as foundational to an environmental ethics may avoid the problems associated with producing the latter from conventional discourse, but at the cost of diluting the non-anthropocentrism that is held to be central to an ecological perspective.

The second point revolves around the problem of potential conflicts between human interests and the interests of the environment, discussed in another context above. One can imagine an immensely wide identification of my 'self' with the non-human world, but still see the survival of my own self as dependent upon a certain amount of 'killing, exploitation and suppression' of that non-human world. Where does that leave the practical implementation of the new ethics that might arise from an 'ecological consciousness'? It certainly seems that Richard Sylvan's demand for 'guidelines as regards day-to-day living' is not satisfied by anything in the ecological consciousness approach. Nor is this a problem confined to some putative 'pre-ecological consciousness era'. There is no suggestion made by this set of deep ecologists that, once a general ecological consciousness has been attained, problems of environmental conflict will 'wither away'. Indeed, Warwick Fox recognizes that conflict between human beings and the non-human world is inevitable: 'my "small" self must meet certain vital needs even at the expense of the vital needs of other (relatively autonomous) entities' (1986a, p. 58). No guidelines are produced, however, for deciding between various sets of 'vital needs', or for deciding what they might be.

The first possible answer to this objection is that guidance is given, via the creation of hierarchies, or 'degrees of intrinsic value' (Mathews, 1991, pp. 122–9), like those outlined in the previous section. The location of entities or collections of entities in these hierarchies will determine which of them are more equal than others in the case of a clash of interests. Of course, there are no agreed criteria for the construction of these hierarchies, so the fine print causes much more trouble than the general rules.

A second and broader answer is that deep ecologists argue that they are in the business not of providing a rule-book, but of advancing a consciousness of identification with the non-human world that would markedly alter the conditions within which any rule-book would be written. Fox makes the point cogently:

> in terms of preserving the nonhuman world, the wider identification approach is more advantageous than the environmental axiological approach in a political or strategic sense because it shifts the onus for justification of one's actions from the person who wants to preserve the nonhuman world to the person who wants to disrupt or interfere with it.
>
> (Fox, 1986a, p. 84)

I think that this is a genuinely significant point to make, and it would certainly have an effect on the environmental ethic that might emerge. Problems of conflict would, of course, remain, but the degree of conflict would be considerably reduced. There is no question but that the non-human world would benefit from a general instilling of an 'environmental consciousness', such as Fox and others have described it. Shifting the onus of justification in this way does not absolve us, of course, from drawing lines of legitimate environmental intervention, but it does mean that the lines will be drawn in very different territory from that which emerges if the onus of justification is not shifted. Put differently, if it is preservation of the non-human world that has to be justified then more environmental intervention is likely to be countenanced than if it is intervention that has to be justified.

However, the next problem – and this is the third point – concerns the generation of this 'wider identification' in people. How are they to be convinced of it? If Robert Aitken is correct when he says that 'Deep ecology ... requires openness to the black bear, becoming truly intimate with the black bear, so that honey dribbles down your fur coat as you catch the bus to work' (in Fox, 1986a, p. 59), then deep ecology would seem to be in deep trouble. The guffaws that generally greet this kind of statement reveal deep ecology's profound problem of persuasion.

To explain: those who now choose to advance the claims of a 'state of being' over a new 'code of conduct' were forced into this position by what they saw as a sense of realism – it was understood that traditional ethical concepts could not do the environmental work required of them. Put another way, they asked: 'Where does an ethics come from?' and came up with the answer: from a given understanding of the way the world is, a metaphysics. The conclusion was to argue for a change in metaphysical perspective towards that described in the first part of this chapter, on the understanding that the desired environmental ethic would be more likely to flourish in this new climate.

However, the metaphysics advanced by deep ecology is (to say the least) taking its time getting a grip, and the self-identification with the non-human world demanded by it is restricted – in 'advanced industrial countries' at least – to isolated pockets of well-meaning radicals. Deep ecology has asked: 'Where does the ethics come from?' and has answered: from a metaphysics. But its long-term problem may lie in finding an answer to the question: 'Where does the metaphysics come from?' because here lies the clue to why the advocacy of a change of consciousness, on its own, is not sufficient. Consciousness is not an independent datum, isolated from the social conditions that nurture it.

Janna Thompson gets closest to the remark that needs to be made: 'Ethical resolution ... presupposes social critique: an attempt to show that present social relations and the goals and desires that spring from them, are unsatisfactory, and that new conceptions of self-fulfilment and happiness are desirable' (Thompson, 1983, p. 98). This social critique ought to be part and parcel of the deep-ecological enterprise, but the ecophilosophers write as though the resolution of philosophical problems were enough to bring about the resolution of practical problems, such as pollution, deforestation and acid rain. Normally, indeed, the social and political context receives no attention at all. Warwick Fox writes: 'This attempt to shift the *primary* focus of environmental philosophical concern from ethics to ontology clearly constitutes a fundamental or revolutionary challenge to normal environmental philosophy. It is (and should be) deep ecology's guiding star' (Fox, 1984, p. 204; emphasis in original). If deep ecology is content to remain in the territory of theory then Fox may be right in his identification of its 'guiding star'. But if it is concerned to turn the theory into practice, it will have to present a programme for social change. This it has so far failed to do.

Anthropocentrism

If there is one word that underpins the whole range of radical green objections to current forms of human behaviour in the world, it is probably 'anthropocentrism': 'the mistake of giving exclusive or arbitrarily preferential consideration to human interests as opposed to the interests of other beings' (Hayward, 1997, p. 51). Concern for ourselves at the expense of concern for the non-human world is held to be a basic cause of environmental degradation and potential disaster. On the one hand, however, the very centrality of this word to the green cause has led to a muddying of its meaning, while on the other, the practical issue of getting the green ideology across has led to contradictory messages from its theorists about anthropocentrism.

As regards the first point, I want to suggest that there is a strong and a weak meaning for the word – meanings that emerge from a reading of the ecophilosophical literature, but that are rarely formally distinguished. My understanding of the weak meaning is referred to by Warwick Fox as having to do with being 'human-centred' (1986b, p. 1). What I call the strong meaning also comes from Fox, and involves seeing 'the nonhuman world purely as a means to human ends' (1984, p. 198). We might refer to these positions as 'human-centred' and 'human-instrumental', respectively. Both of these descriptions were used by Fox with explicit reference to anthropocentrism, but they clearly have different implications.

The first, or weak, sense is more obviously 'neutral' than the second, or strong, sense – and it is truly astonishing how often 'human-centredness' is confused with 'human instrumentalism', usually by those rushing too hastily to find anthropocentric contradictions at the heart of ecocentric thinking. The strong sense carries a notion of the injustice and unfairness involved in the instrumental use of the non-human world. I want to suggest that anthropocentrism in the weak sense is an unavoidable feature of the human condition. This will not do damage to the ecologists' case; in fact it enables them unashamedly to put the human on to the ecological agenda – an agenda from which, for reasons associated with its aims, the centrality of the human being has all but been erased.

The dangers of such erasure have become clear in the theoretical stances and political activities of the North American group Earth First!, a group that has been referred to as 'deep ecology's political action wing' (Reed, 1988, p. 21), and 'the cutting edge of environmentalism' in the American West (Tokar, 1988, p. 134). One article in an Earth First!

journal (engagingly signed Miss Ann Thropy – perhaps the pseudonym of prominent North American Earth First!er Christopher Manes) stated that,

> If radical environmentalists were to invent a disease to bring human population back to sanity, it would probably be something like AIDS … the possible benefits of this to the environment are staggering … just as the Plague contributed to the demise of feudalism, AIDS has the potential to end industrialism.
>
> (quoted in Reed, 1988, p. 21)

Neither is the group all words and no action. Some time ago, Earth First! took to driving nails into the trunks of Californian redwood trees to deter loggers from cutting them down, and at least one lumberjack has been badly injured by his chainsaw kicking out of the trunk and into his neck. I shall have more to say on Earth First! in Chapter 4.

Perhaps the most committed and principled critic (within the ecology movement, broadly defined) of the excesses to which (what he refers to as) biocentrism can lead is Murray Bookchin, from the perspective of what he calls 'social ecology'.

> Whatever its merits, [he writes] the fact is that deep ecology, more than any other 'radical' ecological perspective, blames 'Humanity' as such for the ecological crisis – especially ordinary 'consumers' and 'breeders of children' – while largely ignoring the corporate interests that are really plundering the planet.
>
> (Bookchin, 1991, p. 123)

Bookchin has drawn constant attention to the misanthropic potential within deep ecology and was importantly instrumental in encouraging Dave Foreman – co-founder of Earth First! – to retract some particularly divisive remarks regarding immigration from Mexico to the USA (Foreman, 1991, p. 108; and see Chapter 3).

Social ecology's position on anthropocentrism and biocentrism is to refuse to choose between the two: 'An "anthropocentrism" that is based on the religious principle that the Earth was "made" to be dominated by "Humanity" is as remote from my thinking as a "biocentrism" that turns human society into just another community of animals' (Bookchin, 1991, p. 128). Bookchin prefers to speak of a 'first' and a 'second' nature, with 'first nature' being 'prehuman' (1989, p. 201) and 'second nature' evolving from first nature in the form of the human species. Second nature (humanity) is:

a product of evolution that has the fullness of mind, of extraordinary communicative abilities, of conscious association, and the ability knowingly to alter itself and the natural world. To deny these extraordinary human attributes which manifest themselves in real life, to submerge them in notions like a 'biocentric democracy' that renders human beings and snails 'equal' in terms of their 'intrinsic worth' (whatever that phrase may mean) is simply frivolous.

(Bookchin, 1989, p. 201)

By now it will be clear that while deep ecologists profess a 'biospherical egalitarianism' in principle, most of them find ways of producing a hierarchy of value so as to cope with clashes of interest between species (for instance). Indeed, it will be remembered that biospherical egalitarians often organize these hierarchies around the datum of complexity – one of the features that distinguishes first from second nature in Bookchin's description. In this respect Bookchin and his opponents may not be so far apart.

What finally sets them apart, though, and what makes it hard to regard social ecology as part of a radical *ecocentric* programme (this is not, of course, to deny its radicalism in its own terms) is Bookchin's view that humanity represents a qualitative improvement as far as natural evolution is concerned. 'Selfhood, consciousness, and the bases for freedom' are only dimly visible (if at all) in 'first nature' (Bookchin, 1989, p. 201). Potentially, on the other hand,

an emancipated humanity will become the voice, indeed the expression, of a natural evolution rendered self-conscious, caring and sympathetic to the pain, suffering and incoherent aspects of an evolution left to its own, often wayward, unfolding. Nature, due to human rational intervention, will thence acquire the intentionality, power of developing more complex life-forms, and capacity to differentiate itself.

(Bookchin, 1989, p. 203)

Robyn Eckersley has referred to this as Bookchin's 'evolutionary stewardship thesis' (Eckersley, 1992, p. 154) and she suggests two reasons why this thesis offends ecocentric sensibilities. First, the very idea that nature's unfolding might be 'wayward' does not square with the general ecocentric injunction to 'allow all beings (human and nonhuman) to unfold in their own way' (Eckersley, 1992, p. 156); and the second (connected) reason is that ecocentrics do not purport to know what the direction of evolution is:

> From an ecocentric perspective, it is both arrogant and self serving to make, as Bookchin does, the unverifiable claim that first nature is striving to achieve something (namely, greater subjectivity, awareness, or 'selfhood') that 'just happens' to have reached its most developed form in *us* – second nature.
>
> (Eckersley, 1992, p. 156)

Although Eckersley may overstate somewhat the teleological dimension of Bookchin's thought, it is hard to deny the sense of 'steering' that he gives to humanity's relationship with non-human nature – not that any of this bothers Bookchin too much: '[I]f this [social ecology] be humanism – more precisely ecological humanism,' he writes, 'the current crop of antihumanists and misanthropes are welcome to make the most of it' (Bookchin, 1989, p. 36).

Bookchin aside (if that does not seem too peremptory for a person who has had such a profound influence on North American environmentalism; Bookchin, 1995 and Light, 1998), it would be a mistake to think that deep ecology necessarily leads to Earth First!-type activities and so to reject it on that basis. Chris Reed's assertion (in an article previously referred to) that 'Descent into irrationality has badly damaged American feminism', and that 'The present uproar among environmentalists seems only too likely to repeat the feminists' mistake' (Reed, 1988, p. 21) is not only misguidedly offensive to radical feminism but is also a one-sided reading of the implications of deep ecology. For example, shifting the onus of justification from those who would preserve the non-human world to those who would intervene in it (presented above as implied by deep ecology) hardly justifies the kind of disciplinary violence practised by some members of Earth First! – and nor need it necessarily lead to anti-humanism and misanthropism, *pace* Bookchin, and Bramwell (1994, p. 161).

Be that as it may, the reintroduction of the human on to the green political agenda in a non-anthropocentric way is essential, and so the accusation of anthropocentrism in the strong sense identified above does damage to an ecologist's case, if we accept the ground rule that the reasons given for care for the non-human world are as important as the care itself. What the self-respecting political ecologist has to avoid is a human-instrumental reason. As we shall see shortly, however, this is precisely the sort of reason for changes in behaviour often advanced by the ideologues of ecologism.

In the literature, one finds the weak and strong meanings of anthropocentrism mixed together – sometimes in the same sentence. Richard Sylvan, for example, defines as anthropocentrism any attitude that 'does not move outside a human-centred framework, which construes nature and the environment instrumentally, that is, simply as a means to human ends and values' (Sylvan, 1984a, p. 5). To my mind, and contrary to Sylvan's implication, a 'human-centred framework' does not necessarily mean that it is 'human-instrumental'. Consider, for example, the following statement from Jonathon Porritt: 'For us, it is not enough to protect animals for practical, self-interested reasons alone; there is also a profoundly moral concern, rooted in our philosophy of respect for all that dwells on the planet' (Porritt, 1984a, p. 184). The first half of the sentence represents a rejection of human-instrumentalism, while the second half involves human-centredness ('our philosophy of respect'). There is no contradiction in this, but it does show that there is room for a (weak) form of anthropocentrism in respectable ecological statements.

The reason for this is that weak anthropocentrism is a necessary feature of the human condition. As Tim O'Riordan has pointed out,

> Man's conscious actions are anthropocentric by definition. Whether he seeks to establish a system of biotic rights or to transform a forest into a residential suburb, the act is conceived by man in the context of his social and political culture.
>
> (O'Riordan, 1981, p. 11)

It is this factor that links even the search for intrinsic value with anthropocentrism. The search is a *human* search, and although it may be successful in displacing the human being from centre stage in terms of value, one will always find a human being at the centre of the enterprise, asking the questions. If there were no human beings there would be no such conceptualized thing as intrinsic value, and it is an open question whether there would be any such thing as intrinsic value at all (although see the earlier discussion of value objectivism). In this sense, any human undertaking will be (weakly) anthropocentric, including the green movement itself.

The reason for dwelling on this is that the green movement may be doing itself a disservice by what has been seen as its insistent distancing from the human. In the first place it is self-contradictory. Charlene Spretnak, for example, writes that

> Green politics rejects the anthropocentric orientation of humanism, a philosophy which posits that humans have the ability to confront and solve the many problems we face by applying human reason and by rearranging the natural world and the interactions of men and women so that human life will prosper.
>
> (Spretnak and Capra, 1985, p. 234)

There is evidently a reasonable green rejection of human-instrumentalism here, but also a disturbing hint that human beings should abandon their pretensions to solving the problems they have brought upon themselves. This suspicion is reinforced by comments of the following kind: 'In the long run, Nature is in control' (Spretnak and Capra, 1985, p. 234). If Spretnak really believes this, one wonders why she bothers to write books persuading us of the merits of green politics. The fact of her involvement implies a belief that she has some control, however minimal, over the destiny of the planet.

Overall, of course, it is the generalized belief in the possibility of change that makes the green movement a properly political movement. Without such a belief, the movement's reason for being would be undermined. From this perspective, the recognition that weak anthropocentrism is unavoidable may act as a useful political corrective to the idea that 'Nature is in control': at least it reintroduces the human on to the agenda – a necessary condition for there to be such a thing as politics.

These various confusions regarding anthropocentrism have led to recommendations that it be dropped altogether as a reference point for political ecologists. Tim Hayward, for example, has written that 'blanket condemnations of "anthropocentrism" not only condemn some legitimate human concerns, they also allow ideological retorts to the effect that criticisms of anthropocentrism amount to misanthropy', and he is also keen to avoid the 'conceptual confusion' that often attends attempts to cast anthropocentrism as an 'ethical error' (Hayward, 1997, p. 49). Hayward prefers to use the terms 'speciesism' and 'human chauvinism' which he believes can do the same work as anthropocentrism without the pitfalls he identifies in it. He defines speciesism as 'arbitrary discrimination on the basis of species', and this is indeed a position which all political ecologists will oppose. But how do we know what constitutes 'arbitrariness'? What are the rules for deciding when discrimination on the basis of species is legitimate rather than arbitrary?

Hayward admits to the danger that these rules may be drawn up in such a way as to systematically favour the human species, and this 'human chauvinism' is something that political ecologists would obviously oppose: 'Human chauvinism is appropriately predicated of attempts to specify relevant differences in ways that invariably favour humans' (Hayward, 1997, p. 53). So in place of the single target of anthropocentrism, Hayward has presented us with two: speciesism and human chauvinism. I believe that Hayward has contributed to clearing up some of the conceptual confusion with the distinctions he makes, and there is indeed much less chance of misanthropic interpretations being made of speciesism and human chauvinism than of anthropocentrism. I still concur, though, with Val Plumwood that 'the concept of anthropocentrism is fundamental to the Green critique' (Plumwood, 1997, p. 329), and this is because I do not think that Hayward's concepts can do the transformative work we require of them. Ecologism is a transformative ideology: it seeks to change hearts, minds and behaviour, and an awareness of speciesism and human chauvinism cannot of itself bring about the 'sympathetic moral disposition' (Hayward, 1997, p. 54) towards the non-human natural world that Hayward himself believes is needed.

This is because an awareness of speciesism and human chauvinism *presupposes* the very moral disposition they are supposed to bring about. Anti-speciesists, for example, still work within a human-centred framework in their commitment to root out arbitrary moral reasoning: what determines arbitrariness is the possession by species other than the human of characteristics that humans possess and which are regarded as deserving of moral recognition. Human beings remain the yardstick, and the anti-speciesist is more likely to be driven by a calculating moral rationality than be possessed of a 'sympathetic moral disposition'. But is this objection not covered by the reference to human chauvinism, according to which the specification of morally relevant similarities and differences should not be made in ways that consistently favour human beings? I think not. The logic of opposition to human chauvinism is still anthropocentric in that the similarities and differences referred to are judged in relation to human beings. A sympathetic moral disposition is not best generated by the relational logic of similarities and differences, but by the openness and generosity implicit in taking on 'centrism' – in this case, anthropocentrism. None of this is to say that speciesism and human chauvinism should not be opposed. They most certainly should, but opposing them will involve working with the concept of anthropocentrism rather than without it.

Curiously, though, when it comes to the politics of the green movement, as opposed to its philosophy, there is generally little reluctance to indulge in anthropocentrism – even of the strong variety. In *Green Politics*, for example, Spretnak and Capra talk of 'an understanding that we are part of nature, not above it, and that all our massive structures of commerce – and life itself – ultimately depend on wise, respectful interaction with our biosphere'. And if that is not a clear enough expression of a human-prudential argument the authors add: 'Any government or economic system that ignores that principle is ultimately leading humankind into suicide' (1985, p. 28).

Again, Jonathon Porritt writes that the 'ecological imperative ... reminds us that the protection of the Earth's natural systems is something we all depend on', and that 'The fact that thousands of species will disappear by the turn of the century is not just an academic irritation: our own survival depends on our understanding of the intricate webs of life in which we're involved' (1984a, pp. 98–9). In fact, Porritt goes as far as to make human-instrumentalism the lever for engineering the changes that ecologism recommends: 'A re-interpretation of enlightened self-interest is … the key to any radical transformation' (ibid., p. 117).

The same strong anthropocentric message comes through loud and clear in Green Party manifestos. The German Greens' seminal 1983 manifesto stated that

> Encroachment on natural habitats and the extermination of animal and plant species is destroying the balance of nature *and along with it the basis of our own life*. It is necessary to maintain or restore a bio-logically intact environment, *in order to ensure the humane survival of future generations*.
>
> (*German Green Party Manifesto*, 1983, p. 29; emphasis added)

And on the next page we find a perfect expression of the strong anthropocentric principle: 'We must stop the violation of nature in order to survive in it' (*German Green Party Manifesto*, 1983, p. 30).

The manifesto of the Green Party of England and Wales is less explicit but equally clear: 'The relentless pursuit of economic growth has brought *humankind* to the brink of a disaster which is unprecedented in history' (*Manifesto for a Sustainable Society*, 1999, PB101, emphasis added), and: 'The overriding, unifying principle is that all *human* activities must be indefinitely sustainable' (ibid., PB303, emphasis added), with the answer to the question: 'Sustainable for whom?' supplied by the italicized words.

The list of examples is endless, and they all demonstrate the same point: that the politics of ecology do not follow the same ground rules as the radical forms of its philosophy I suggested earlier in the chapter that, for ecophilosophers, the reasons for the care of the non-human world are at least as important as the care itself. For ecophilosophers, care should be disinterested. This principle appears to have been abandoned (or at least suspended) by the majority of the green movement's political ideologues.

Several reasons for this might be advanced, among which is the reason of convenience – i.e. that for the purposes of communicating the basic idea of care for the 'natural' world, short cuts may have to be taken. This is the approach outlined by Warwick Fox in the following lengthy but worthwhile quote:

> Consider the following. If you ask me to try to tell the 'average per-son' in one sentence why I think we ought to care about some non-

human 'being' (whether alive or not), then the simplest thing for me to say, given our present cultural context, is along the lines: 'Because it has all these uses for us'. However, if I wish to get a little closer to what I really want to say, but at the same time take care to speak in terms that others will immediately understand rather than in terms that might sound alien to them (and, hence, alienate them), then I will probably say something along the lines: 'Because it has value in itself'. Unless we have a lot more time to talk, the last thing I am going to say *given the present cultural context* is the first thing I want to say: 'Because it is part of my/our wider Self, its diminishment is My/Our diminishment'. In other words, given the constraints of culture, desire to persuade, and limited time in which to try to communicate something clearly, my *popular* statement of 'basic principles' will, while reflecting my deepest views, nevertheless be an unreliable or superficial guide to the way in which I would elaborate these views in formal, philosophical terms.

(Fox, 1986a, pp. 71–2; emphasis in original)

On this reading, the purveyors of human-prudential reasons for the care of 'nature' can always say that they do so only for tactical reasons – that the end of persuasion is more important than the means of achieving it. At one level this collapses into an issue of the intellectual consistency of individuals, but at another, a profoundly important political question is raised: 'Will human-prudential reasons do the job for the environment that is required of them?' Put another way, does the use of human-prudential reasons (as means) endanger the desired end of a hands-off approach to the environment?

Presumably the answer of 'ecological consciousness' supporters to these questions would be, respectively: no and yes. The whole point of developing a perspective which goes beyond (what I have defined as) a strong anthropocentric principle is that such a principle only serves to reinforce the attitude which radical greens are concerned to invalidate – that which has the universe revolving around the human being. Warwick Fox's argument is that only the development of an ecological consciousness will turn the tables in favour of the environment, such that the onus of persuasion is on those who want to destroy, rather than on those who want to preserve. The best that can be said of human-prudentialists, from the point of view of the deep ecologists, is that they will get some of the job done, albeit at the cost of ditching the totality of the enterprise. I shall return to these important strategic issues in the Conclusion.

I think it would be wrong to jump to the conclusion, however, that this disagreement counts towards a disqualification of ecologism's political ideologues from the ecological camp. My strong sense, in any case, is that, although political ecologists might publicly give human-instrumental reasons for care for the environment, they are likely to have been motivated to do so by considerations of the intrinsic value variety. There is little point in trying to draw up a definitive list of requirements for deep-ecological membership. Much more interestingly, the differences between the philosophy of deep ecology and its political manifestation are symptomatic of a failure of the philosophy to make itself practical.

I should mention in passing that this failure has accounted for some famous political casualties – none more so than Rudolf Bahro, who left the German Green Party in June 1985 over the issue of animal experimentation. Bahro's position was one of uncompromising opposition to animal experimentation, for recognizably deep-ecological reasons. He complained that the German Green Party

> has no basic ecological position; it is not a party for the protection of life and I know now that it never will be, for it is rapidly distancing itself from that position. Yesterday, on the question of animal experiments, it clearly came down in favour of the position taken by the speaker who said, more or less: 'If even one human life can be saved, the torture of animals is permissible.' This sentence expresses the basic principle by which human beings are exterminating plants, animals and finally themselves.
>
> (Bahro, 1986, p. 210)

The sentence Bahro quotes also expresses a form of strong anthropocentrism that would be rejected by deep ecologists. The 1985 German Green Party's acceptance of the principle of animal experiments, and Bahro's consequent departure from the Party, are a concrete expression of ecophilosophy's failure to make itself practical.

Nor do I mean by this simply that the recommendations of ecophilosophy are impractical or Utopian. I want to make the more far-reaching point that ecophilosophy has not paid enough attention to the practical relations among people, and between people and their environment, that make its recommendations impractical. Perhaps I can make this clearer by referring to Karl Marx's *Eighth Thesis on Feuerbach*, which runs as follows: 'Social life is essentially *practical*. All mysteries which mislead theory to mysticism find their rational solution in human practice and in the comprehension of this practice' (in Feuer, 1976, p. 285; emphasis in original).

While not wanting to endorse everything Marx has to say, I think Marx's thought here points us in the right direction. The idea is that there are things about the world that are hard to understand ('mysteries'), and that their resolution can take on an inadequate theoretical form ('mysticism'). In our present context, I would argue that the environmental crisis is the 'mystery' and that ecophilosophy – in all its various forms – is the 'mysticism'. Marx's thesis goes on to point out that adequate understanding lies in the comprehension of the social life and its practices that give rise to the problem, or 'mystery'. Further, that the tendency towards 'mystical' solutions is a function of those very forms of social life (i.e. the present ones), and thus that both the avoidance of 'mysticism' and the final resolution of the 'mystery' will depend upon changes in social practice. If this is correct, and if I am justified in interpreting ecophilosophy in this light, then ecophilosophy's failure to address the issue of social practice will disqualify it from ever formulating a satisfactory solution to the problems that have given rise to it.

This is what I meant when I said above that 'the differences between the philosophy of deep ecology and its political manifestation are symptomatic of a failure of the philosophy to make itself practical'. This is not to say that ecophilosophy's embracing of the practical would immediately resolve all conflicts of theory or practice, but it would make radical disagreements of the type that forced Bahro to leave the German Green Party unlikely. The reason is that a practical philosophy would have a strategy for social change built into it, a programme around which activists could work and within which disagreements would be over tactics and not over strategy.

The 'changes in social practice' to which I have just referred are very much conceived within the ecology movement to be the concern of its political rather than its philosophical 'wing'. It is this tendency towards the separation of the theoretical from the practical – or better, the refusal explicitly to link them – that I would criticize in ecophilosophy. However, if it is also true to say that successful practical resolutions are associated with successful theoretical resolutions, then the *lacunae* in ecophilosophy will have profound practical (political) ramifications. Discussion of this point will take us both further into this book (see Chapter 4), and towards the heart of ecologism as a political ideology.

3   The sustainable society

Limits to growth

Amid the welter of enthusiasm for lead-free petrol and green consumerism it is often forgotten that a foundation-stone of radical green politics is the belief that our finite Earth places limits on industrial growth. This finitude, and the scarcity it implies, is an article of faith for green ideologues, and it provides the fundamental framework within which any putative picture of a green society must be drawn. The guiding principle of such a society is that of 'sustainability' (now one of the most contested words in the political vocabulary; Dobson, 1998, Chapter 2), and the stress on finitude and the careful negotiation of Utopia that it seems to demand forces political ecologists to call into question green consumerist-type strategies for environmental responsibility. In this respect, it is the limits to growth thesis, together with the ethical conclusions to be drawn from ecocentrism, that divides light-green from dark-green politics.

Much has already been written on the limits to growth issue, and I do not see it as my task here to rehearse all of the arguments to which the notion has given rise. I do think it important, though, to stress its centrality to the green position I am describing and to take this opportunity to point out the features of the limits to growth thesis that are most often referred to in green discussions. Greens have all along been confronted with rebuffs to their belief in limits to growth, and as their responses to these criticisms have developed it has become easier to identify what they are prepared to jettison in the thesis and what they feel the need to defend.

It turns out that there are three principal thoughts related to the limits to growth thesis that have come to be of prime importance to the radical green position. They are, first, that technological solutions (broadly understood; i.e. solutions formulated within the bounds of present economic, social and political practices) will not in themselves bring about a sustainable society; second, that the rapid rates of growth aimed for (and often achieved) by industrialized and industrializing societies have an exponential character, which means that dangers stored up over a relatively long period of time can very suddenly have a catastrophic effect; and third, that the *interaction* of problems caused by growth means that such problems cannot be dealt with in isolation – i.e. solving one problem does not solve the rest, and may even exacerbate them. These three notions will be discussed in more detail very shortly, but first (principally for the uninitiated) the strategy and conclusions of the original *Limits to Growth* report ought briefly to be noted. The description and assessments that follow are primarily based on the 1974 report, although I have included references from the 1992 sequel where it seems appropriate. In one or two of these cases it is the sense of the two reports that is identical, rather than the quoted words.

The researchers pointed to what they described as '5 trends of global concern': 'accelerating industrialisation, rapid population growth, widespread malnutrition, depletion of nonrenewable resources, and a deteriorating environment' (Meadows *et al.*, 1974, p. 21). They then created a computerized world model of the variables associated with these areas of concern, i.e. industrial output per capita, population, food per capita, resources and pollution; and programmed the computer to produce pictures of various future states of affairs given changes in these variables. From the very beginning it was understood that such modelling would be rough and ready, and the Club of Rome (the name given to the informal association of scientists, researchers, industrialists, etc., that carried out the research) anticipated later criticisms of inaccuracy and incompleteness by admitting that the model was 'imperfect, oversimplified and unfinished' (Meadows *et al.*, 1974, p. 21; and 1992, p. 105). From our perspective, the important point to make is that greens have generally been unperturbed by criticisms of the detail of the various limits to growth reports, and have rather relied upon the general principles and conclusions of these reports.

The first computer run, then, assumed 'no major change in the physical, economic, or social relationships that have historically governed the development of the world system' (Meadows *et al.*, 1974, p. 124; 1992, p. 132). This, in other words, was a run in which business carried on as usual. In this case the limits to growth were reached 'because of nonrenewable resource depletion' (Meadows *et al.*, 1974, p. 125; 1992, p. 132). Next, the group programmed a run in which the resource depletion problem was 'solved' by assuming a doubling in the amount of resources economically available. In this case collapse occurred again, but this time because of the pollution brought about by the spurt in industrialization caused by the availability of new resources. The group concluded that 'Apparently the economic impetus such resource availability provides must be accompanied by curbs on pollution if a collapse of the world system is to be avoided' (Meadows *et al.*, 1974, p. 133; 1992, p. 134). Consequently, the next computer run involved not only a doubling of resources but also a series of technological strategies to reduce the level of pollution to one quarter of its pre-1970 level (Meadows *et al.*, 1974, p. 136; 1992, p. 168). This time the limits to growth are reached because of a food shortage produced by pressure on arable land owing to its being taken for 'urban-industrial use' (Meadows *et al.*, 1974, p. 137; 1992, p. 168).

And so the experiment progresses, with the world model programmed each time to deal with the immediate cause of the previous collapse. Eventually all sectors have technological responses filled in:

> The model system is producing nuclear power, recycling resources, and mining the most remote reserves; withholding as many pollutants as possible; pushing yields from the land to undreamed-of heights; and producing only children who are actively wanted by their parents.
>
> (Meadows et al., 1974, p. 141; 1992, p. 174)

Even this does not solve the problem of overshoot and collapse:

> The result is still an end to growth before the year 2100 [2050 in the 1992 report, p. 174]. In this case growth is stopped by three simultaneous crises. Overuse of land leads to erosion, and food production drops. Resources are severely depleted by a prosperous world population (but not as prosperous as the present [1970] US population). Pollution rises, drops then rises again dramatically, causing a further decrease in food production and a sudden rise in the death rate.
>
> (Meadows et al., 1974, p. 141)

and the next sentence of the group's conclusion on the computer's final run helps distance environmentalism from ecologism and provides the intellectual springboard for radical green political strategy: 'The application of technological solutions alone has prolonged the period of population and industrial growth, but it has not removed the ultimate limits to that growth' (Meadows *et al.*, 1974, p. 141). In the words of the 1992 report, 'This is a society that is using its increased technical capacity to maintain growth, while the growth eventually undermines the effects of these technologies' (Meadows *et al.*, 1992, p. 174).

This, then, brings us to the first of the three notions associated with the limits to growth thesis that I suggested above are essential to the theory and practice of political ecology: that technological solutions cannot provide a way out of the impasse of the impossibility of aspiring to infinite growth in a finite system. Irvine and Ponton point out that

> technological gadgets merely shift the problem around, often at the expense of more energy and material inputs and therefore more pollution. Favourite devices such as refuse incineration, sulphur extractors in power stations and catalytic converters in cars cost money and energy while at the same time generating new pollutants.
>
> (Irvine and Ponton, 1988, p. 36)

This will most likely appear heretical to those familiar with light-green, environmental politics, which bases itself precisely upon this sort of strategy, but it is at just these points that ecologism distinguishes itself most clearly from environmentalism.

So if the sustainable society is not, on the face of it, going to be full of environment-friendly technological wizardry, what *will* it be like? Part of the answer is provided by Garrett Hardin's definition of a 'technological solution': 'one that requires only a change in the techniques of the natural sciences, demanding little or nothing in the way of change in human values or ideas of morality' (quoted in Meadows *et al.*, 1974, p. 150). It follows that if the green movement believes technological solutions to the limits to growth problem to be impossible, then it will have to argue for more profound changes in social thought and practice – changes in human values and ideas of morality. These changes will involve accommodating social practices to the limits that surround them, and abandoning the Promethean (in this context, technological) attempt to overcome them. It is in this kind of respect, once again, that the dark-green sustainable society is different from the environmentalist one, and why the latter can sit only uncomfortably with the former. All of this is a result of the idea that technological solutions can have 'no impact on the *essential* problem, which is exponential growth in a finite and complex system' (Meadows *et al.*, 1974, p. 45).

And this is the second notion that political ecologists have rescued from the debate over limits to growth, making it central to their argument as to why present industrial practices are unsustainable: the idea of exponential growth. Meadows *et al.* claim that all of the five elements in the Club of Rome's world model experience exponential growth, and explain that 'A quantity exhibits *exponential* growth when it increases by a constant percentage of the whole in a constant time period' (Meadows *et al.*, 1974, p. 27; emphasis in original). In quantitative terms this is easily demonstrated by placing rice grains on the squares of a chess board, with one on the first square, two on the second, four on the third, sixteen on the fourth, and so on. The numbers build up very fast, and while the twenty-first square will be covered with over 100,000 grains of rice, the fortieth will require about 1 million million (Meadows *et al.*, 1974, p. 29; 1992, p. 18).

The central point is that such growth is deceptive in that it produces large numbers very quickly. Translated to the arena of industrial production, resource depletion and pollution, what seems an innocuous rate of use and waste disposal can quickly produce dangerously low quantities of available resources and dangerously high levels of pollution. Greens often point to the staggeringly rapid growth in industrial production this century and ask the (increasingly less rhetorical) question: 'Can this be sustained?' Thus, Irvine and Ponton note that 'In a mere blink on the timescale of human evolution, industrial society has been depleting and impairing Earth's "supply system" at a phenomenal rate', and that 'Americans, for example, have used more minerals and fossil fuels during the past half-century than all the other peoples of the world throughout human history' (Irvine and Ponton, 1988, pp. 24–5).

Greens believe, simply, that present rates of resource extraction and use – a '3 per cent growth rate implies doubling the rate of production and consumption every twenty-five years' (Ekins, 1986, p. 9) – and the production of waste and pollution necessarily associated with them, are unsustainable. They further believe that the nature of the rate of growth produces a false sense of complacency: what appears to be a safe situation now can very quickly turn into an unsafe one. A relevant French riddle for schoolchildren goes like this:

> Suppose you own a pond on which a water lily is growing. The lily plant doubles in size each day. If the lily were allowed to grow un-checked, it would completely cover the pond in 30 days, choking off the other forms of life in the water. For a long time the lily plant seems small, and so you decide not to worry about cutting it back until it covers half the pond. On what day will that be? On the twenty-ninth day, of course. You have one day to save your pond.
>
> (Meadows *et al.*, 1974, p. 29; 1992, p. 18)

The 1992 report, indeed, makes much of this effect by running computer scenarios in which the necessary policies for sustainability are implemented in 1975, 1995 and 2015 respectively (Meadows *et al.*, 1992, pp. 202, 198, 204). It will come as no surprise to hear that 1975 would have been best, and that waiting until 2015 will mean a very bumpy first hundred years of the twenty-first century.

The third and final aspect of the limits to growth thesis that has become central to the radical green position is that of the interrelationship of the problems with which we are confronted. It should already have become clear from the description of the Club of Rome's computer runs that solving one problem does not necessarily mean solving the rest, and our refusal to confront the complexity of the global system and to draw the right conclusions for action (or inaction) from it is why most greens believe our attempts to deal with environmental degradation, in particular, to be insensitively inadequate. 'What matters,' write Irvine and Ponton, 'is not any particular limit, which might be overcome, but the total interaction of constraints, and costs' (1988, p. 13). Change in one element means change in the others: nuclear power might contribute to solving problems of acid rain but it still contributes to global warming, and chemical fertilizers help us grow more food but simultaneously poison the water courses.

Fundamentally, this is a problem of knowledge, in the context of which green ideologues adopt a predominantly conservative stance:

> One of the worst changes that industrialism has made to pollution is not the addition of individual new pollutants, but their combined effects ... Some half a million chemicals are in common use; about another thousand are added each year. Yet we know next to nothing about their interaction and combined effects, and the scale of the problem suggests that we never will.
>
> (Irvine and Ponton, 1988, p. 34)

The implied impossibility of knowing enough is crucial to the green suggestion that we adopt a hands-off approach to the environment. If we cannot know the outcome of an intervention in the environment but suspect that it might be dangerous, then we are best advised, from a green point of view, not to intervene at all. In a less radical form this has become known in policy-making circles as the 'precautionary principle' (O'Riordan and Cameron, 1994). In this respect, green politics opposes drawing-board social design and thus falls in the realm of what is generally considered to be conservative politics – siding with Edmund Burke against Tom Paine, so to speak (see Chapter 5 for more on the relationship between ecologism and conservatism).

So radical greens read off three principal features of the limits to growth message and subscribe to them and their implications wholeheartedly: technological solutions cannot help realize the impossible dream of infinite growth in a finite system; the exponential nature of that growth both underpins its unsustainability and suggests that the limits to growth may become visible rather quicker than we might think; and the immense complexity of the global system leads greens to suggest that our present attempts to deal with environmental problems are both clumsy and superficial.

At the root of all this, of course, is the most profound belief of all: that there *are* limits to growth. The most common criticism of the *Limits to Growth* report is that its predictions as to the likely exhaustion of raw materials (for example) have been proved wildly wrong. This is a point most famously put by Julian Simon and Herman Kahn in their *The Resourceful Earth* (1984), and more recently in an engaging debate between Julian Simon and Norman Myers on various aspects of the limits to growth thesis (Myers and Simon, 1994): 'Conventional "green" beliefs are massively contradicted by the scientific evidence' (Simon in Myers and Simon, 1994, pp. xvii–xviii). Greens have learned to accept the detail of these criticisms while continuing to subscribe to the general principle of the limits to growth thesis. Thus, a contributor to Bunyard and Morgan-Grenville's compilation recognizes that the original report underestimated both the amount of resource reserves to be discovered and the ability of the system to cope in terms of the production of synthetic substitutes, etc., but continues:

> The simple fact is that if we go on using up the earth's nonrenewable resources (its oil, coal, minerals) at the rate we are now, and misusing the earth's renewable resources (its fertile soil, clear water, forests) at the rate we do now, then at some stage in the future the whole system is going to fall apart.
>
> (Bunyard and Morgan-Grenville, 1987, p. 327)

This is the starting-point for thoughts about the sustainable society: that aspirations of ever-increasing growth and consumption cannot be fulfilled because, 'To spread such [American] consumption levels to the rest of the world's expanding numbers would require over 130 times the world output of 1979' (Irvine and Ponton, 1988, p. 25). Thus, 'The concept of scarcity is fundamental … It is rooted in the biophysical realities of a finite planet, ruled and limited by entropy and ecology' (Irvine and Ponton, 1988, p. 26). Dark-green politics is based upon a fundamental commitment to the principle of scarcity as an insurmountable fact of life and the consequent limits to growth imposed by a finite system. In this respect, to hint that radical green thinking is damaged by hitching itself to the *Limits to Growth* report – because of its self-fulfilling prophecy of doom, programmed to collapse by dint of Malthusian reasoning – is rather to miss the point. Green thinkers do believe that present industrial practices are programmed to collapse by virtue of their internal logic, and in this respect they are persuaded by the fundamental message of the limits to growth thesis.

It is worth stressing here a point made in the Introduction: that this 'scientific' element in the green position pushes it well beyond a merely romantic response to the trials and tribulations of industrial society. Greens propose a sustainable society not merely because they think, in terms of some bucolic fantasy, that it would be more pleasant to live in. They believe that science is on their side. This has given rise to a radical green economics that was presaged at the beginning of the century by the so-called 'energy economists' – a story told by Anna Bramwell (1989). She points out that as long ago as 1911 Wilhelm Ostwald wrote that 'the free energy accessible can only decrease, but not increase' (in Bramwell, 1989, p. 64). The most influential contemporary champion of the economics based upon this kind of observation is American economist Herman Daly. Green economics are rooted in our ecological circumstance in a very fundamental way: '[O]ur dependence on the natural world takes two forms – that of a source of low-entropy inputs and that of a sink for high-entropy waste outputs' (Daly, 1992, p. 34).

Daly notes that the first law of thermodynamics states that 'we do not produce or consume anything, we merely rearrange it' – so we cannot produce resources, we can only use them, and they will eventually run out. The second law – that of entropy – has it that 'our rearrangement implies a continual reduction in potential for further use within the system as a whole' (Daly, 1977b, p. 109). This also implies that there is a limit to the use we can make of scarce resources, as well as pointing out that waste (high entropy) is a necessary product of the extraction and use of resources (low entropy). The limits to growth notion is thus the practical reason, as it were, why greens argue for the necessity of a sustainable society. They also present 'social' and 'ethical' reasons (Daly in Ekins, 1986, p. 13), which will be pursued as the chapter progresses. Now, though, we are in a position to sketch the parameters within which dark-greens believe any picture of the sustainable society would have to be drawn.

Possible positions

Various responses to the problem of sustainability are possible, both in political-institutional terms and also in terms of the social and ethical practices that a sustainable society would need to follow. By no means all of the 'solutions' that have been presented over the years are green in the sense in which I think we ought to understand the word – i.e. in the sense in which ecologism has become a political ideology in its own right. In drawing the boundaries for ecologism, we find ourselves excluding from its meaning a number of political postures that have been wrongly associated with it. This has the effect, of course, of narrowing down the range of thoughts and practices that we can link with radical green politics, and thus makes clearer the territory within which it most properly moves.

To my mind no one in this context has been able to (or has had to) improve upon the typology provided by Tim O'Riordan in his book *Environmentalism* (1981, p. 307). O'Riordan suggests that in political-institutional terms there are four principal postures available. First, there is the possibility of a 'new global order', arranged so as to deal with the problems of global co-ordination presented by the international nature of the environmental crisis. Supporters of this position typically claim that the nation-state is both too big and too small to deal effectively with global problems and bemoan the lack of efficacy of the United Nations, which, nevertheless, seems to be the kind of organization on which they would base their new global order. O'Riordan refers to people like Barbara Ward and René Dubos (1972) as supporters of this view, to whom we might now add Gro Harlem Brundtland, after her Brundtland Report of 1987. The United Nations Earth Summit of 1992 was the most spectacular example to date of UN-sponsored attempts to deal with global environmental problems; more governments than ever before were brought together to discuss the issues, and five separate agreements were signed. Although the Summit's success was equivocal (Grubb *et al.*, 1993), 'global order' enthusiasts drew some succour from its achievements.

The second position is described as 'centralized authoritarianism'. This position also takes seriously the existence of an environmental crisis, and its supporters believe that, because no one is likely to succumb voluntarily to the measures needed to deal with it, they will have to be made to do so. The locus of authority is generally seen as the governments of nation-states, and in this respect no major political-institutional changes are held to be necessary. Governments would merely decide upon a course of action leading to sustainability (perhaps protectionism, rationing, population control and restriction of immigration) and would put it into effect regardless of opposition. O'Riordan refers to William Ophuls ('whatever its specific form, the politics of the sustainable society seem likely to move us along the spectrum from libertarianism toward authoritarianism'; 1977, p. 161) and Garrett Hardin as exemplars of this position.

The third position described by O'Riordan is that of the 'authoritarian commune', which is distinguished from the previous position by the scale on which the sustainable society would operate. Institutional structures would be broken down, the locus of decision-making would (in principle) be devolved, but social structures would, of necessity, remain hierarchical. The model, says O'Riordan, is that of the Chinese commune, and he also refers to Heilbroner's *An Enquiry into the Human Prospect* (1974) as a prototype for this kind of thinking. Some might put Edward Goldsmith, co-author of *A Blueprint for Survival* (1972) and editor of *The Ecologist*, in this bracket, but although he appears traditionally hierarchical in some respects – particularly in the context of relations within the family – his support (for example) for forms of participatory democracy disqualifies him from full membership of the authoritarian commune canon.

The final possibility referred to by O'Riordan in his typology is the 'anarchist solution'. He makes his meaning clearer by writing that 'The classic ecocentric proposal is the self-reliant community modelled on anarchist lines' (1981, p. 307). This shares the commune perspective with the previous position and thus envisages a major shift in the focus of authority and decision-making, but differs from it in adopting a left-liberal stance on relations within the community. In political terms at least (and often in material terms as well), O'Riordan's 'anarchist solution' is fundamentally egalitarian and participatory.

How are we to know which of these possibilities – or which combination of them – is properly descriptive of the political-institutional arrangements associated with ecologism? One approach would be to survey what members of the green movement and sympathetic academic backers have actually said about social arrangements in the sustainable society. Although in the Introduction I dissociated the present description of ecologism from explicit links with any real-life political manifestation of it (party or movement), it is impossible to avoid reference to named individuals, whose perspective is – inevitably – partial and particular. In what follows, then, my discussion of the sustainable society will draw upon views expressed by both activists and academics in and around the green movement.

One common theme in the debate is that there is no one form of society which is singularly appropriate to or suitable for sustainability. Martin Ryle has written importantly that '[E]cological limits may limit political choices, but they do not determine them ... A society adapted to ecological constraints ... could take widely varying forms' (Ryle, 1988, pp. 7–8). This is a point of view recently endorsed by Luke Martell, who writes that

> while ecology implies some forms of social and political arrangements rather than others it also draws on older traditions to work out which are preferable on these grounds and to answer non-environmental questions to do with issues such as justice and liberty.
>
> (Martell, 1994, p. 159)

(Many greens will of course blench at the suggestion that environmental issues have nothing to do with justice and liberty.)

Although the indeterminacy of ecological criteria for social ones seems to be the dominant opinion at present, there are alternative views. What is crucial for understanding green politics in relation to other forms of political thought is that the non-human natural world always provides the principal context for deciding questions of political-institutional 'design':

> an ecocentric approach regards the question of our proper place in the rest of nature as logically prior to the question of what are the most appropriate social and political arrangements for human communities. That is, the determination of social and political questions must proceed from, or at least be consistent with, an adequate determination of this most fundamental question.
>
> (Eckersley, 1992, p. 28)

This general statement hides at least three possible types of position, each of which is consistent with Eckersley's lexical ordering. First, social principles are sometimes deduced from ones found in 'nature'. I remarked on the difficulties associated with deriving lessons from nature in Chapter 1, and John Barry provides a useful reminder: 'non-human nature gives us no determinate prescriptions about how we ought to live, despite the attempts of some deep ecologists and bioregionalists to argue otherwise' (Barry, 1994, p. 383). Second, some radical greens urge us to adapt our social aspirations to the constraints and opportunities provided by a closer relationship with the land of our immediate surroundings – this is a kind of 'materialist ecologism'. I shall have more to say on this shortly under the heading of 'bioregionalism'. Third, there is the view that dealing with the multi-layered and interrelating nature of environmental problems implies that political institutions should somehow 'match' the layers and approximate as far as possible to the interrelations.

Nothing in Eckersley's statement commits her, of course, to deriving social and political arrangements from 'natural' ones (indeed, she explicitly opposes such a position: 1992, pp. 59–60), but there is a suggestion that some arrangements would *not* be consistent with proper understanding of 'our proper place in the rest of nature'. This seems to imply, in turn, that some social and political arrangements have unsustainability (to use a shorthand description) built into them. If they do, then this also implies that some arrangements could have positive repercussions for sustainability and that, therefore, Ryle is overstating his case in claiming that a society adapted to ecological constraints could take 'widely varying forms'.

In sum, we might say that the political and social options available are narrowed down by recognizing, first, that some ways of life are more sustainable than others, and, second, that some institutional forms are more likely to deal effectively with environmental problems than others. As regards the second, Ryle suggests that it is possible to imagine a sustainable 'authoritarian or post-capitalist society' (Ryle, 1988, p. 7). There is, though, some evidence to suggest that democratic institutions and a 'quite heavily circumscribed market economy that is scaled down in terms of material-energy throughput' (Eckersley, 1992, p. 184) are more conducive to sustainable living than Ryle's putative capitalist authoritarianism. Authoritarianism is found wanting because the information flows needed for effective policy-making are missing, because in the long term, authoritarian regimes lack legitimacy (Dryzek, 1987, and Paehlke, 1988, for example), and because capitalism needs curbing due to its 'expansionary dynamics' (Eckersley, 1992, p. 121) and the short-termism associated with market logic.

These considerations suggest that there is something about ecologism – despite Martell's objection (1994, p. 159) – that pushes it irrevocably towards the left of the political spectrum, and this view is strengthened if we make a distinction between the *objectives* of ecologism and its informing *principles*. Most of those who argue for a non-determinate relationship between ecology and socio-political form focus upon the objective of sustainability. They then argue that the green stress on this objective leaves them (greens) open to the charge that it (the objective) takes precedence over the means of arriving at it. If it could be shown that authoritarianism was more effective in this sense than democracy, then that would be enough to privilege authoritarianism ahead of democracy.

I have already suggested that the conclusion that authoritarianism is more functional for sustainability than democracy is quite likely wrong, and if we focus, in any case, on principles rather than objectives, then linking ecologism with authoritarianism seems even more implausible. As I pointed out in Chapter 1, Robyn Eckersley argues that ecologism is fundamentally emancipatory in its focus on the self-determination of all entities, including humans (Eckersley, 1992, pp. 53–5). This stress on self-determination outlaws authoritarianism as a matter of principle; on this reading it makes no more sense to say that ecologism is a friend of authoritarianism than it would do to say that liberalism is a friend of authoritarianism. (I shall say more on the relationship between authoritarianism, democracy and ecologism in the next chapter.)

In my view; then, there is considerably less room for manoeuvre within ecologism as far as social and political arrangements are concerned than commentators such as Ryle and Martell suggest. This is not to say, though, that the relationship between ecologism and socio-political form is univocal: there is plenty of room within a broadly left-emancipatory framework for disagreement. So much will be clear from what follows.

More problems with growth

'The notion that the living standards of the rich countries are attainable by all countries is pure fantasy,' write Irvine and Ponton (1988, p. 21), thus suggesting that there are physical limits to growth. As noted above, though, greens also typically believe that there are social and ethical limits to growth. It has been argued, for example, by some green economists that indiscriminate growth exacerbates problems that it is intended to solve – particularly in the context of inflation and unemployment. It is suggested that unemployment is significantly the result of technological advances that reduce the labour/output ratio. The traditional idea that rates of unemployment can be brought down only by increased growth is challenged at two levels: first, that further growth and subsequent investment in the same direction (i.e. labour-saving technology) can result only in more unemployment, not less; and second, that the rates of necessary growth projected by traditional political interests are unsustainable anyway. Either way unemployment in a growth-oriented economy at a British (or comparable) level of development is liable to structural increase, despite temporary fluctuations. The social costs of unemployment are unacceptable, say greens, and the aspiration of unlimited growth, being part of the problem, can hardly be a part of the solution.

At the same time greens argue that the economics of growth are inherently inflationary. In the first place, and building on the position that scarcity is a fundamental and unavoidable datum on a finite planet, they suggest that as resources are depleted there will inevitably be upward pressure on prices. Similarly, the costs of economic growth (some of its 'externalities'), which have, up until now, been largely ignored, will soon have to be taken into account and charged for. This, too, will increase the cost of living. Paul Ekins writes that 'environmental "goods" (e.g. clean air, pure water), which at a lower level of economic activity were effectively "free", will come to have an economic cost, resulting in further inflationary pressure' (1986, p. 11). Indeed, among traditional neo-classical (but pro-environment) economists, the 'internalization of externalities' has come to be seen as the best way forward for environmental protection (see, for example, Pearce *et al.*, 1989).

From a green perspective, then, the problems of inflation and unemployment are (or will be) the products of growth and so cannot be solved by more of it. And the point above about the coming necessity of including the cost of cleaning up dirty water in economic projections also serves to illustrate green concerns about traditional ways of measuring the strength of national economies. An increase, for example, in the Gross National Product (GNP) is invariably seen as a good thing, but, as Jonathon Porritt points out, 'Many of those goods and services [measured by GNP] are not beneficial to people: increased spending on crime, on pollution, on the many human casualties of our society; increased spending because of waste or planned obsolescence; increased spending because of growing bureaucracies' (Porritt, 1984a, p. 121).

More particularly, Paul Ekins (1986, pp. 32–5) points to four reasons why greens (and not a few others) consider GNP to be an inadequate measure of the health of an economy. First, it ignores the production that takes place in the non-monetarized part of the economy – household work, social work such as caring for the old and sick that takes place within the family, home-based production and the myriad networks of production and exchange associated with the underground, or 'black', economy. The value of such informal production in some countries has been calculated at some 60 per cent of GNP (Ekins, 1986, p. 34). Second, GNP calculations give us no idea of the distribution of production or its fruits. Third, they give no indication, either, of the sustainability of the economic practices that contribute to production. For example, the American farming system generates huge profits (for some farmers) but is highly inefficient in terms of the ratio between the energy that is put into the system and the calorific value of the food it produces. Greens would question the wisdom of using economic indicators that pay no mind to the future viability of the system that they are measuring. Lastly, as pointed out above in the context of the clean water debate, GNP ignores the costs of production – particularly the environmental costs.

In the light of these criticisms, the fact that GNP is still the principal indicator of the health of national economies is, for greens, symptomatic of the myopia induced by what they will see as an obsession with economic growth. In their view, the success of a system of production and exchange can only really be judged once alternative indicators are developed. Victor Anderson has suggested that a start could be made by including 'unpaid domestic labour, non-money transactions outside the household, and environmental deterioration' in the calculation, as well as starting with the net national product rather than the gross national product – 'i.e. GNP minus capital depreciation' (Anderson, 1991, p. 39). From a green point of view, expenditure on environmental protection and on compensation for environmental damage, the costs of excessive urbanization and centralization (such as travel and trade costs) and the money spent on dealing with what greens see as the problems brought about by 'industrial society' all should be removed from GNP calculations so as to give a measure of the quality of life as well as its quantity.

Even this Adjusted National Product (ANP), though, argues Anderson, would not provide an adequate picture of welfare in any given society because of its one-dimensional concentration on economic factors. He suggests that financial indicators need to be accompanied by two further sets which he calls 'social' and 'environmental' indicators (Anderson, 1991, pp. 55–64 and 65–74). The former include factors such as primary school enrolment figures, illiteracy, mortality and unemployment rates, and telephones per thousand people (Anderson, 1991, p. 61). The latter include deforestation and population figures, carbon dioxide emissions and energy consumption data (Anderson, 1991, p. 74). Anderson's own deployment of these indicators across fourteen countries at various stages of development leads him to the following conclusion: '[S]ocial conditions are generally improving, and in the short term this is likely to continue … In the medium term, environmental deterioration threatens to put these social improvements into reverse' (Anderson, 1991, p. 91). All of this has led Jonathon Porritt, in typically epigrammatic style, to say that: 'progress in the future may consist in finding ways of reducing GNP' (Porritt, 1984a, p. 121).

It is in this last respect that the physical, social and ethical objections of greens to the economy and society of indiscriminate growth come together: such an economy and such a society, they say, are not very nice places in which to live. Side-stepping the obvious objection that societies where there is no growth at all are hardly a delight either, greens claim that we are stunted ethically by the growth economy's refusal to take the quality of life of future generations seriously and by its easy preparedness to take the Earth as resource rather than as blessing. We produce indiscriminately and consume voraciously, and our status and aspirations are largely judged and dictated by the wealth at our disposal. Greens believe that lives in the growth economy will tend away from the elegant and towards the grubby and materialistic. Conversely, they suggest that a society orientated around sustainable growth would be a less greedy and more pleasant place in which to live, and if this seems hard to credit, then greens might quote John Stuart Mill as a temporary bulwark against disbelief:

> It is scarcely necessary to remark that a stationary condition of capital and population implies no stationary state of human improvement. There would be as much scope as ever for all kinds of mental culture, and moral and social progress; as much room for improving the Art of Living and much more likelihood of its being improved.
>
> (in Meadows *et al.*, 1974, p. 175)

Questioning consumption

Political ecologists argue, then, for a contraction in economic growth or, more accurately, in what economist Herman Daly calls 'throughput' (1992, p. 36). The components of throughput are resource depletion, production, depreciation (involving consumption) and pollution. Of these four, it is probably production that receives most attention when commentators consider the bases and implications of the sustainable society, but it seems to me that consumption provides the most used starting-point for discussion. In the first place, this is because the other three terms are founded upon the existence and persistence of consumption: consumption implies depletion implies production implies waste or pollution. And second, the picture of the Good Life that the political ideology of ecologism paints for us is differentiated from most other pictures precisely because of its arguing for less consumption. Not only does this mark off ecologism from most other political ideologies but it also helps to distinguish it from light-green environmentalism. Jonathon Porritt, for example, writes in dark-green rather than light-green mode when he says that 'A low-energy strategy means a low-consumption economy; we can do more with less, but we'd be better off doing less with less' (1984a, p. 174). In this context, to concentrate on consumption and its implications is both to help mark out ecologism's proper territory and to keep in mind that in this respect at least it comprises 'a sharp break with the principles of the modern era' (Ophuls, 1977, p. 164).

As with growth, the green questioning of consumption has both a pragmatic and an elegiac content. Irvine and Ponton suggest that 'an attitude of "enough" must replace that of "more" ' (1988, p. 15), and Porritt, likewise, argues that 'It's time for the economics of enough' (1984a, p. 125), not only because they feel that present rates of consumption are physically unsustainable but also because they are unseemly. They balk at the production and purchase of what they consider to be unnecessary items, and press for a life based on 'voluntary simplicity' (Porritt, 1984a, p. 204). The 'middle way between indulgence and poverty' (Porritt, 1984a, p. 204), which would be the way of the sustainable society, might be uncomfortable for some: 'Of course people will still have washing-machines (as long as they are energy-efficient). But electric toothbrushes and carving-knives? That's another matter!' (Bunyard and Morgan-Grenville, 1987, p. 335).

Essential, then, to ecologism's picture of the sustainable society is reduced consumption (in profligate 'advanced' industrial countries, at any rate), and equally essential is the idea that, while this might involve a reduced material standard of living, such sacrifice will be more than made up for by the benefits to be gained. Greens will always distinguish between quantity and quality: 'in terms of crude material wealth, we're not likely to get any wealthier. But ... what matters now is the quality of wealth' (Porritt, 1984a, p. 124). In similar vein, Edward Goldsmith reckons that the specious satisfactions of consumption can and should be replaced by 'Satisfactions of a non-material kind ... social ones' (1988, pp. 197–8), and for Bunyard and Morgan-Grenville (or one of their contributors) the sky is the limit:

> Judged by illusory standards of wealth we might well be 'poorer' in a Green future – but we would, in reality, have a higher standard of living, better food, healthier bodies, rewarding work, good companionship, cleaner air, greater self-reliance, more supportive communities and, above all, a safer world to live in.
>
> (Bunyard and Morgan-Grenville, 1987, p. 335)

Given the centrality of reduced consumption to the dark-green project, for all the reasons given above, it is surprising that so few of ecologism's theorists (as far as I am aware) have paid much serious attention to the role of advertising in reproducing the habits and practices of consumption that they seek to criticize. Irvine and Ponton prove themselves exceptions to this general rule in pointing out that 'Linking mass production and mass consumption is the advertising industry' (1988, p. 62). It seems to me that in this respect there may be a political strategy lurking in marketing's murky entrails – exposure of the social irresponsibility (from the point of view of sustainability) of the advertising industry would be a concrete way of raising the issue of consumption (well beyond, and in opposition to, the phenomenon of green consumerism) and making clearer what a sustainable society might look like. As Irvine and Ponton go on to say:

Notions such as durability, reduced or shared consumption, or substi-
tuting non-material pleasures for the use of objects, conflict with the
requirements of mass marketing. Advertising is tied to an expanding
economy, the one thing that we, living on a finite planet, must avoid.
(Irvine and Ponton, 1988, p. 63)

In this sense, basic nostrums of the green movement come together in
the same place: the finitude of the planet, the need to restrict growth, the
consequent need to reduce consumption and the necessity for calling into
question the practices (in this case advertising) that help reproduce the
growth economy.

Questioning consumption: need

Reducing material consumption is an integral part of ecologism's project
and so the green movement has a profound political and intellectual
problem on its hands. It is faced, in the first place, with persuading
potential supporters that this is a desirable aspiration, and it is saddled
with a series of intellectual arguments for its position that presently
appear too weak to do the job required. The assertion, noted above, that
a society organized around reduced consumption just *would* be more
pleasurable to live in seems unlikely – in present circumstances – to cut
the necessary ice. Likewise, the most favoured alternative strategy, the
building of a theory of need, is notoriously difficult to carry out. How did
Bunyard and Morgan-Grenville, above, arrive at the conclusion that
washing machines are legitimate objects but that electric toothbrushes are
not? There is evidently a theory (or more likely an intuition) of need at
work here, but how is it to be persuasively expressed? Paul Ekins, for one,
thinks that it is important for the green movement to answer this query –
'The question of human needs is of absolutely central significance to the
New Economics' (Ekins, 1986, p. 55) – but most expressions of theories of
need are far too vague to be of much use: 'needs being those things that
are essential to our survival and to civilized human existence, wants being
the extras that serve to satisfy our desires' (Porritt, 1984a, p. 196).

The problem with such a formulation is that, while it gives us an idea
of the general differences between needs and wants, it does not help us
concretely to fill out their content. At the same time, to be able to fill out
their content in any universal sense presupposes that 'fundamental human
needs are finite, few and classifiable' (Ekins, 1986, p. 49). The obvious
objection to this – that needs are historically and culturally mediated –
can be partly met by saying that

common sense, along with some socio-cultural sensitivity, surely points to the fact that the needs for Subsistence, Protection, Affection, Understanding, Participation, Creation and Leisure have existed since the origins of *homo habilis* and, undoubtedly, since the appearance of *homo sapiens*.

(Max-Neef, 1992, p. 203)

Max-Neef goes on to talk of the distinction between 'needs' and 'satisfiers' – needs are permanent and satisfiers are contingent and therefore open to negotiation (Max-Neef, 1992, pp. 206–7).

But how far does this help? The distinction just pushes the problem back one place. We might all be able to agree on certain 'basic needs' (food, drink, clothing, shelter) but the 'satisfiers' are another matter, and they are precisely what have to be negotiated. As Jonathon Porritt remarks, 'We all need to get from A to B; some people insist they can manage such a feat only in the back of a Rolls Royce' (1984a, p. 196). Just what size car is acceptable? Is a car acceptable at all?

If the needs/wants problem seems presently intractable, it is enough to notice for our purpose – that of identifying the principal features of the radical green sustainable society – that the emphasis on reduced consumption brings up the question sooner or later, and that therefore the distinction between needs and wants is one of the intellectual features of the various pictures of such a society. At the same time, the sense of scarcity that informs the whole discussion also generates another characteristic of the sustainable society to which most of its supporters will subscribe: a tendency towards the egalitarian distribution of the material wealth that is available. Thus, more fully, Irvine and Ponton explain that 'If there are limits to the needs for which society can provide, their fair distribution is even more urgent ... Limiting differentials between people is as essential as limiting economic growth and technological innovation' (Irvine and Ponton, 1988, p. 80). In this respect, the sustainable society of dark-green politics approximates closely to socialistic conceptions of equality in calling for reduced differentials, although it is clear in other respects that the stress on equality of opportunity means that there will be room for differentials, 'fairly' arrived at.

Questioning consumption: population

So we can identify a green belief in the benefits and necessity of reducing levels of material consumption, and the problems associated with convincing enough of us (for it to make any appreciable difference) to do so. But greens have another way of reducing consumption – one that does not involve intricate argumentation. Porritt is most clear in this respect: 'In terms of reducing overall consumption, there's nothing more effective than reducing the number of people doing the consuming' (1984a, p. 190). Greens are aware that some people in some countries consume much more than other people in other countries, and that therefore it is far too simplistic to argue for across-the-board reductions: 'Per capita energy consumption in the United States is two and one-half times the European average and thousands of times that of many Third World countries' (Tokar, 1994, pp. 75–6). Nevertheless, the option of population reduction is rather more contentious than it is elegant, constituting as it does a specific aspect of the general green position that even present population levels are unsustainable, let alone projected future levels. Experience suggests that this message is a difficult one to swallow for very many people.

The 1999 Green Party of England and Wales *Manifesto for a Sustainable Society* states that 'growth in human numbers is probably the greatest long-term threat to achieving ecological stability either locally or throughout the world' (1999, P 100). It is certainly central to most radical green pictures of the sustainable society that population levels would be lower than they presently are, although there is disagreement about what levels actually would be sustainable. Irvine and Ponton put the level for Britain at about 30 million people, which is (as they say) about half its present level (1988, p. 22). Bunyard and Morgan-Grenville, however, suggest that Britain could sustain 55 million people more or less self-reliantly – but only if we could all first be converted to vegetarianism (1987, pp. 94–6). Edward Goldsmith has put the globally sustainable figure at 3,500 million ('and probably a good deal less'; 1972, p. 57), which means somehow losing about 1,800 million of the present world population (Lutz, 1994, p. 465).

And, of course, this is exactly the problem: how to 'lose' 1,800 million people. In the furthest reaches of some groups associated with the green movement, draconian measures for solving this problem have been advanced. As reported in Chapter 2, the Earth First! group in the United States of America has suggested that epidemics such as AIDS should be allowed to run their course so as to help rid us of excess population. These are the sorts of pronouncements that have hampered the green movement's attempts to get its population policies taken seriously; indeed, there appears to be a sense in which the mere mention of population control brings to mind bloodied seal pups, quickly followed by the suggestion that this is not for human beings.

At the same time, the left has been fighting a running battle with Malthus and his supporters ever since 1792 and the publication of *An Essay on the Principle of Population*, and they will generally respond to the green position by arguing that starvation is caused primarily by uneven distribution of resources rather than by their absolute limitation. Greens will take note of this response, but in the same way in which they will point to the absolute limits on resource extraction despite temporary respites gained by our ingenuity in extracting them, they will also suggest that there are limits to the population that can be sustainably and comfortably maintained on a finite planet.

Despite the contributions of groups such as Earth First!, greens usually suggest that population control and reduction, although considered absolutely necessary, are a matter for negotiation rather than imposition. Thus the *Green Party Manifesto for a Sustainable Society* rejects 'repressive or coercive population control measures' (1999, P 100) and Arne Naess in his Schumacher Lecture of 1987 recognized that reaching a sustainable population might take hundreds of years, because 'It remains vitally important to reject coercive measures as an unacceptable and morally repugnant infringement of human rights' (Porritt, 1984a, p. 193). The kinds of tactic that have therefore been suggested within the green movement are summed up by Irvine and Ponton:

> There could be payments for periods of non-pregnancy and non-birth (a kind of no claims bonus); tax benefits for families with fewer than two children; sterilization bonuses; withdrawal of maternity and similar benefits after a second child; larger pensions for people with fewer than two children; free, easily available family planning; more funds for research into means of contraception, especially for men; an end to fertility research and treatment; a more realistic approach to abortion; the banning of surrogate motherhood and similar practices; and the promotion of equal opportunities for women in all areas of life.
>
> (Irvine and Ponton, 1988, p. 23)

With respect to the last point, the authors stress that 'There is a happy correlation between women's liberation and population control' (Irvine and Ponton, 1988, p. 23), and the 1994 World Population Conference in Cairo broadly endorsed such a view. As for the rest, while it is clear that there are sticks as well as carrots at work (and that measures such as 'sterilization bonuses' have often proved unwieldy, offensive and open to abuse), such tactics are a far cry from the culling feared by the greens' opponents and recommended by some deep ecologists.

However, it would be wrong so easily to absolve green strategy with respect to population control from any potential connection with repression. It has been suggested by some of the movement's supporters that communities (whether nation-states or some other political-institutional formation) will need to be protected from population growth by some form of immigration control. This was most notoriously suggested by Garrett Hardin in the wake of his development of the lifeboat ethic, which had it that if there was enough room for only ten people to survive in a lifeboat then the eleventh (generally read as Third World populations) would have to be thrown out. This is not standard fare in the green movement today, but it has its echoes, I suggest, in some remarks about immigration control.

Dave Foreman, co-founder of Earth First!, has been berated for saying in a notorious interview that 'letting the USA be an overflow valve for problems in Latin America is not solving a thing. It's just putting more pressure on the resources we have in the USA' (in Bookchin and Foreman, 1991, p. 108). Although he has publicly retracted this statement, he still has '[A] little troll in the back of [his] brain [which] keeps whispering nagging questions. Who is really being helped by unlimited immigration? Is it sustainable? Does it actually exacerbate social and ecological problems here and in Latin America?' (in Bookchin and Foreman, 1991, p. 109). In Britain, Jonathon Porritt announced that 'The strictly logical position, as far as ecologists are concerned, is to keep immigration at the lowest possible level while remaining sensitive to the needs of refugees, split families, political exiles etc.' (1984a, p. 191), and Edward Goldsmith recommended that 'a community must be relatively closed' (1988, p. 203). The repressive tribalism and exclusion that this could generate is absolutely clear in Goldsmith: 'a certain number of "foreigners" could be allowed to settle but again ... they would not, thereby, partake in the running of the community until such time as the citizens elected them to be of their number' (1988, p. 203).

These remarks make rather a nonsense of some other green positions, such as that 'Greens celebrate the diversity of culture in a multi-cultural society', and that 'our goal is equality of opportunity for members of all ethnic communities' (*British Green Party Manifesto*, 1987, pp. 14–15). It is hard to see how Porritt could have his way of keeping immigration at the lowest possible level and at the same time argue that this should '*in no way* be discriminatory in terms of race or colour' (1984a, p. 191; emphasis in the original). Immigration controls just do discriminate in terms of race or colour (or in terms of difference, generally). Some would argue that the really pressing problem (for greens) is not immigration but that of stabilizing and then reducing the exploding world population.

Questioning consumption: technology

Pretty soon, discussion of the green sustainable society raises the issue of the role and place of technology. To the extent that green politics is a challenge to the norms and practices of contemporary science and society, to the extent that it will blame scientific development (in a certain direction) for many of the ills it believes we now suffer, and to the extent, finally that it attacks the belief that more of the same will cure those ills, technology is always under the critical green microscope. It is this, of course, that has led those outside the movement (and not a few, it has to be said, within it) to view it as anti-technological and therefore (a non sequitur) as a call to return to a pre-technological age.

This is far too simplistic. The most that can be said, I have concluded, about the green movement's attitude to nineteenth- and twentieth-century technology (which is what I shall principally mean by 'technology' from now on) is that it is ambivalent and that, more specifically, it depends on the kind of technology you are talking about. Rudolf Bahro of Germany for instance, was (before his death in 1998) pretty much against most forms of technology; Jonathon Porritt is in favour of certain sorts, but generally likes to remain agnostic; and Brian Tokar of the USA is suspicious of it. What can be said, it seems to me, is that wholehearted acceptance of any form of technology disqualifies one from membership of the dark-green canon; thus André Gorz and Alvin Toffler, for instance, in substantially basing their Utopias on technology, do not adopt radical green stances towards it. Put differently, although much attention has been focused on green attitudes to technology, greens are likely to want the spotlight turned elsewhere: more specifically towards the moral (and sometimes spiritual) changes that they conceive to be necessary for the practice of sustainable societies. We should remember that greens are forever suspicious of the 'technological fix', and to this extent suspicion towards technology in general is a fundamental feature of the green intellectual make-up.

We can see how this works for greens by their distinguishing between what Edward Goldsmith calls the 'real world' and the 'surrogate world' – the former comprising things like trees and topsoil, and the latter being the world that we make or fashion (1988, pp. 185ff.). Greens will most usually gravitate towards what they conceive to be the authenticity of the 'real world' and would probably like to have it stay mainly as it is. Robert Goodin gives an account of this sort of sentiment in terms of a 'green theory of value'. As we saw in Chapter 2, Goodin's theory 'links the value of things to some naturally occurring properties in the things themselves' (1992, p. 24), and the upshot of this is that the traditional English village is more valuable than a modern megalopolis such as Los Angeles. This is not so much because St Mary Mead (Goodin's example, drawn from Agatha Christie) is 'natural' (evidently it is not) but because of the 'modesty of its creation' (Goodin, 1992, p. 52). This could be read as a privileging of the real world against the surrogate one, and green attitudes to technology must be seen in this context. Allaby and Bunyard have captured the picture well: 'to the environmentalist nuclear power is almost certain to be unacceptable, overseas travel by jet aircraft is likely to raise moral qualms, and microprocessors are viewed with a distinct feeling of unease' (1980, p. 63).

This ambivalence can be instructively expressed by referring to the issue of recycling. Evidently the technology exists to recycle large amounts of 'waste' material (newspapers, bottles, etc.) and make it useful again. This is probably the kind of activity most often associated with green politics, and it is true that members of the green movement will often base their pictures of the sustainable society on such strategies: 'We have already suggested that the key to pollution control is not dispersal but recycling' (Goldsmith, 1972, p. 43), and, 'District Councils will be required to recover for recycling at least 60 per cent of recyclable domestic waste within 5 years [of the election of a Green government]' (*Green Party Manifesto for a Sustainable Society*, 1999, NR 412).

In the wider context of the green demand for reduced consumption, however, this is clearly not enough, and some greens will be worried that excessive reliance on recycling will shift the onus away from the recognition that more profound changes are required. The emphasis should be on reducing consumption rather than recycling that which has already been consumed. Thus, in a formulation to which I have already referred:

> The fiction of combining present levels of consumption with 'limitless recycling' is more characteristic of the technocratic vision than of an ecological one. Recycling itself uses resources, expends energy, creates thermal pollution; on the bottom line, it's just an industrial activity like all the others. Recycling is both useful and necessary – but it is an illusion to imagine that it provides any basic answers.
>
> (Porritt, 1984a, p. 183)

Greens will insist that in this connection Porritt's basic answers can be provided only by 'A reduction in the total amount of resources we are consuming' (Irvine and Ponton, 1988, p. 28), and by answering the following questions (and particularly the second) from Brian Tokar in the affirmative: 'If something cannot be manufactured, built or grown without causing irreparable ecological damage, can't we strive to create something to take its place, or simply decide to do without it?' (1994, p. 80). The option of doing without things (which is not, interestingly, mentioned in the 1999 *Green Party Manifesto for a Sustainable Society*) is a direct result of radical greens demanding reduced consumption – a demand that consistently recognizes that even appropriate use of technology is a holding operation rather than an assault on the principal issues.

While there is some ambivalence over the green attitude to technology's capability of dealing with the problem of limited resources, there is even more disagreement over its general role in the sustainable society. We might wonder, for instance, what kinds of technology will be allowed in order to cope with the demands of defending green societies from potential or actual aggressors. Some green thinkers will side-step the issue, of course, by arguing that sustainable societies will be basically peaceful ones anyway. Others will advocate non-violent civil resistance, drawing on practices followed, for example, during the 1980s anti-nuclear actions and demonstrations. This is fine as long as one is not fired upon, or is prepared to die defenceless if one is.

But most green scenarios for defence involve some variation of the 'hedgehog principle' – that the attacked population makes itself as prickly and uncomfortable for the invading forces as possible: 'A high enough level of non-cooperation, civil disobedience and sabotage,' suggests Brian Tokar, 'should be sufficient to make any country ungovernable' (1994, p. 128). This may be true, but civil disobedience and sabotage in the face of an aggressor willing to use force, if they are not to be enormously wasteful of human life, can make high-technology demands. How far would a green society be prepared to go along the road of weapons technology and its associated spin-offs?

Again, it has been suggested more positively that, far from being a *bête noire*, technology can make more palatable the transition to, and practice of, more localized and frugal forms of living. One of the major fears of observers outside the green movement is that its picture of localized politics smacks of a petty parochialism, which would be both undesirable and unpleasant to live with. But would not information technology reduce the likelihood of this? Is this not precisely the sort of thing that Edward Goldsmith was thinking of when he wrote of 'the technological infrastructure of a decentralised society' (Goldsmith, 1972, p. 86)? Greens will often be heard contending that one of the beauties of modern technology is that it is ideally suited to decentralized forms of politics, and the vision of the computer terminal in every home is just one expression of this. Jonathon Porritt, for one, appears enthusiastic about the possibilities as he advocates 'smaller, more self-reliant communities': 'with modern communications technology, there need be no fear of a return to the mean-minded parochialism of pre-industrial Britain' (1984a, p. 166). In this respect we would seem entitled to agree with William Ophuls when he contends that 'The picture of the frugal society that thus emerges resembles something like the city-state form of civilization, but on a much higher and more sophisticated technological base' (1977, p. 168).

However, it would be wrong to leave green thoughts on the general role of technology in the sustainable society at this Toffleresque level. Just as Porritt worries about the resource use and waste associated with recycling technology, so others in the movement worry about the environmental implications of his information technology society: many of the processes involved in microchip production, for example, are anything but environmentally benign. Brian Tokar observes that 'electronics manufacture, underneath its clean facade, is a series of dangerous chemical processes' (Tokar, 1994, p. 80), and these processes involve the creation of more and more compounds of which the 'natural' world has no evolutionary experience, so reducing the likelihood of their being safely broken down. Tokar continues: 'The "information society" does not use any fewer goods; it simply seeks to better hide the consequences of their production' (Tokar, 1994, p. 81). In this respect, some greens will always adopt an attitude of suspicion towards the so-called surrogate world.

Energy

If reduced consumption rather than more technological devices is the answer to the problems raised by the absolute scarcity of resources, then greens will point out that the same must apply to the use of energy. Energy is, of course, a resource, and, to the extent that present global energy policies rely principally on non-renewable sources of energy, it is also a limited resource. Nuclear power itself is produced from the limited resource of uranium and so seems unlikely to solve the problems brought about by resource scarcity. At the same time, while actual resource levels might be quite high, *available* non-renewable energy resource levels will be somewhat lower. This is because, in the first place, the cost of extraction (it is argued by greens) will eventually reach unacceptable heights; and second, there must come a point where, as Herman Daly puts it, it will cost as much energy 'to mine a ton of coal as can be got from a ton of coal' (1977b, p. 111).

Beyond the problem of the limits of non-renewable energy resources, greens are also typically wary of the use of such resources for the environmental damage they can cause. Nuclear energy is potentially highly polluting, the problems of disposing of even low-level waste (often referred to as the nuclear industry's 'Achilles' heel') have not been satisfactorily solved, and nuclear power stations under normal operating circumstances might just be a source of leukaemia. Likewise, fossil-fuel power stations notoriously contribute to the greenhouse effect and are one of the causes of acid rain. Technological abatement of these latter problems is possible: 'Strict pollution controls would reduce the environmental effects of burning hydrocarbons to less than 20 per cent of their present level' (Bunyard and Morgan-Grenville, 1987, p. 158), but such strategies are subject to the same kind of criticism advanced by Jonathon Porritt in connection with recycling.

In the face of the perceived disadvantages of relying for energy on limited stocks of polluting and dangerous non-renewable resources, greens usually base their energy strategy around renewable sources of energy, conservation of energy – 'The most important energy source of all is conservation' (Porritt, 1984a, p. 175) – and reduced consumption, of both energy and the durable objects that it helps us produce. Renewable energy sources are argued to be desirable because they are in principle unlimited (although notoriously difficult to capture and store in any great quantities), they are relatively environmentally benign, and they are suited to the decentralized forms of living often recommended by political ecologists. In all these respects they speak to the basic demands of the green sustainable society. It is worth remarking, however, that in one respect they do not. The technology associated with renewable energy sources (windmills, barrages) is often highly complex and, in the case of the production of solar cells, polluting. Remembering the objections to the technologies associated with recycling and information technology, we can see that the issue of alternative energy sources provides us with yet another specific example of the ambivalence with which greens will view the role of technology.

Few greens pretend, however, that the energy policy referred to above will produce the fantastic quantities of energy presently required, let alone cope with the dizzying projections associated with the developing nations: 'Dreams of powering the current lifestyles of the industrialized countries from alternative energy sources are illusory' (Irvine and Ponton, 1988, p. 53). This means that demand for energy will have to lessen beyond the reductions brought about by price increases and improved conservation policies. At this point, the green assertion that sustainability will involve reducing material consumption meets the energy problem. Reduced energy use, for dark-greens, involves reduced production, and reduced production involves reduced consumption. The point is that 'we can satisfy our needs today from these sources [wind, water, sun] without robbing future generations of their energy supply' (Irvine and Ponton, 1988, p. 55), but we cannot satisfy what greens would regard as our greed. Once again, the distinction between needs and wants is raised, and once again we see that the green picture of the sustainable society is buttressed by the necessity and desirability of reduced material consumption.

Trade and travel

Consistent with the principles of self-reliance and communitarian decentralization that inform some versions of the sustainable society, greens have unfashionable views on the issues of trade and travel. Before discussing this in a little detail it is important to be clear that self-reliance is not the same as self-sufficiency and that greens go to some lengths to distinguish the two. Despite green politics often being identified with the self-sufficiency commune movement (quite properly in a sense, given that many of its members practise such self-sufficiency and that some of its major theorists – e.g. Rudolf Bahro – come very close to envisaging green societies in this way), my understanding is that green politics is most generally seen to be organized around principles of self-reliance rather than self-sufficiency.

What is the difference? Self-sufficiency can be described as 'a state of absolute economic independence', while self-reliance is best understood as 'a state of relative independence' (Bunyard and Morgan-Grenville, 1987, p. 334). In terms of the importance of the notion of self-reliance to the politics of ecology, Paul Ekins goes so far as to claim that, along with theories of need (already covered) and a reconceptualization of work (see below), it is one of the three pillars of the New Economic framework (1986, p. 97). According to Johan Galtung, the basic rules that the theory of self-reliance gives rise to are:

> produce what you need using your own resources, internalising the challenge this involves, growing with the challenges, neither giving the most challenging tasks' positive externalities to somebody else on whom you become dependent, nor exporting negative externalities to somebody else to whom you do damage and who may become dependent on you.
>
> (in Ekins, 1986, p. 101)

On this reading, trade is something to be carried out as an exception rather than as a rule. There is nothing in the theory of self-reliance that forbids trade, but it certainly aims to shift the onus of justification away from those who would reduce it and on to those who would maximize it.

It would be wrong, then, to characterize greens as recommending complete economic independence – they are perfectly aware that 'There are always goods or services that cannot be generated or provided locally regionally or nationally' (Ekins, 1986, p. 52). The ground rule, however, would be that 'self-reliance starts with the idea of producing things yourself rather than getting them through exchange' (Ekins, 1986, p. 104). Imagining this rule being followed amounts to imagining an important part of the economic and political framework within which a green sustainable society would operate.

Trade is viewed with suspicion by greens on four grounds. In the first place (not necessarily a green reason) it is a site of the exercise of political and economic power and an easy way to exchange self-determination for dependence; second, it encourages frippery and helps to turn wants into needs (do we need kiwi fruits? but, then, do we need tea?); third, patterns of trade end up being notoriously wasteful of resources, as (for example) tomatoes are grown on the island of Guernsey, exported, and then sometimes shipped back for consumption; and fourth, reliance on one or two products for export can render economies vulnerable to a drop in prices or a general worsening of the terms of trade.

It is this last point that leads Johan Galtung to suggest that, if trade is to take place, 'one field of production – production for basic needs [food, clothing, shelter, energy, health, education, home defence] – should be carried out in such a way that the country is at least potentially self-sufficient, not only self-reliant' (in Ekins, 1986, p. 102). In this way populations would be shielded, at least in terms of necessities, from the vagaries of the market. As a result of these views on trade, green economic practice would be built substantially around protectionism: 'it's clear that selective protection of the domestic economy will be needed to establish its sustainable basis, and to encourage the country to become far more self-sufficient than it is at present' (Porritt, 1984a, p. 135).

Understanding this will help us to understand why much-vaunted 'green' politicians such as Norway's Gro Harlem Brundtland have a long way to go before embracing a radical green programme. In this context she argues that 'protectionism is one of the aspects of confrontation [between nations] which needs to be abolished ... The advantages of free trade for the countries of the North and South ought to be evident' (Brundtland, 1989, p. 5). In the present political climate, particularly since the GATT agreement reached in 1994 and despite the ferocious opposition to the World Trade Organisation talks in Seattle in 1999, this is standard fare, and it provides a further illustration of the way in which political ecology sets its face against dominant paradigms.

Likewise, supporting the green argument for reduced trade we find the central notions of reduced consumption (if you can't produce it, think about doing without it first, and only trading for it second), and a theory of need that hopes to sustain the view that in many instances the trade to which we have become accustomed is an unwarranted indulgence. If life under these circumstances sounds like reproducing the styles of life most often associated with developing countries, then the green position on trade (and not a few of their other recommendations) reflects Rudolf Bahro's view that 'With a pinch of salt one might say … the path of reconciliation with the Third World might consist in our becoming Third World ourselves' (1986, p. 88).

Part of the effect of protectionism, of course, would be to throw communities back on to their own resources, and this is entirely in line with the green plan of creating a political life founded upon communitarian decentralization. This plan also affects the green position on travel: one of the characteristics of the radical green sustainable society is that people would travel less. Arne Naess in his 1987 Schumacher Lecture referred to the principle of 'limited mobility' and William Ophuls, too, believes that personal mobility would be limited in such a society (1977, p. 167). In the first place this is because greens consider present travel practices to be wasteful of resources. Rudolf Bahro, especially, was particularly difficult to coax on to an aircraft for this reason.

Second, and more importantly, greens argue for reduced mobility as a part of their hopes for generating supportive, satisfying relationships in their decentralized, self-reliant communities. From this point of view travel involves dislocation of the ties that hold such communities together, and so endangers the emergence of the 'sense of loyalty and involvement' (Porritt, 1984a, p. 166) that, for greens, will be one of the prime benefits of decentralized communitarian life. The sustainable society is substantially about living 'in place' and developing an intimacy with it and the people who live there; travel, on this reading, is too expansive and too centrifugal an occupation.

Work

Paul Ekins refers to 'a reconceptualisation of the nature and value of work' as one of the principal pillars of the green economic and social framework (1986, p. 97), and it is certainly true that ecologism can be marked off from most other modern political ideologies by its attitude to the subject. Political ecologists have a specific view on the value of work and they also question the dominant tendency to associate work with paid employment. Such an association can lead us to believe that if a person is not in paid employment then they are not working. This, for greens, is simply untrue, and their renegotiation of the meaning of work leads them to suggest ways of 'freeing' it from what they see as restrictions founded on the modern (and archaic) sense that work is just paid employment. This will become clearer shortly, but first a word needs to be said about how greens value work itself.

One of the most common scenarios for advanced industrial societies in this context is the workless future. This is a familiar story – one that begins in automated car factories and suggests that technological advances will eventually enable us to enjoy more or less labourless production across vast swathes of the industrial process. In this future the only problem would be how best to use the increased leisure time created by clean and automated production. Greens have peered into this future and they do not like what they see.

In the first place, they will claim that it pays no mind whatever to the problems of sustainability on a finite planet. Second, to the extent that this future is already with us, political ecologists will object to the unemployment that automated production appears to cause, and they typically reject claims that other industries (service, 'sunrise') will take up the employment slack caused by industrial reconversion. Third, such a future (given the present general antipathy to redistribution) would most likely produce a society split between the highly paid monitors of machinery and the stunted recipients of social security payments pitched at a level designed to discourage indolence. Finally, greens look at the burgeoning leisure industry and see its consumer-oriented, environmentally damaging, industrialized and disciplined nature as a threat to the self-reliant, productive practices that the green Good Life holds out for us.

But beyond even all this, greens will be sceptical (at the very least) of the workless future because they think work is a good thing to do. In this respect they are part of a tradition that has it that work is a noble occupation, that it uplifts the spirit and helps create and reproduce ties with one's community – even helps to create oneself. This view has it that work is an obligation both to oneself and to one's society and that this obligation has to be redeemed. Thus Jonathon Porritt, for example, states:

> I must confess to being revolutionary in a very old-fashioned way when it comes to work. The statement of Thomas Aquinas, 'There can be no joy of life without the joy of work', just about sums it up for me.
>
> (Porritt, 1984a, p. 127)

He continues: 'I'm one of those who consider work to be a necessity of the human condition, a defining characteristic of the sort of people we are'; and finally 'Far from universal automation "solving our economic problems", I believe it would so impair our humanity as to make life utterly meaningless' (Porritt, 1984a, p. 127).

This is evidently another respect in which green politics clearly confronts the dominant post-industrial vision. Automated production is precisely one of the features of that vision and while Porritt (at least) hedges his bets just a little – 'One undisputed advantage of microprocessors is that they will enable machines to do jobs that are boring, unhealthy, unpleasant and dangerous' (Porritt, 1984a, p. 129) – the general understanding of the green position is that it advocates that the emphasis be in principle on labour-intensive production. It should be noted that, in the wider context of the green sustainable society and the reasons for its necessity (limits to growth), this is not simply because work is a fulfilling thing to do, but because it will become a standard requirement: 'With more people and fewer resources, the capital/labour ratio must start shifting back towards labour-intensive production' (Porritt, 1984a, p. 129). In other words, as the price of resources goes up (as greens believe it will do, in the context of scarcity), the amount of capital available for reinvestment in labour-saving machinery will go down. This, it is held, will swing the balance back in favour of more labour-intensive production. For all these reasons, then, the dark-green sustainable society will be more labour-intensive than the one we presently occupy.

The green favouring of work will evidently lead political ecologists – like most other people – to bemoan the existence of unemployment, but greens add a twist to the expected story. They will claim that, while there is clearly unemployment, that does not mean that there is no work being done. At the root of this judgement lies the belief that work should not be seen as synonymous with paid employment. Greens (and, once again, not a few others) point out that enormous amounts of work are done that do not register as work, precisely because the tasks do not take the form of paid employment. Examples of this would be work done by women (mainly) in the home, caring for the sick and elderly outside the institutions of care, and work done in the so-called 'informal' economy.

A concrete example of an attempt to make all this visible is Victor Anderson's suggestion that the 'money value of unpaid domestic labour' and of 'non-money transactions outside the household' should be included in Adjusted National Product (ANP) improvements on Gross National Product (GNP) calculations (1991, p. 39). This, incidentally, also rather gives the lie to Mary Mellor's claim that 'The male-orientation of futurist green thought lies in its tendency to see life and work as separate, as alternatives' (1992b, p. 244).

Greens point out that this distinction between work and paid employment is not merely of semantic importance. The modern tendency of associating reward and status with paid employment results in employers and potential employees looking to the sectors of production traditionally associated with paid employment when it comes to strategies for dealing with unemployment. In other words, the unemployed look for work in paid employment and employers try to place them in such employment. The green approach to problems of unemployment, in contrast, is to concentrate on those areas where work has always been done, but where it is frowned upon, if not actually criminalized. Nothing, evidently is solved by semantically collapsing the distinction between work and paid employment, but greens argue for a series of policies that would practise such a collapse.

Most generally, the green argument is prefaced by the belief that traditional solutions to the problems of unemployment (like more growth) are doomed to failure either because of the context of a finite planet or because the technological infrastructure that has been built up is actually designed to reduce places of paid employment. Irvine and Ponton are clear about the implications: 'In these circumstances slogans about "No Return to the 30s" and "Jobs for All" are irrelevant if not downright reactionary' (1988, pp. 66–7). Political ecologists will go on from here to say that the work that is done in the informal economy must be liberated and decriminalized, and that policies presently designed to prevent people from working in the informal economy should be abandoned and replaced by policies that will encourage them to work there. In this sense, collapsing the distinction between work and paid employment means collapsing the distinction between the formal and the informal economy.

The reasons greens give for why the potential of the informal economy is presently not fully realized revolve around the role played by current systems of social security and the assumptions that inform them. Greens point out that most social security systems deter people from doing work on a part-time, irregular basis (i.e. just when it 'shows up') because benefits are likely to be withdrawn – in other words, it is not always financially worthwhile to work. Second, rises in income can also lead to the withdrawal of benefits, leading to what has been called the 'poverty trap' (*Green Party Manifesto for a Sustainable Society*, 1999, EC 753). For these two reasons, work in the informal economy, the conditions of which bear little relation to the rigid structures of paid employment, is effectively discouraged. Furthermore, most social security systems (and certainly Britain's, based on Beveridge's 1942 proposal) have been designed around the assumptions of a growth economy and a system of reward based on the existence of practically universal paid employment. Once those assumptions no longer hold (and greens believe that they do not), the social security system based upon them must come into question too.

Beyond these points, greens are often critical of the means-testing that is part and parcel of current social security strategies and, associated with this, they are offended by the conditionality of awards and the repercussions this has: 'There are far more unclaimed benefits than illegal claims, though we have not seen many teams of investigators seeking out non-claimants' (Irvine and Ponton, 1988, p. 84). The solution most often canvassed in green literature to the problems associated with present social security systems, and particularly the way in which they help marginalize the informal economy, is a minimum income scheme (MIS) or guaranteed basic income scheme (GBIS).

The general form of the GBIS is simply expressed. According to the 1999 *Manifesto for a Sustainable Society*, it would be 'sufficient to cover basic needs ... [and] be paid to all adult citizens and will not be withdrawn as income rises. Those payments due to children under school leaving age will be payable to a parent or legal guardian' (1999, EC 750, 752). Likewise, Anne Miller writes that

> A Basic Income Scheme would aim to guarantee each man, woman and child the unconditional right to an independent income sufficient to meet basic living costs. Its main purpose would be the prevention of poverty, as opposed to mere poverty relief.
>
> (quoted in Ekins, 1986, p. 226)

Advocates of the GBIS claim that it has distinct advantages with respect to the drawbacks and anomalies of standard social security systems. First, people will not be discouraged from taking part-time, irregular work, because no drop in benefit will be involved; second, small rises in income will not affect benefit payments either; and third, the system would be much simpler to administer than most present ones. More generally, flexible working patterns would be encouraged, leading (it is hoped) to the liberation of the informal economy and its recognition as a site of respectable employment. At the same time, greens hope that the GBIS would help to break down what they consider to be an insidious distinction in status between those employed and those unemployed.

Ever since their inception (and greens are not the only ones to have argued for guaranteed basic income schemes – Milton Friedman has been associated with them too, for example) such schemes have been highly controversial. In the first place, people ask how much the weekly or monthly payment would actually be. Obviously to give figures would be pointless, but, according to Irvine and Ponton, 'To be politically attractive, the level of basic income must save people from poverty. Beyond that, it is a matter of careful calculation of what society can afford' (1988, p. 73). The *Green Party Manifesto for a Sustainable Society* rather elliptically states that payments would be 'high enough to enable people to choose their own patterns and types of work' (1999, EC 751). Some on the left have criticized this kind of proposal on the grounds that payments would likely be so low as to further institutionalize poverty rather than relieve it. But even if greens accept that payments might not be as high as some would like, they will maintain that the GBIS's effect of opening up the informal economy and allowing for flexible patterns of work would mean that very few people would remain at GBIS levels of income – and that, if they did, it could be more meaningfully called a voluntary decision than is presently the case.

Yet it is not, of course, only a matter of calculation, as Irvine and Ponton suggest, but also of negotiation (and this is the second point to be made), because GBIS proposals are thrown into the political market-place at a time when social security systems funded by compulsorily raised taxes are under severe intellectual attack. Thus the notion of 'political attractiveness' to which they refer is ambiguous. Those who believe that social security systems encourage idleness will see the GBIS as the height of folly – no need to work at all. Greens are convinced, however, that the vast majority of people will work, and they will argue fully that at the lower end of the pay-scale the removal of the part-time, unemployment and poverty traps will positively encourage people to work.

The third standard criticism of all guaranteed basic income schemes is that they would be too expensive to put into operation. In response, advocates of such schemes usually take the redistributive bull by the horns and admit that high earners would be expected to finance the GBIS through paying high taxes: one is faced with a graduated income tax system of the type that is currently so out of favour, at least in liberal democratic polities. At the same time, greens can point to all sorts of other taxes that would be levied in the sustainable society: taxes on inputs to the production process, taxes on outputs, resource taxes and consumption taxes (*Green Party Manifesto for a Sustainable Society*, 1999, EC 700, 701, 702, 710, 711) – all of which they claim would help raise sufficient revenue for the GBIS. Then they will refer to the savings made in administering such a simple system in comparison with the sums spent on present systems, and lastly they will suggest that tax revenues would increase anyway given the increase in earnings created by more people working.

It seems clear that, in the context of funding, much depends on being able to negotiate higher taxes for higher earners, and in the short term this may be the GBIS's principal drawback. As suggested above, the political culture in most liberal democracies has shifted away from seeing social justice in terms of redistribution, and towards something like Robert Nozick's entitlement theory of justice. This theory has it that you are entitled to what you justly own (e.g. money earned through work) and that it cannot be legitimately taken from you without your consent. From this point of view, taxation is a form of robbery. This, I suggest, is the view that most generally informs attitudes towards taxation today, and funding the GBIS would involve confronting it. This task has proved beyond the capabilities of the left (which now seems largely to have abandoned the job in any case) over the last fifteen years and there are no signs, either, that political ecologists have taken this particular problem of persuasion seriously enough.

Two further issues related to the GBIS remain to be raised, both of which bear on the question of how much such schemes have to do with the green sustainable society anyway. Readers who have taken in the rest of the chapter might feel that the GBIS sits unhappily with the rather radical picture painted up until now of the sustainable society. The GBIS is radical in the sense that it would be a far-reaching extension of present practices, but the point of the green sustainable society as I have been led to see it is that it constitutes a substantial break with present practices. On this reading, we might suggest that there is too much in the GBIS that is 'of this world' to see it as part of a deep-green solution to sustainability.

Boris Frankel (1987) sounds the first alarm in this regard when he asks what political structures greens advocate for administering the GBIS. He argues that the centralized nature of such structures stands in tension with the decentralist impulse of many green programmes. He implies, in other words, that decentralist greens want it both ways – they seek decentralized forms of political life on the one hand and, on the other, they want to institutionalize social practices that are only possible through a high degree of planning and the centralization that this implies. I suspect that such greens will reply that the administration of (and revenue-raising for) the GBIS will just have to be carried out centrally, but that this does not negate the principle that 'nothing should be done at a higher level that can be done at a lower' (Porritt, 1984a, p. 166). GBIS administration, on this view, does have to be carried out at a 'high level', and that is that. How far one considers this to be a heresy within the green canon will depend upon how strict one is in one's interpretation of the meaning of decentralization in the green political programme. I shall return to this point below.

More serious in this respect, perhaps, is the objection that the productive system on which the GBIS depends to produce the fabulous amounts of wealth needed to fund it (i.e. the present productive system) is elsewhere described by greens as being in decline and is unsustainable anyway – that is where green politics begins, in fact. Put more bluntly: as productivity declines and tax revenues dwindle, where will the money to pay for the GBIS come from? From this perspective, the GBIS looks like a social-democratic measure grafted unsustainably on to the ailing post-industrial body politic, rather than a radically green measure in the spirit of solutions to the problems of sustainability raised by the spectre of limits to growth. At the very least, greens will find themselves back with the problem of negotiating the redistribution of decreasing amounts of material wealth. Just what social security measures in the green sustainable society would look like I don't know, but the guaranteed basic income scheme seems to depend too much on the habits and practices of the society that greens would like to replace to provide the answer

At the beginning of this chapter I suggested that the limits to growth notion represents the starting-point for radical green politics. The notion is indispensable for understanding ecologism, if only because it points us in the direction – at the outset – of the radical prescriptions for political and social life that the green sustainable society involves. If it were simply a question of eating healthy food, living in a lead-free environment or using biodegradable detergent, then environmentalist strategies such as green consumerism would probably do the job. But greens suggest that green consumerism is no more sustainable – in the long run – than grey consumerism: both are subject to limits to growth. This state of affairs needs to be addressed by a specifically different set of habits and practices from those that we presently follow, and green consumerism is too tied in to present rates of depletion, production, depreciation (involving consumption) and pollution to constitute the new set of habits and practices that dark-greens say we need.

I also suggested that of these four terms – collected together under Herman Daly's umbrella term 'throughput' – consumption was the one on which to focus attention in order best to see from where green prescriptions take off. The urge to reduce consumption as a response to the limits to growth thesis leads to the development of theories of need, the recommendation to reduce population levels, the questioning of the 'technological fix', the support for sustainable sources of energy – and all this is underpinned by the proposal for a self-reliant society, the ground rule for which is provided by Porritt: 'All economic growth in the future must be sustainable: that is to say it must operate within and not beyond the finite limits of the planet' (1984a, p. 120). Having sketched the most important features of one way of life of the sustainable society, from a radical green point of view we are now in a position to consider the (broadly speaking) political-institutional characteristics of such a society: what will it look like?

Bioregionalism

When I considered the possible responses to the limits to growth thesis nearer the beginning of the chapter, I proposed that we accept Tim O'Riordan's fourfold classification: the 'new global order', the idea of 'centralized authoritarianism', the 'authoritarian commune' and the 'anarchist solution'. At the time I resisted the temptation of saying that one or another of these possibilities came closest to describing what a green sustainable society would look like, and limited myself to arguing – more generally – that sustainable societies cannot take just any form, and that unregulated markets and authoritarian regimes were likely to be dysfunctional for sustainability as well as contradictory of a basic green principle regarding the autonomous development of self-renewing systems. I also pointed out that one of the responses to the 'anything goes' school of thought was to say that an ecological principle for social life might be that the best social arrangements are those that involve an embeddedness in the 'natural' world. I can now push this further by considering the notion of bioregionalism.

The general principles of what Kirkpatrick Sale has called the 'bioregional paradigm' (Sale, 1985, pp. 41–132) are simply expressed.

> We must get to know the land around us, learn its lore and its potential, and live with it and not against it. We must see that living with the land means living in, and according to the ways and rhythms of, its natural regions – its bioregions.
>
> (Sale, 1985, p. 56)

There are 'ecoregions' of 'perhaps several hundred thousand square miles' (ibid.), smaller 'georegions' of a few tens of thousands of square miles, and 'morphoregions' (he has also called these 'vitaregions'; Sale, 1984, p. 227) of 'several thousand square miles' (Sale, 1985, p. 58). Living bioregionally involves identifying bioregional boundaries and living (for the most part) with what those territories provide in the way of, for example, 'given ores and minerals, woods and leathers, cloths and yarns' (Sale, 1985, p. 75). Bioregionalists have identified these regions and have names for them: there is a land along the California coast, for example, known as Shasta (Tokar, 1994, p. 73).

Within these bioregions people would live in communities, because 'If one were to look for the single basic building block of the ecological world, it would be the community' (Sale, 1985, p. 62). Sale suggests that the 'human animal' has historically favoured communities of 500–1,000 people for face-to-face contact and 5,000–10,000 'for the larger tribal association or extended community' (ibid., p. 64). Communities much bigger than this are regarded as undesirable because they cannot be sustained on their own resources.

The bioregional community would seek to 'minimise resource-use, emphasise conservation and recycling, [and] avoid pollution and waste' (Sale, 1984, p. 230), and all of this would be aimed at achieving sustainability through what Sale calls self-sufficiency. The bioregionalist is likely to be even less keen on trade than the advocate of self-reliance, and Sale himself sees self-sufficiency as centred on a 'full-scale morphoregion' so as to ensure 'a wide range of food, some choice in necessities and some sophistication in luxuries, [and] the population to sustain a university and large hospital and a symphony orchestra' (1985, pp. 74–5). We would, however, be likely to do without some things: 'some bioregions would have to steel themselves for significant changes from their omnivorous and gluttonous habits of the present: noncitrus regions would need to look to other sources of vitamin C, for example' (ibid., p. 75). In general, bioregionalists will claim that the oft-cited problems associated with the unequal endowment of regions with natural resources simply do not, in fact, arise: 'there is not a single bioregion in this country [the United States of America] that would not ... be able to provide its residents with sufficient food, energy, shelter, and clothing, their own health care and education and arts, their own manufactures and crafts' (ibid.).

Bioregionalists will usually insist that land be communally owned because the fruits of nature are fruits for everyone, and they will urge that polities follow the natural world's example and abhor systems of centralized control. Consequently, they advocate 'the spreading of power to small and widely dispersed units' (Sale, 1985, p. 91). Associated with this is the idea that nature's lesson as far as social relations are concerned is one of equality, or what Sale calls 'complementarity' (ibid., p. 101). The claim is that 'stratification and hierarchy within specific sub-groups in the animal world is extremely rare' (ibid., p. 98), and that, on the basis that what is good for the 'natural' world is good for us as a part of it, hierarchy should not be institutionalized in politics either. One further principle of bioregionalism, that of diversity, will be treated shortly; it has destabilizing possibilities for the picture presented so far.

The guiding principle of bioregionalism, then, is that the 'natural' world should determine the political, economic and social life of communities, and that the messages that nature gives off are best read through ecology rather than, say, through social Darwinism: 'by a diligent study of her [nature] … we can guide ourselves in constructing human settlements and systems' (Sale, 1984, p. 225). Sustainability for bioregionalists and those who draw their inspiration from them is seen as presaged upon reducing the spiritual and material distance between us and the land:

> We must somehow live as close to it [the land] as possible, be in touch with its particular soils, its waters, its winds; we must learn its ways, its capacities, its limits; we must make its rhythms our patterns, its laws our guide, its fruits our bounty.
>
> (Sale, 1984, pp. 22–5)

No doubt Kirkpatrick Sale's general picture of bioregionalism and the exhortation just quoted both sound extremely far-fetched, but it will probably inform many of the postures struck by even the least mystical of greens. In this particular context nearly all of them will bemoan the lack of knowledge of the land so typical of the industrialized human being. They will deplore our ignorance of where our food comes from and how it grows, and suggest that the pre-packaged produce on supermarket shelves is both a symptom and a cause of our dangerous distance from the land. In this sense, both they and the bioregionalists will urge us to 'live in place' – to accommodate our lives to the environment in which we live, rather than resisting it.

Agriculture

In this respect, beyond the claims of bioregionalism itself but clearly informed by it, agriculture will always have a special place in the theory and practice of the green sustainable society and a particular sort of agriculture at that: 'the problem of how we feed ourselves [is] arguably the most vital component of a Green ecological strategy' (Tokar, 1994, p. 63). This is so in two ways. First there is the relatively well-known point that the green movement considers present agricultural practices (what they would call 'industrial agriculture') to be unacceptable because unsustainable. Intensive chemical-based farming is held to pollute water-courses, to encourage erosion, to produce tasteless food of low nutritional value, to bring about salinization of the land through irrigation, to upset ecological balances through insensitive pest control, and to bore us with its monocultural panoramas.

But the green point pushes past this rather pragmatic attachment to sustainable agriculture. Brian Tokar introduces the idea with the thought that organic farming, in place, would strengthen 'bioregional awareness' (1994, p. 64). Jonathon Porritt is more explicit. He suggests that the importance of sound agriculture goes beyond producing healthy food on a sustainable basis; rather,

> its implications for a change in the attitude of people to the planet are highly significant. It binds people to the natural processes of the Earth and, with the use of appropriate technology, creates a sense of harmony that is sorely lacking.
>
> (Porritt, 1984a, p. 180)

In this respect, agricultural practices in the green society are charged with the essential task of providing the site at which our rifts with the 'natural' world are to be healed, and that is why Brian Tokar invests it with such importance. Spirituality ghosts dark-green politics; green politics is a filling of the spiritual vacuum at the centre of late-industrial society, and the land itself is the cathedral at which we are urged to worship. Peter Bunyard's message is instructive: 'The search for self-sufficiency is, I believe, as much spiritual and ideological as it is one of trying to reap the basic necessities of life out of the bare minimum of our surroundings' (in Allaby and Bunyard, 1980, p. 26).

In the light of all this we should not be surprised to see that other consequences of sustainable agriculture – such as its labour-intensive nature – have something more than a pragmatic content. Goldsmith claims that 'A rough calculation suggests that it would suffice to increase the agricultural labour force in the UK by four or five times, to enable this country to forgo much of the input of machinery and chemicals which have been introduced over the last thirty years' (Goldsmith, 1988, p. 197). This urge to produce a population of 'part-time peasants' (Ophuls, 1977, p. 167) is both necessary and desirable, from a green point of view. It is necessary because sustainable agriculture involves less machinery and therefore more hands, and it is desirable because it is where theory becomes practice – agriculture is, indeed, the praxis of green politics.

Diversity

One principle of Kirkpatrick Sale's bioregional society has been held over because it is one of the points at which the wider green movement's notion of the sustainable society will begin to diverge from the bioregional project. The principle is diversity, and the point is that to talk of a generic 'bioregional society' (as I have been doing) is a misrepresentation. More accurately we have to speak of bioregional *societies* – not only in the obvious numerical sense, but also in terms of their informing political, social and economic characteristics.

Sale writes bluntly that it is not necessarily the case that each bioregional society 'will construct itself upon the values of democracy, equality, liberty, freedom, justice, and other suchlike desiderata' (1984, p. 233), and Arne Naess in his 1987 Schumacher Lecture agreed with this. This may seem peculiar, given Sale's commitment, expressed above, to the notions of equality and political participation, both derived (in contested fashion) from principles of the science of ecology, but there is evidently a tension between the demands of 'complementarity' and diversity. When diversity is privileged, one is obliged to admit to (and underwrite) the possibility that

> truly autonomous bioregions will likely go their own separate ways and end up with quite disparate political systems – some democracies, no doubt, some direct, some representative, some federative, but undoubtedly all kinds of aristocracies, oligarchies, theocracies, principalities, margravates, duchies and palatinates as well.
>
> (Sale, 1984, p. 233)

At this point the wider green movement is likely to lose its bioregional nerve. Its members will want to subscribe to Sale's declaration that 'Bioregionalism ... not merely tolerates but thrives upon the diversities of human behaviour' (ibid., p. 234), but, as images of slavery and sexism come to mind, misty eyes will snap into focus and greens will remember that they are as much the heirs of the Enlightenment tradition as its committed critics. They most certainly believe that 'their model of post-industrialism will maximise democracy, freedom, tolerance, equality and other rationalist values which made their appearance in Europe a few hundred years ago' (Frankel, 1987, p. 180), and in this respect the bioregional imperative of diversity is tempered by the desire to universalize messages most often associated with liberal democracy.

Decentralization and its limits

Many green stories of the sustainable society are written in the language of decentralization, often to the point where the decentralist impetus takes the final form of communal types of living. Rudolf Bahro is probably the person most normally linked with full-blown commune recommendations for the shape of the green society, and the reasons he gives for favouring communes echo those given by Sale. In the first place, communes are not 'economically expansive'; as Edward Goldsmith puts it, 'to deploy a population in small towns and villages is to reduce to the minimum its impact on the environment' (1972, p. 64). Next, they provide an obvious focus for political decentralization. Third, they are what Bahro calls 'anthropologically favourable', i.e. they correspond more 'to human nature, among other things by avoiding both the neurotic-making family and the alienating big organization' (1986, pp. 87–8). In this respect Goldsmith goes even further: 'it is probable that only in the small community can a man or woman be an individual' (1972, p. 63). Communes therefore provide the site on which personal relationships become fulfilling, and where people will learn to live 'in place' (according to, and not against, their environment).

In this respect, green politics inserts itself in a tradition that is as long as history and embroils itself in debates that will be most familiar to the modern reader in the context of the theory and practice of communitarian anarchism. Some greens (and particularly bioregionalists) bring a novel perspective to bear on this debate in two respects: first, the idea that communal living is somehow 'read off' from the 'natural' world – that it is a natural way of living, and in this sense responds to the demand for sustainability; second, they are also likely to suggest that something like a federation of communes is the only viable political-institutional form for the sustainable society to take.

In this sense they will suggest that other political forms are more susceptible to environmental irresponsibility and that this is therefore a very practical reason (in view of the long-term project of sustainability) for supporting the commune option. This is why Goldsmith claims that decentralization is proposed, not 'because we are sunk in nostalgia for a mythical little England of fêtes, olde worlde pubs, and perpetual conversations over garden fences' (1972, pp. 61–2), but for more hard-headed reasons. The idea is that resource problems are best solved by bringing points of production and consumption closer together – we should no longer be talking of producers and consumers but of 'prosumers'. It is often argued that greens have no reasons of their own (as opposed to reasons borrowed from other political traditions) for arguing for one particular political form rather than another. This is wrong: all greens of whatever tint will argue that political-institutional design should be guided by environmental and/or ecological realities. In Goldsmith's case there is the suggestion that there are environmental benefits to be derived from political decentralization – a green-sounding argument if ever there was one. From this point of view cities produce too much pollution, degrade neighbouring land through the demands of waste disposal, make 'excessive demands on natural resources' (Stoett, 1994, p.

339), and prevent their inhabitants from acquiring a sense of their dependence on the natural world.

All this, though, is by no means accepted by everyone. It is argued, on the contrary, that essential services can be supplied more cheaply for people living in close proximity, and that environmental degradation can be more effectively dealt with in bounded spaces. Moreover, the Amazonian experience suggests that a rush to the countryside can have devastating consequences under the wrong conditions. Notwithstanding these debates, the other arguments surrounding green communitarianism are familiar: 'Is it practical?', 'Would such a life be stultifying?', 'What would the relationships between communes look like?' and so on. Certainly many will feel uncomfortable at the implications of arbitrary justice implied by Edward Goldsmith's suggestion that 'crime' be controlled 'through the medium of public opinion' by subjecting the offender to 'ridicule' (1972, p. 135), and will agree with André Gorz that:

> communal autarky always has an impoverishing effect: the more self-sufficient and numerically limited a community is, the smaller the range of activities and choices it can offer to its members. If it has no opening to an area of exogenous activity, knowledge and production, the community becomes a prison ... only constantly renewed possibilities for discovery, insight, experiment and communication can prevent communal life from becoming impoverished and eventually suffocating.
>
> (quoted in Frankel, 1987, p. 59)

The themes of confinement and surveillance at which Gorz hints haunt some green texts surreptitiously – 'Many in the informal economy who do not now disclose their income ... would find that in the new system the risks of tax evasion outweigh gains', for example; Irvine and Ponton, 1988, p. 73 – and while this is probably not surprising given the puritanical tenor of much of the green programme, it is an aspect of green politics that (on the face of it) can offend the modern liberal sensibility. It seems to me that either green politics as a project will suffer because of this, or it will usefully refer to it as just one more example of the self-denial that sustainable living requires of us. I once knew an anarchist who was surprisingly military about getting people up in the early morning before meetings to wash and clean their teeth. Equally surprisingly, this exercise was generally accepted with good grace because somehow it all seemed part of the necessary preparations for the brave new world that the anarchists were seeking to usher in.

Many greens, though, will respond to the practical or ethical objections to commune living by falling back on a more loosely conceived notion of political decentralization: the reasons remain the same, but the form is different. The basic rule once the commune option has been set aside, according to the 1999 *Green Party Manifesto for a Sustainable Society*, is that 'nothing should be done centrally if it can be done equally well, or better, locally' (PG 100). This amounts to a call for what Schumacher famously called 'appropriateness', and often turns in green hands into a commitment to local politics and some form of participatory democracy: 'Greens believe that many more decisions should be taken at the local level, encouraging greater participation and accountability', and, in a statement typical of advocates of participatory democracy, 'voting is the beginning and not the end of one's democratic commitment' (Bunyard and Morgan-Grenville, 1987, pp. 319, 320). As far as this last is concerned, Brian Tokar refers to New England town meetings as the *locus classicus* of face-to-face democracy in action, as well as to 'ancient Greek democracy, the Parisian sections of the French Revolution, pre-Revolutionary Boston and the anarchist city of Barcelona during the Spanish Civil War' (1994, p. 105).

This much is clear, and probably familiar. Familiar, too, are the questions normally asked of such a picture, and they have been forcefully put by Boris Frankel (1987) and more recently by Luke Martell (1994). Their principal difficulty with the green decentralist picture revolves around how such a decentralized society is to be co-ordinated, in both the political and the economic spheres. They argue that the green decentralist programme is unrealistic for three principal reasons. First, not everything that we might reasonably expect from a green society can be produced locally; second, dealing with the environmental problems that the green movement has identified requires the kind of planning and co-ordination that can only be provided by centralized political structures; and third, such structures are needed to organize the redistribution required by the greens' egalitarian project. I suggest that greens (or rather some of them, depending on what their picture of a sustainable society looks like) are perfectly able to accept these points, within the framework provided by their maxim that no decision should be taken at a higher level that can be taken at a lower level.

With respect to the first issue, Martin Ryle argues that it is not possible to make 'fridges, bicycles [or] kidney dialysis machines' in 'domestic enterprises or craft workshops' (Ryle, 1988, p. 23) – or at least certainly not to the standard required for the safe operating of complex equipment. Chinese experiences of decentralized production during the 'Great Leap

Forward' under Mao suggest that even relatively uncomplicated goods are hard to produce adequately.

Second, Ryle points out that 'ecological restructuring' as opposed to 'environmental protection through piecemeal legislation' (Ryle, 1988, p. 63) will involve planning, and concludes that, although one might prefer to have no state:

> If one is honest about the objectives which an ecologically enlightened society would set for itself, it is difficult to avoid concluding that the state, as the agent of collective will, would have to take an active law-making and -enforcing role in imposing a range of environmental and resource constraints.
>
> (Ryle, 1988, p. 60)

On this reading, planning is essential if the green programme is to be realized, and such planning can be devised and carried out only by centralized political structures. Ryle makes the interesting further point that, if it could be successfully argued that environmental problems can be relieved only by intervention, it might be possible more generally to turn the tables on the free-marketeers: 'the idea of an ecological transformation of the economy can itself play a part in renewing the legitimacy of political interventions in the market' (Ryle, 1988, p. 66). Boris Frankel adds that redistribution with a view to egalitarianism presupposes centralized structures too:

> Until individuals and groups accept the unpalatable news that stateless, decentralized, moneyless, small-scale communes or other informal alternatives are not viable without the complex administrative and social structures necessary to guarantee democratic, participation, civil rights and egalitarian co-ordination of economic resources, there is not much hope of strong coalitions between labour movements and new social movements.
>
> (Frankel, 1987, p. 270)

Greens might make two responses to these remarks. In the first place, some of them will say that it is a caricature of their position to imply, as Ryle and Frankel do, that they seek entirely stateless societies. They will say that only the bioregionalists and the extreme commune theorists would subscribe to that, and that although they influence the movement's thinking it would be wrong to argue that their position is exhaustively representative of the movement's as a whole. This is not to say that the movement doesn't exhibit confusion on this score, and there are clearly problems associated with the programme of seizing central power and then giving it away again, but this is not the same as suggesting that the green movement is innocent of the need to plan. Robyn Eckersley is a representative ecocentrist who is quite clear about the need for states in bringing about and maintaining a sustainable future (Eckersley, 1992, pp. 183–5).

Decentralist greens, though, might put their same argument a different way. They can also say that, rather than pushing for the abolition of the centralized state, the movement is merely asking that the ground rules for decision-making be changed. Presently the onus of justification is on those who would have decision-making locally based, and ecologists would like to see this reversed. In other words, the current norm is for decisions to be taken at high levels, while under a green regime decisions would be taken at low levels unless it were expressly necessary for them to be taken higher up. In this context the kinds of decision and the types of production to which Frankel and Ryle refer (income or resource distribution and kidney dialysis machines) are precisely those that would justifiably correspond to higher levels according to the green maxim. In this sense, the socialist critique of green forms of organization enables us to clarify the radical green position rather than undermine it.

We must recognize, of course, that the problems of co-ordination that underpin many of the criticisms of green decentralization do not arise in the most extreme versions of bioregionalism because contact between communities would not be institutionalized. Or rather, different problems would arise, in the sense that relations between and within communities could not legitimately be universalized and regulated. Frankel wonders in this regard (with reference to Bahro) whether the relationships between decentralized communes would not simply 'grow into capitalist markets with all the inherent qualities of inequality, exploitation and so forth' (Frankel, 1987, p. 56). But while this could be a problem for Enlightenment enthusiasts, Kirkpatrick Sale and his supporters might consider it merely to be part of life's rich pattern: the outcome of allowing for diversity.

However, if we assume that connections between communes are to be institutionalized, then the relations between local and 'national' levels need to be carefully spelt out. My reading of the green ideologues' approach to this problem (to the extent that they have dealt with it at all) is that they end up where they do not want to be: with a more weighty 'national' framework than some of them would like. Taking the economic arena as an example, greens are typically opposed to the workings of the market as they characterize it. For them, the market unsustainably and therefore irresponsibly encourages consumption, and it most usually is prepared to answer only short-term questions. This, in the context of limits to growth (which by its nature, according to greens, demands long-term thinking), is unacceptable. The problem in our context is that, if the market is to be fettered, who is to do the fettering? More obviously, if greens demand long-term policies, we might argue that they will have to be planned and co-ordinated. Once again, who is to do the planning and co-ordinating if not some supra-community political agency (Martell, 1994, pp. 58–62)? As Frankel puts it,

> would a Green post-industrial society minimize or maximize social planning? If it minimized social planning and relied predominantly on market mechanisms, then all the major difficulties of market socialism would appear. If the new society maximized planning, then how would this be possible without national state institutions?
>
> (Frankel, 1987, p. 55)

In response to these questions, there is a definite trend in green thinking now towards an understanding that environmental problems need to be dealt with at all the levels at which they occur, and that political institutions must both correspond to these levels and integrate between and across them. Edward Goldsmith, above, argued that there are good ecological reasons for decentralization; this position recognizes that ecologies are regional, national and international as well as local, and seeks to match this ecological diversity with political-institutional diversity. So Robyn Eckersley writes that 'the ecoanarchist defence of local sovereignty provide[s] no firm institutional recognition of the many different layers of social and ecological community that cohere *beyond* the level of the local community' (Eckersley 1992, p. 182). From this point of view, the state plays 'a vital role in controlling the operation of market forces and in laying down the framework for a socially just and ecologically sustainable society' (ibid., p. 194). Moreover, it is clear that many of the global environmental problems with which we are faced are international in nature. Sometimes these are best dealt with through negotiations between sovereign states, sometimes through international agencies such as the United Nations, and sometimes through supranational bodies with supranational powers, such as the European Union. The (tenuous but relevant) relationship between the statist view (represented by Eckersley) and Sale's bioregionalism is that they both seek to match political forms with ecological realities, but the statist view differs in retaining the nation-state as the fundamental political unit, with the authority both to make laws in respect of its own populations and to enter into negotiation with other nation-states in the international arena.

Eckersley, in sum, argues that decentralist greens are crucial to the creation of an ecocentric *culture*, but that they have relatively little to contribute to more precise questions of institutional design (1992, p. 182).

Once again it is worth stressing, though, that the commune perspective can provide a by-pass of such questions. For Frankel, Bahro takes just this option in that he 'has an idealized image of communal life where there is little need for extensive government-run "social wage" programmes as these jobs and roles will be performed by mutual self-help within the confines of "basic communes" ' (Frankel, 1987, p. 87). If this option is not taken, though, greens will respond to Frankel's question in the following way: 'we're talking about establishing at the national level the minimum legislative framework necessary for the maintenance of ecological principles, leaving the details to be determined locally' (Bunyard and Morgan-Grenville, 1987, p. 319). This is a delicate balancing act. The Green Party of England and Wales' evident commitment to decentralization is tempered by the recognition that 'Given the scale of much activity in the world today, it is clear that not all decisions can be made locally' (*Manifesto for a Sustainable Society*, 1999, PG 103). These are considerable responsibilities, and it is Martell's (for example) belief that appropriateness in the context of dealing with environmental problems involves a positive bias to centralization given the problems involved in co-ordinating the actions of plural and self-interested actors (Martell, 1994, pp. 54–5).

This suspicion is certainly borne out in the case of Irvine and Ponton. Loosely, they suggest that central government should be involved in taxing resource-intensive products, providing subsidies for energy conservation, and enforcing performance standards on products (Irvine and Ponton, 1988, p. 31). More specifically, this seems to result in a plethora of government institutions, miles removed from the light touch apparently guaranteed by the original decentralist project:

> A department of resource conservation and planning would be a necessary agency to look after the measures that require government action. It would, for example, plan how much of a particular mineral was needed in a given year while a ministry of land use would determine the best sites for extraction. The ministries of environment protection and of health would ensure that this was done in ways which had the least impact on place and people.
>
> (Irvine and Ponton, 1988, p. 31)

This sounds much more like a parody of a heavy-industrial command economy than a recipe for post-industrial decentralized sustainability.

In sum, the possible political arrangements in a sustainable society seem to range all the way from radical decentralization to a world government. Ecologism, though, is a transformative political ideology: transformative of people and the way they think about, relate to and act in the non-human natural world. The problems associated with transformative ideologies of any sort were flagged by Jean-Jacques Rousseau as long ago as 1762 when he opened his *The Social Contract* with the words: 'My purpose is to consider if, in political society, there can be any legitimate and sure principle of government, taking men as they are and laws as they might be' (Rousseau, 1762/1968, p. 49). Pretty soon he realized that the society he had in mind would not work so long as men remained 'as they are', and so he introduced a *deus ex machina* in the form of a 'Lawgiver' whose job was to 'change human nature' (ibid., p. 84). Transformative greens are in much the same position as Rousseau: the raw material is inadequate to the task at hand. Greens are asked political-institutional questions, and they have to answer them. Taking 'men' (and the societies that have spawned them) as they are, decentralized politics seems ineffective and naive. Taking 'men' (and their modes of production and consumption) as they might be, though, decentralized politics is the preferred radical green form – and for some of these radical greens, indeed, decentralized politics is the ecological equivalent of Rousseau's Lawgiver: the source of the transformation of human nature.

4   Strategies for green change

The Schwarzes ask: 'How do we start? By what imaginable transition can we move from here to a green future? Can the immense gap at least be narrowed, between the Green-thinking dreamers and the present reality?' (Schwarz and Schwarz, 1987, p. 253). Ecologism provides us with a critique of current patterns of production and consumption, and the Schwarzes' 'Green-thinking dreamers' have painted pictures of the sustainable society that they would like us to inhabit. Two of the classic requirements of a functional definition of 'ideology' are thus far fulfilled by ecologism: it has a description (which is already an interpretation) of 'political reality', and it has a prescription for the future, which amounts to a description of the Good Life. In the light of the space between the former and the latter, the primary question addressed in this chapter is: 'What is ecologism's strategy for social change?' The subsidiary question posed is: 'Will this strategy (or these strategies) do the job required of them?'

The first point to note about ecologism and social change is that until recently very little serious thinking had been done about it. Boris Frankel once rightly observed that 'one reads very little about how to get there from here' (1987, p. 227), and it is noticeable how many conversations about green politics very soon dry up when the issue of change is broached. Several reasons for the lack of material might be advanced.

In the first place there is the belief that the changes required are so far-reaching that nothing short of an environmental catastrophe could produce the political will needed to bring them about: 'it is quite "unrealistic" to believe that we shall choose simplicity and frugality except under ecological duress' (Daly, 1977a, p. 170). Second, among more optimistic observers there has been a tendency (noted in Chapter 1) to believe that the delivery of the message of impending catastrophe would be enough to generate social change. After all, how could a humanity aware of the threat to its existence fail to act in its own best interests? This certainly seems to have been the line taken in the original *Limits to Growth* report: 'We believe that an unexpectedly large number of men and women of all ages and conditions will readily respond to the challenge and will be eager to discuss not if but how we can create this new future' (Meadows *et al.*, 1974, p. 196). Contrary to its authors' expectations, however, the publication of their report has not of itself produced the changes for which they argue.

It is often the immaturity of the ideology that is held responsible for its not having got to grips with the issue of social change: green thinkers have had their work cut out simply describing our environmental malaise and convincing us of their arguments. It follows, from this perspective, that the very newness of the ideology is the reason for its current lack of a strategy that might be productive in the light of the ends it proposes. Now that the foundations are more or less in place, it is held, the strategy will follow. This argument would be more persuasive if ecologism really did have no strategy for social change. The point is, rather, that it does have various strategies, but there is a suspicion that they have been found wanting – it is not as though its strategies are correct and that they just need more time to work. Jonathon Porritt sets the agenda for this chapter:

> Though the environmental movement has indeed been growing in strength over the past few years, so that its influence is now greater than it has been since the early 1970s, this has not brought about the kind of fundamental shift that one might have anticipated.
>
> (in Goldsmith and Hildyard, 1986, p. 343)

Porritt goes on to argue that this is because the green movement has founded its project on reform of the system rather than its 'radical overhaul'. This might be true, but it simply pushes the problem back one space and the problem remains: how is the radical overhaul to be brought about? It must be stressed that 'radical overhaul' is what we are talking about in the context of ecologism. No one would dispute that significant improvements to the environment can be brought about by parliamentary party and pressure group activity – it would be a mistake to underestimate the achievements of groups like Friends of the Earth, brought about by high levels of commitment and undeniable expertise. Similarly, many governments are now (to a greater or lesser degree) committed to environmental policies. However, Porritt's concern at the lack of change is based on his desire for a 'fundamental shift' and it is this objective that provides the backdrop for this chapter.

I intend to organize most of the discussion around the distinction between parliamentary and extra-parliamentary political activity. There is evidently nothing particularly novel about this, although the very fact that this turns out to be the most fruitful way of approaching the issue is symptomatic of the general theme of ecologism and social change: that liberal democratic politics and the spaces in which it allows one to act constitute the parameters for the majority of ecological political action. This mention of liberal democracy allows us to consider, first, the most over-arching issue of green social change: the ongoing debate regarding authoritarianism and democracy.

Democracy and authoritarianism

Accusations of authoritarianism are never far from the surface where green social change is concerned. In the early days of the contemporary environmental movement, North American writers such as Heilbroner (1974) and Ophuls (1977) appeared to argue that the environmental crisis was so dire that no one could reasonably be expected to accept voluntarily the kinds of measures that would be needed to deal with it, and that therefore only strong government – even authoritarian government – would do. More recently, as the influence of the catastrophist tendency in green politics has declined, attention has turned to the kinds of values held by political ecologists, and it has been suggested that the political-ecological belief that there is a right way to live the green Good Life is incompatible with the value pluralism normally associated with (liberal) democracy. There are, then, both pragmatic and ethical roots to the palpable tension between radical green objectives and the democratic process. In recent years a good deal of attention has been paid to this tension, and a number of ways of lessening it have been suggested (Mathews, 1995; Doherty and de Geus, 1996a; Lafferty and Meadowcroft, 1996a). Some have wondered why greens have felt so obliged to defend their democratic credentials – 'greens can ask why they should find new grounds for their adherence to democracy different from those advanced by socialists and liberals' (Barry, 1996, p. 119) – but both the 1970s authoritarian tendency in some environmental political theory and the corrosive association of 'nature politics' with some forms of fascism (Bramwell, 1989) are enough to put both greens and their opponents continually on their democratic guard.

The underpinning source of the tension between radical green objectives and democracy is the apparently *imperative* nature of the former: 'To the extent that the realization of certain green principles – like dealing urgently with over-population – is seen as essential, we are dealing with an imperative that has a no-real-choice quality' (Saward, 1993a, p. 64). This sounds incompatible with the democratic resolution of problems:

'ecological value-sets often contain a considerable tension between advocating certain essential policy outcomes and valuing (direct) democratic procedures' (ibid.). And indeed, some early environmental political theorists, particularly in North America, appeared to eschew democratic processes in favour of the 'right' kind of ecological outcomes. It needs to be said, though, that even the villains of the piece, such as Heilbroner and Ophuls, were never as clear in their rejection of democratic procedures as their detractors have claimed. Two examples from William Ophuls will make this evident.

First, Ophuls does indeed write that 'As the community and its rights are given increasing social priority, we shall necessarily move from liberty toward authority, for the community will have to be able to enforce its demands on individuals' (Ophuls, 1992, p. 285). But he also says that 'this authority need not be remote, arbitrary, and capricious. In a well-ordered and well-designed state, authority could be made constitutional and limited' (ibid., p. 286). Second, Ophuls does seem to endorse 'a movement away from egalitarian democracy toward political competence and status', but he is careful to say that the values that inform competence should be arrived at by 'common consent' (ibid., p. 286), and he also writes that 'extreme centralization and interdependence ... should give way to greater decentralization, local autonomy, and local culture' (ibid., p. 291). Ophuls concludes by saying that 'The essential political message of this book is that we must learn ecological self-restraint before it is forced upon us by a potentially monolithic and totalitarian regime or by the brute forces of nature' (ibid., p. 297). A few swallows do not make a summer, of course, but these examples serve to illustrate the care with which we need to treat 'green authoritarian' claims. If indeed, as Saward suggests, 'Ophuls represents the clearest credible example of the authoritarian tendency in green political theory' (Saward, 1993a, p.71), then the tendency would appear to be equivocal.

We need to be clear, in any case, not to confuse anti-*liberal* elements in green thought with anti-*democratic* ones. I have written at length in the next chapter on the relationship between liberalism and ecologism, but it is worth recalling here that a large part of Heilbroner's and Ophuls' prescription for salvation consisted in – as Bob Paehlke puts it – 'a sense of social unity uncharacteristic of liberal, individualistic societies' (Paehlke, 1988, p. 293). The social unity of which they speak is not at all incompatible with democracy, of course, but it may indeed be in tension with the individualism associated with liberalism.

So one form of the green imperative is pragmatic, as it were. This is to say that drawing on the dire warnings found in texts such as *The Limits to Growth* (Meadows *et al.*, 1974), some writers drew the conclusion that ecological catastrophe could only be averted by authoritarian means. The other form of green imperative is more ethical, or value-oriented, in origin. Bob Goodin has argued persuasively that what drives environmental political thought and action is the 'green theory of value' to which we referred in Chapter 2. According to this theory, something is 'especially valuable' if it has 'come about through natural rather than through artificial human processes' (Goodin, 1992, p. 30). The task of the political ecologist, then, is to work for the preservation of this 'natural value' through time. Goodin carefully distinguishes between this theory of value and a putative green 'theory of agency', and the crucial issue for us is the relationship between them. Can a particular theory of agency be derived from the green theory of value? No, says Goodin. As we have seen, he argues that what 'lies at the core of green thinking ... is an abiding concern that natural values be promoted, protected and preserved'. So

> Given that as the logical primitive in their moral system, I think we would have to say ... that it is more important that the right things be done than that they be done in any particular way or through any particular agency.
>
> (Goodin, 1992, p. 120)

Where there is a clash between green values and any particular way of bringing them about, the former should take precedence:

> In cases of conflict ... the green theory of value – and the ends that it would have us promote – simply must, within the logic of the greens' own theory, take priority over the green theory of agency, and the principles of right action, agency and structure that that would recommend.
>
> (Goodin, 1992, p. 120)

Goodin himself deploys this distinction to argue against greens endorsing only radical lifestyle change as a means of bringing about green objectives. On Goodin's reading of what green politics is about, the sustaining of natural value is more important than ' "clean hands" principles of personal rectitude' (Goodin, 1992, p. 123), and if this means doing boring things like voting for green political parties, then so be it. But his radical distinction between a green theory of value and green theories of agency can be read in more equivocal ways, for if it is true that 'it is more important that the right things be done than that they be done in any particular way or through any particular agency', then *any* form of agency would seem to do as long as it brings about the right results. As it happens, Goodin himself endorses democratic means of bringing about green ends:

> green theory treats individual human beings as agents who naturally are, and morally ought to be, autonomous and self-governing entities. Politically, that pretty directly implies the central theme of the green political theory of agency: the importance of the full, free, active participation by everyone in democratically shaping their personal and social circumstances.
>
> (Goodin, 1992, p. 124)

But if getting the right thing done is more important than how it gets done, why should greens not endorse authoritarian means to green ends? At root, 'the core green concerns are consequentialistic' (Goodin, 1992, p. 120), and this *consequentialism* is in tension with the *proceduralism* of democracy.

As well as the nature of the 'green imperative', two further sources of the tension between ecological problems and democratic processes deserve mention – *time* and *space*. We are increasingly aware that policies in the present will have an impact on those in the future – even those yet to be born. From the point of view of the standard democratic four- or five-year cycle this is a problem, since governments generally have an eye on short-term policies for short-term gain. Colin Tudge's view that 'we cannot claim to be taking our species and our planet seriously until we acknowledge that a million years is a proper unit of political time' (Tudge, 1996, p. 371) puts current legislature cycles around the world into some sort of perspective. Similarly, the dynamics of political accountability cannot easily be made to work in the environmental context: 'how can politicians be brought to book for decisions whose consequences will only be fully felt long after the individuals concerned have retired from the political stage?' (Lafferty and Meadowcroft, 1996b, p. 7).

As for 'space', it is well known that many environmental problems are of an international character: global warming, by definition, is an issue that affects many nations rather than just one or two of them. This raises particular problems for the democratic process because democratic structures are, almost without exception, based on the nation-state. I shall say more about these issues of time and space below.

A number of reactions and responses to the authoritarian-ism/democracy conundrum have been given in recent years, and in no special order I outline seven of them in what follows. First, there is the possibility that the distinction drawn between green consequentialism and democratic proceduralism is too sharp. This is to say that consequences matter for democracy and procedures are important for greens. Consequences matter for democracy because some consequences may be inimical to democracy itself. This is sometimes referred to as democracy's 'self-bindingness', according to which democracy 'restricts itself, or proscribes certain types of outcome, in order to preserve itself' (Saward, 1993a, p. 66). The kind of outcome it might proscribe in our context is ecological catastrophe, since that would undermine the conditions for the practice of democracy itself. John Dryzek refers to this as a 'generalizable interest', and remarks that 'The continuing integrity of the ecological systems on which human life depends could perhaps be a generalizable interest par excellence' (Dryzek, 1990, p. 55). If a democratic procedure resulted in an outcome that threatened the integrity of ecological systems, it could legitimately be proscribed for self-binding reasons. I have pointed out elsewhere, though, that this is not a conclusive argument in favour of the compatibility of green objectives and democratic procedures, since 'just as democracy is self-bound not to endorse decisions that endanger the practice of democracy, so is authoritarianism – a sustainable society is as much a generalisable interest for authoritarians as it is for democrats' (Dobson, 1993b, p. 138).

From the other end of the problem, the end according to which procedures must matter for greens, Robyn Eckersley has sought to connect ecologism and democracy in much the same way as liberalism and democracy are connected: through building on the observation that 'liberal support for democracy flows from the liberal principles of autonomy and justice' (Eckersley, 1996, p. 222). In particular, the liberal principle of autonomy 'respects the rights of individuals to determine their own affairs' (ibid.), and if we were to read ecologism not in consequentialist terms but in terms of a 'broader defence of autonomy (let us say, for the moment, the freedom of human and non-human beings to unfold in their own ways and live according to their "species life")' then 'the connection between ecology and democracy would no longer be contingent' (ibid., p. 223). Both the 'preconditional' and the 'principle' approaches, then, call into question the sharp distinction normally drawn between green consequentialism and democratic proceduralism, and show that in this regard, at least, there may be more common ground than is often assumed.

A second argument for bringing ecologism and democracy into line turns on the indeterminacy of green objectives. The 'green theory of value' to which we have had cause to refer takes us some way towards deciding what is important for greens, but calculations of that value in any determinate and final sense are perhaps impossible to make. 'Natural value' and 'sustainability' are both contested ideas, and according to John Barry the achievement of the latter 'makes democracy a core, non-negotiable, value of green political theory' (J. Barry, 1996, p. 117), since because of the 'essential indeterminateness and normative character of the concept of sustainability ... it needs to be understood as a discursively "created" rather than an authoritatively "given" product' (ibid., p. 116). Michael Jacobs points out that this creative and open-ended articulation of the meaning of sustainability

> involves reasoning about other people's interests and values (as well as one's own) and the weight which should be given to them; about the application of and conflict between ethical principles in particular circumstances; and about the nature of the society one wishes to create or sustain.
>
> (Jacobs, 1997, p. 219)

For Jacobs,

> This suggests that where public [environmental] goods are at issue, the appropriate kind of value-articulating institution is not a private survey, but some kind of public forum in which people are brought together to debate before making their judgements. That is, the institution should be *deliberative* in character.
>
> (Jacobs, 1997, p. 220)

It is a very short step from here to the idea that the appropriate sorts of institutions for determining the nature of green objectives and the means for achieving them are democratic ones.

A third, family-related, suggestion for bringing green and democratic thought into alignment relies on an argument from pragmatism regarding the truth: 'democracy can be justified rationally precisely because of the impossibility of incontrovertible proof of anything' (Saward, 1993a, p. 76). Given that we can never be certain of anything, the most justifiable means of policy- and decision-making is one which takes turns around a problem and makes provision for reassessing the solution on a regular basis. With its public debate, accountability and periodic elections, this is democracy in all but name. In our context, Saward points out that 'Politics without certainty – indeed, politics as a substitute for certainty – has strong echoes in green political thinking' (Saward, 1993a, p. 77). The 'precautionary principle' (referred to briefly in Chapter 3) has indeed become a byword in green policy-making circles, and while there is no reason why authoritarian regimes could not adopt the precautionary principle of decision-making, the supposedly *provisional* nature of decisions taken in democracies makes them a more appropriate context for the 'epistemological pragmatism' of which we are talking.

The fourth argument takes an alternative view of the truth question. Despite the inherent uncertainty of decision-making, particularly in the environmental context, it can still be argued that some decisions are better – more in line with 'the truth' – than others. The question is, what is the best way of producing these better decisions? John Stuart Mill wrote that 'the opinion which it is attempted to suppress by authority may possibly be true. Those who desire to suppress it, of course deny its truth; but they are not infallible' (Mill 1859/1972, p. 79). This is an argument for open decision-making of the type normally associated with democratic consultation, and it should perhaps be endorsed by greens – even those with a determinate view of what the truth is:

> To the degree that there is a determinate answer about the 'right' values and the 'right' kind of society in which to live (and greens, in the round, believe that there is), then greens should be committed to democracy as the only form of decision-making that ... will necessarily produce the answer.
>
> (Dobson, 1996a, p. 139)

A fifth argument derives from the putative environmental benefits of a particular sort of decentralized face-to-face democracy. As Doherty and de Geus point out, and as we had cause to observe in Chapter 3, 'From an ecological standpoint greens view decentralisation as essential because it is less wasteful of resources, giving priority to local production and consumption rather than the production and transport of goods for a global market' (Doherty and de Geus, 1996b, p. 3). In one direction, this train of thought actually leads to bioregionalism, and as we saw in Chapter 3, bioregionalism is not necessarily democratic. But there are connections in democratic theory and practice between decentralization and participation, and to this degree there may be quite specific ecological arguments for localized democracy.

Finally, there are two sorts of argument from historical experience. The first of these rests its case on the respective environmental records of 'democratic' and 'authoritarian' societies in the belief that these records count decisively in favour of the former. The empirical strength of this claim cannot be assessed here, and we should certainly enter the caveat that the undoubtedly poor record of those regimes usually referred to as authoritarian in this context (i.e. the Soviet Union and its Eastern European neighbours) may have been due to factors other than their authoritarianism. Nevertheless, Lafferty and Meadowcroft speak for many when they write that

> it may be that acute environmental crises are more readily (or perhaps only) amenable to authoritarian solution. The response here must be that ... neither theory nor practical experience suggest that authoritarian regimes are likely to best democracies at resolving environmental problems over the long term.
>
> (Lafferty and Meadowcroft, 1996b, p. 3)

The second of these arguments from historical experience picks up on Bob Paehlke's observation that, at precisely the same time as the theoreticians of 'green authoritarianism' such as Heilbroner and Ophuls were peddling their wares, early environmental *activists* were favouring 'openness and participation in environmental administration' (Paehlke, 1988, p. 292). More recently, Doherty and de Geus point out that greens just turn out mostly to have been participatory democrats: 'In their organisation green parties and many grassroots green groups have tried to counter what they see as the dominance of political organisations by bureaucracies and leaders' (Doherty and de Geus, 1996b, p. 5). This defence of the existence of 'green democracy' is sociological rather than political-theoretical, however: a statement of what is (or has been) rather than what ought to be. On this reading, the relationship between ecologism and democracy is contingent rather than necessary, based on the sociological origins of ecologism rather than its theoretical foundations:

> Historically and sociologically the ideas on democracy of most of the Western European green parties developed from the models provided by the New Left in the late 1960s and from the practices of the new social movements in the 1970s and 1980s. The challenge to the bureaucratic character of modern government, and the call for self-management were unifying elements of the discourse of the New Left.
>
> (Doherty and de Geus, 1996b, p. 5)

All of these remarks on the possible connections between green and democratic thinking should be accompanied by the thought that there are many types of democracy, and the difference this can make to the compatibility question is considerable. For example, Michael Saward points out that the tensions he identifies between green objectives and democratic procedures are most marked in the context of *direct* democracy where the participatory proceduralism of democracy is at its height. In *representative* democracy it is understood that the representative has room for manoeuvre, and is entitled to take decisions on behalf of her or his constituents. Here, says Saward, the 'tensions [between green imperatives and democratic procedures] would be lessened' (Saward, 1993a, p. 70). In other words, the more democracy is understood to be government *for* the people rather than *by* the people, the more compatible with the objective-driven nature of green thinking it becomes.

Similarly, the empirical record suggests that some types of democracy are more amenable to environmental problem-articulation than others:

> the link between altruism and environmentalism may explain why the smaller social democracies of northern Europe – Norway, Sweden, the Netherlands – have been more active in promulgating policy discussions about environmental issues which involve regulation of market externalities and making the distributional costs of environmental programmes more transparent.
>
> (Witherspoon, 1996, p. 65)

All of this suggests that a full account of the troubled relationship between ecologism and democracy would require a cross-tabulated assessment of compatibility across *all* possible types of ecologism and *all* possible types of democracy. Such an assessment is beyond the scope of this book (and quite possibly beyond the capabilities of its author, too), but enough has been said to show that any equating of ecologism with authoritarianism needs to be treated with great caution.

One more type of 'green democracy' problem remains to be considered. Environmental problems have brought 'new constituencies' on to the political agenda, constituencies whose interests are affected by environmental change, but which are not easily represented through traditional democratic structures and their boundaries. Such constituencies include 'away country' nationals (e.g. Scandinavians affected by British acid rain), future generations, and parts of the non-human natural world. The question is: assuming that the interests of these constituencies should be represented democratically (a large assumption which is discussed in detail in Dobson, 1996b), how might institutions be appropriately redesigned? Two broad, and very different, answers have been given to this question. The first, from Bob Goodin, trades on the possibility of the interests of these constituencies (and particularly those of future generations and non-human nature) being 'encapsulated' in those of present human beings (Goodin, 1996, p. 841) in much the same way as the interests of very small children are regarded as encapsulated in those of their parents. Goodin is aware that this model has a disreputable past:

'Slaves' and servants' interests were, in just such ways, encapsulated within those of their master,' he says. Likewise, 'Pre-Edwardian wives, having no independent legal personality apart from that of their husbands, saw their interests incorporated within those of their husbands' (ibid., p. 842). But, he goes on, 'Both in the cases of young children and of future generations, the model of "incorporated interests" seems legitimate largely because it seems inevitable' (ibid., p. 843).

In my view there are three problems with Goodin's suggestion for 'enfranchising the earth'. First, and most damaging, it is not democratic: if it was not democratic for Edwardian wives to have their interests incorporated in those of their husbands, then the same must apply to the case of present and future generations. Second, 'encapsulation' is not the only method of representation available to us, and third, there is no guarantee that present people will 'internalize [the] interests' (Goodin, 1996, p. 844) of future generations and of non-human nature in the required way – and if they don't, then encapsulation will not bring about the benefits it promises. An alternative strategy is to have proxy representatives, elected by proxy constituencies, to represent 'directly' the interests of future generations and non-human nature in national and transnational legislatures:

> The proxy would function in exactly the same way as any democratic electorate. It would, in the first place, 'be' the future generation electorate, and candidates for representing the interests of future generations would be drawn from it. These candidates would fight election campaigns, outlining their objectives as far as furthering the interests of future generations are concerned … The proxy electorate would consider the various candidates' merits and then choose its preferred candidate(s) through a democratic election. The successful candidates would then sit in the democratic assembly alongside present generation representatives.
>
> (Dobson, 1996b, p. 132)

This form of enfranchisement is not without its difficulties, many of which are discussed elsewhere (Dobson, 1996b), but such a system would avoid the non-democratic implications of encapsulation, and while it would not quite *guarantee* that the interests of future generations and non-human nature were taken into account, the democratic discipline of accountability – provided by elections, and absent in encapsulation – would help to focus minds appropriately. At present, though, environmentalists and political ecologists have to work with legislatures that are composed in much more traditional ways, and I shall now examine the extent to which they can expect their objectives to be realized through national parliaments.

Action through and around the legislature

Green movements in most countries are attached to recognizably green parties which seek election to national legislatures. Green movements in all countries that have them see it as at least part of their role to try to influence the legislative process, either while policy is being drawn up, while bills are being debated, or during their execution. The principal assumption behind both kinds of activity (broadly speaking, party political activity and pressure group activity) is that the liberal-democratic decision-making process and the economic structures with which it is engaged are sufficiently open to allow the green agenda to be fulfilled through them. It seems to be accepted that even if a green party is not elected to government then sufficient pressure can be brought to bear on the incumbents to bring about a sustainable society:

> The Government ... must intervene, using the full range of sticks and carrots at its disposal, to address the root causes of our current crisis, not the symptoms. Through legislation, direct regulation, changes in the taxation system, subsidies, grants, loans, efficiency standards, the Government has it in its power to effect the sort of transition I am talking about.
>
> (Porritt, 1984a, p. 133)

The great majority of green literature on the issue of strategies for political change is written in the same vein. Peter Bunyard and Fern Morgan-Grenville's *The Green Alternative* (1987) is typical, and the following constitutes a representative sample of the advice given (my emphasis added in each case):

> If we act immediately, through *lobbying local councils* and rallying support amongst the community, we may be able to save areas of beauty for ourselves and the rest of humanity.
>
> (p. 1)

> We should *lobby Parliament* and voice concern that our money, via taxes, is being used to perpetrate policies that are ultimately destructive.
>
> (p. 30)

We must make our own voices heard through, for instance, *informing our MPs*.

(p. 4)

write to your MPs.

(pp. 58, 89)

It is important to understand that these are not isolated examples of the kind of strategy advanced by the green movement. On the contrary, at this level the movement's prescriptions rely extremely heavily on operation within the liberal-democratic framework. The question is: Is such reliance advisable given the radical political and social change that ecologism proposes?

The first problem for any green party (in some countries, and certainly in Britain) is that of getting elected in the first place – by which I mean not necessarily being elected to government but garnering sufficient votes to gain even minimal representation in the legislature. In Britain, the first-past-the-post system, in which the candidate in a given constituency with the most number of votes takes the seat, militates notoriously against small parties. The results of such a system were most obviously on view in the 1989 European elections, when the British Green Party gained 15 per cent of the popular vote and yet won no seats in the Strasbourg Parliament. (What a difference ten years can make. In the 1999 European elections, run on a form of proportional representation, the British Green Party won just 5.8 per cent of the national vote, and yet returned two members – Jean Lambert and Caroline Lucas – to the European Parliament.) It is still extremely hard to imagine the British Parliament with even one green representative, let alone with sufficient members to be able to enter into coalition with one of the major parties. Of course, most members of the Green Party in Britain are aware of this, and the parliamentary candidates I have talked to are evidently serious about political power but see their role principally in educative terms. The platform provided by elections is used to 'get the message across'. Of course, not all countries make it so difficult for small parties to taste electoral success, and shortly I shall consider the situation where a green party does have representation in a national legislature.

In any case, a green party's political problems clearly do not end with getting elected. It would be faced with confronting and overcoming the constraints imposed by powerful interests intent on preventing the radical political and social change that a radical green government would seek. Even at the level of relatively minor changes, opposition would most likely be intense. Werner Hülsberg, for example, discusses the notion of a green government taxing resource-intensive industries and observes that 'the question of power is largely ignored in this approach' (Hülsberg, 1988, p. 182), and that '[it is] clear that attempts at structural reform would be met with an investment strike and flight of capital' (ibid., p. 183). The central question in this context is whether a sustainable society can be brought about through the use of existing state institutions.

It has been argued that from two points of view the answer would seem to be 'No'. In the first place, political institutions are not best seen as neutral instruments that can be used by just any operator to achieve just any political ends. Political institutions are always already tainted by precisely those strategies and practices that the green movement, in its radical pretensions, seeks to replace. An instance of this would be the way in which political institutions (in the Western world at least) have come to embody the principles of representative forms of democracy. These institutions represent the formal abandonment of notions of mass participation in political life; they are indeed 'designed' to preclude the possibility of massive regular participation.

The exclusive nature of these institutions, which is constitutive of them, makes it impossible for them to be used for inclusive ends. If they were to be inclusive, in the sense of participatory, then they would be something other than they are. On this reading, participatory politics demands the radical restructuring (if not the abolition) of present institutions rather than their use in the service of participation. Attempts to press them into such service will necessarily result in the progressive dilution of the original project. Jonathon Porritt has argued that 'the taking of power from below, by this process of self-empowerment, must be combined with the passing down of power from above' (1984a, p. 167), or as the 1999 *Green Party Manifesto for a Sustainable Society* puts it: 'Parliament's role in the first five years of a green government will be ... to devolve functions to more local bodies' (AD 203). It has been suggested that this is a Utopian strategy, not because greens are as likely to be corrupted by power as anyone else (although this is a respectable argument), but because the institutions Porritt proposes to use already have centralization built into them.

Second, we have to take into account the point that political change is a matter of political and economic power. Even if we assume a green party in government, we are still left with the problem of powerful sources of resistance in other institutions such as the bureaucracy, the financial centres and so on. The Die Grünen Sindelfingen programme of January 1983 expressed the hopeful belief that the desire for a different kind of life and work will grip the majority, and that this majority will be strong enough to demonstrate clearly to the opposing minority the superiority of an economic system whose goal is not itself but ecological and social need.

(Hülsberg, 1988, p. 127)

Hülsberg himself cogently observes that, in this formulation, 'The question as to what would happen if the "opposing minority" could not be convinced is simply avoided' (ibid., p. 127).

I promised earlier to discuss the situation of a green party that had significant representation in a national legislature, so as to illustrate the problems encountered there. Die Grünen in Germany provide us with a set of experiences to which we can usefully refer. In the federal elections of 1983 they obtained 5.6 per cent of the vote and entered the Bundestag, increasing their share of the vote to 8.3 per cent in the next election of January 1987. In the 'reunification election' of 1990, the shared East and West German vote plummeted to 1.2 per cent (with the West German party losing all its seats; Jahn, 1994, p. 313), rising again to 7.3 per cent (49 seats, third largest party in the Bundestag) in 1994, falling slightly to 6.7 per cent for Bündnis90/die Grünen (47 seats and a share in a coalition government with the Social Democratic Party) in 1998. The 1994 and 1998 results, indeed, call the bluff of those who (like Anna Bramwell) had virtually written the party off:

> Since 1980 the Green Party [in Germany] has described a parabola. In the first election after reunification (December 1990) support for the post-unification Greens dropped sharply, and although the Greens retained support in Hesse, there is little doubt that the underlying drive behind their party is diminishing.
>
> (Bramwell, 1994, p. 133)

Subsequent events have rather proved her wrong.

The metaphor of colonization allows us to theorize some of the experiences of Die Grünen since 1983, for in two specific contexts the party has been colonized by the demands and temptations of parliamentary activity. In the first place, enormous amounts of energy have been expended over the issue of whether to make tactical alliances with other political parties so as to influence policy in a more extensive way. From a radical point of view, Petra Kelly's is the crucial observation: 'If the Greens end up becoming merely ecological Social Democrats, then the experiment is finished – it will have become a waste' (in Spretnak and Capra, 1985, p. 152). Any green party operating in the parliamentary sphere will be faced, at some level of administration, with the possibility of coalition, and the German greens have been increasingly prepared to practise coalition politics (even of the 'traffic light' variety – red-yellow-green; Poguntke, 1993, p. 398). Kelly's warning is clear: that dealings with other parties are undertaken at the risk of dilution of radical green principles. In this sense, the demands of parliamentary politics can contribute to a wearing down of the green project and the consequent likelihood of the abandonment of the project as originally conceived. The tremendous tensions within the German Green Party during the 1999 Kosovo crisis are evidence of this. Joschka Fischer, leading light in the party, was German Foreign Minister during the crisis, and he had to weather a considerable storm from those within his own ranks opposed to NATO intervention in the crisis.

On the other hand, Robert Goodin has pointed out that 'realist' greens

> are, as it were, in the same position as the missionary confronting many starving mouths and only a few morsels of food: they would dearly love to satisfy all, but they are only able to satisfy a few: still it is better that few be satisfied than none.
>
> (Goodin, 1992, p. 110)

As we saw above, this follows from Goodin's (contested) view that the green theory of value is 'distinctively consequentialistic' (Goodin, 1992, p. 111), and that any green theory of political agency should be the servant of the theory of value. The point of green agency, then, is to bring about green consequences, and consequences override agency in the event of conflict. Goodin has been congratulated for sorting out 'woolly green claims about grass-roots democracy and decentralisation' (Saward, 1993b, p. 511), but there remains the worry that too many green good intentions will be given up along the path of compromise. Some radical greens will argue that this is what has happened in the second instance regarding the German greens to which I want to refer: the struggle over the rotation system of delegates elected to the Bundestag. Under the original system, green representatives elected to the Bundestag would serve only two years and then give way for the next two years to understudies who were originally hired as 'legislative assistants' (Spretnak and Capra, 1985, p. 39). The reason given for this principle reflects the fear of colonization: 'Because a person's thinking is affected by the way she or he lives, eight, or even four years in the Bundestag – or a state legislature – machine would be very destructive' (ibid.). At the same time, the rotation system was intended to be a visible sign of green refusal to concentrate political power in the hands of relatively few individuals. Objections to the principle were derived from the demands of working effectively in the Bundestag: rotation was held to prevent the emergence of influential 'personalities', and it reduced expertise.

From 1983, commitment to rotation and the principles it embodies waned and in May 1986 it was formally abandoned. This is not because the principles in themselves were found wanting but because they were unworkable, as originally conceived, in the context of parliamentary politics: 'Under the pressure of political developments, naive notions of rank and file democracy are now a thing of the past' (Hülsberg, 1988, p. 123). In similar vein Spretnak and Capra state that 'the rotation principle for elected officials has proven to be more trouble than it is worth for the Greens in West Germany' (1985, pp. 188–9). The general upshot has been that

> after more than a decade of experience with their experimental attempt at institutionalising direct democratic structures within the framework of representative democracy, the Greens have moved somewhat towards the established parties ... the structural impera-tives of the political system have taken their toll.
>
> (Poguntke, 1993, pp. 395–6)

The question is: How far can radical green politics be achieved through the parliamentary context if its 'structural imperatives' demand the progressive abandonment of the principles of such politics?

In 1985 Rudolf Bahro, then the most famous 'fundamentalist' in Die Grünen, left the party. He argued that by then the party had 'no basic ecological position' because 'what people are trying to do ... is to save a party – no matter what kind of party; and no matter for what purpose. The main thing is for it to get re-elected to parliament in 1987' (1986, p. 210). Bahro is here articulating the experience of a fundamentalist green who has seen the party colonized by the demands of the very system that it originally sought to overcome. His conclusion ran as follows:

> At last I have understood that a party is a counterproductive tool, that the given political space is a trap into which life energy disap pears, indeed, where it is rededicated to the spiral of death. This is not a general but a quite concrete type of despair. It is directed not at the original project which is today called 'fundamental', but at the party. I've finished with it now.
>
> (Bahro, 1986, p. 211)

The problem that has informed this discussion of the possibility of promoting green change through the parliamentary process centres on the difficulty of bringing about a decolonized society through structures that are already colonized – structures that are deeply (perhaps irremediably) implicated in the *status quo* that green politics seeks to shift. This is not a new problem: socialists have been debating the issue for over 150 years. I think it important to reiterate it in this context, though, because it points up the tension between the radical nature of the green project and the piecemeal strategy that has often been advanced to bring it about. Indeed, if one focused solely on the parliamentary strategy one could be forgiven for thinking that the green movement had no radical project beyond environmentalism at all, so far is this strategy removed from any radical pretensions. Raymond Williams has pointed out the dangers of the 'practical surrender of the real agenda of issues to just that version of politics which the critique has shown to be defective and is offering to supersede' (1986, pp. 252–3). This is the point of the general critique of the parliamentary road to the sustainable society.

Most people in the green movement who argue for change through liberal-democratic political structures will also support other forms of action. The rest of this chapter will be taken up with discussing these other options, under the four headings of lifestyle, communities, direct action and class.

Lifestyle

The general principle behind both lifestyle and community strategies is that changes of consciousness and changes in behaviour are mutually reinforcing. Lifestyle change concerns changes in the patterns of individual behaviour in daily life. Typical examples of this would be: care with the things you buy, the things you say, where you invest your money, the way you treat people, the transport you use, and so on.

During the late 1980s there was a veritable explosion in the popularity of green lifestyle changes in Britain. Home ecology, among certain sections of the community at least, was all the rage. Retailers picked up and reinforced this trend and the major supermarket chains fell over themselves to stock their shelves with environmentally friendly goods. Products in green packets sold significantly better than similar products packaged in any other colour. In this context, green rapidly becomes the colour of capitalist energy and enterprise. From the point of view of lifestyle changes, the spaces for political action are in principle infinite – even the toilet is a potential locus for radical politics, for as John Seymour and Herbert Girardet inform us: 'A quarter of all domestic water in most countries goes straight down the toilet. Every time somebody flushes the toilet about 20 litres of water are instantly changed from being pure to being polluted' (Seymour and Girardet, 1987, p. 27). They offer concise advice: 'If it's brown wash it down. If it's yellow let it mellow' (Seymour and Girardet, 1987, p. 27). I suppose that's one way to start a revolution. Although recessions have taken their toll on the green consumer somewhat, as people buy the cheapest rather than the greenest washing-up liquid, green consumption still exists. If anything, its relative invisibility is due to its success rather than its failure – it is now so much a normal part of the product parade that we don't notice it as much as we used to.

The lifestyle strategy has been around for a long time in the green movement and it has spawned an enormous number of books and pamphlets on practical action to avert environmental decay. Back in 1973 Fritz Schumacher wrote, 'Everywhere people ask: "What can I actually *do?*" The answer is as simple as it is disconcerting: we can, each of us, work to put our own inner house in order' (1976, pp. 249–50). The theme is consistent: that personal transformation leads to altered behaviour; which in turn can be translated into sustainable community living: 'The only possible building blocks of a Greener future are individuals moving towards a Greener way of life *themselves* and joining together with others who are doing the same' (Bunyard and Morgan-Grenville, 1987, p. 336).

The positive aspect of this strategy is that some individuals do indeed end up living sounder; more ecological lives. More bottles and newspapers are recycled, more lead-free petrol is bought, and fewer harmful detergents are washed down the plughole. The disadvantage, though, is that the world around goes on much as before, ungreened and unsustainable – certainly in terms of Porritt's desire for a 'radical overhaul', which I took as my rubric for this chapter. In the first place, one has the problem of persuading sufficient numbers of people to lead sustainable lives for it to make a difference to the integrity of the environment. It is evidently hard to predict just how far the message will spread, and how many people will act on it, but it seems unlikely that a massive number of individuals will experience the conversion that will lead to the necessary changes in their daily behaviour.

At the same time, many of the proposals for change of this sort ask us to alter our behaviour at particular points in our daily life and then allow us back on the unsustainable rampage. There is nothing inherently green, for example, in green consumerism, briefly referred to above. It is true that consumer pressure helped bring about a reduction in the use of CFCs in aerosol sprays. It is true that the Body Shop will supply you with exotic perfumes and shampoos in reusable bottles and that have not been tested on animals. It is true that we can help extend the life of tropical rainforests by resisting the temptation to buy mahogany toilet seats. There is also evidence that consumer resistance in Europe to genetically modified (GM) foods is damaging GM companies, as Europe's largest bank (Deutsche Bank) advises its major investors to sell their shares in GM companies because consumers do not want to buy their products (*Guardian*, 25 August 1999, p. 1). All of this helps the environment, but none of it – absent other strategies – can bring about the radical changes envisaged by ecologism.

First, it does nothing to confront the central green point that unlimited production and consumption – no matter how environmentally friendly – is impossible to sustain in a limited system. The problem here is not so much to get people to consume soundly but to get them – or at least those living in profligate societies – to consume less. The Body Shop strategy is a hymn to consumption: in their contribution to the Friends of the Earth Green Consumer Week leaflet (12–18 September 1988) they urged people to 'wield their purchasing power responsibly' rather than to wield it less often. It is this that makes green consumerism environmental rather than radically green.

Second, it has been pointed out that 'there are masses of people who are disenfranchised from this exercise of power by virtue of not having the money to spend in the first place' (*Green Line*, no. 60, March 1988, p. 12). Third, parts of the green movement feel consumerism to be too grubby and materialistic a means to lead us reliably to the stated end of a society of 'voluntary simplicity'. This is the point behind Porritt and Winner's observation that 'A crude, consumer-driven culture prevails, in which the spirit is denied and the arts are rejected or reduced to a privileged enclave for the few' (Porritt and Winner, 1988, p. 247) and, more generally, that 'it is ... worth stressing that the underlying aim of this green consumerism is to reform rather than fundamentally restructure our patterns of consumption' (ibid., p. 199). Once more we are forced to recognize the difference between environmentalism and ecologism: the strategy of green consumerism, in its call for change substantially in line with present strategies based on unlimited production and consumption, is a child of the former rather than the latter

The strategy of change in individual habits leading to long-term social change takes no account, either, of the problem of political power and resistance to which I referred in the previous section. It is perhaps unrealistic to assume that those forces that would be positively hostile to sustainability will allow present forms of production and consumption to wither away. Of course, this is much less of a problem if the green movement has in mind only some form of attenuated environmentalism, but if (once again) it is serious about the desire to usher in a radically ecocentric society then it will eventually be forced to confront the issue of massive resistance to change.

What seems common to these lifestyle strategies as I have treated them is that they mostly reject the idea that bringing about change is a properly 'political' affair – they do not hold that green change is principally a matter of occupying positions of political power and shifting the levers in the right direction. In Chapter 1 I noted that spirituality is of greater importance to the green perspective than is probably publicly realized, and this has made a significant impression on some activists in the movement with regard to how change might come about. Rudolf Bahro's writings from the period of his increasing disillusionment with Die Grünen and the parliamentary strategy are the *locus classicus* of what we might tentatively call the 'religious approach' to green change.

The general point behind the religious approach is that the changes that need to take place are too profound to be dealt with in the political arena, and that the proper territory for action is the psyche rather than the parliamentary chamber. Marilyn Ferguson has recommended the use of 'psychotechnologies' (Ferguson, 1981) to bring about calmer, gentler, more 'green' states of consciousness, and the Findhorn community in Scotland bases its activities on the belief that this is indeed the right path to change. Such an approach takes seriously the point made above – namely, that political opposition to radical green change will be massive – and side-steps it. Bahro talks expressively of needing to take 'a new run-up from so far back that we can't afford to waste our time in the mock battles which are so typical of Green committees' (1986, p. 159), and the change he envisages is the 'metaphysical reconstruction' advocated by Jonathon Porritt and David Winner (1988, pp. 246–9). Ultimately, this approach involves a rejection of political strategies, normally understood, on the basis of the belief that profound shifts of direction are carried out only by those motivated by what we might loosely call a religious, rather than a material, sensibility: 'The differentiation between the creative forces and the forces of inertia does not take place economically or sociologically but rather psychologically and in the last instance religiously' (Bahro, 1986, p. 94). Such a belief, in Bahro's case, is based upon a particular reading of history:

> If we take a look in history at the foundations on which new cultures were based or existing ones essentially changed, we always come up against the fact that in such times people returned to those strata of consciousness which are traditionally described as religious.
>
> (Bahro, 1986, p. 90)

More recently, but in similar vein, Bahro wrote that '[T]he new order exists first of all in heads and hearts' (Bahro, 1994, p. 304), and more specifically: '[I]t seems to me that to take up Tantric and Indian initiation praxes ... guides us ... in the direction of solving the problem of the Megamachine' (ibid., p. 299).

This is, of course, in direct opposition to any theory that has it that political and social change is primarily generated through people identifying their immediate material (widely understood) interests and acting to satisfy them. (For an empirically informed assessment of the role of 'psychotechnologies' in social change, see Seel, 1999, Ch. 6.) Bahro's contention causes him to take completely seriously the idea that Porritt's metaphysical reconstruction will involve revisiting the historical experience to which he refers: 'We need a new Benedictine order,' he writes (Bahro, 1986, p. 90). Part of his enthusiasm for the Benedictine experience lies in its having taken a communal form, and we have already seen him (in Chapter 3) arguing that the sustainable society will be founded upon small-communal life. But for our present purposes the content of Benedictine life is more important than the context within which it was lived. Very significantly, Bahro writes that 'the monastery was not meant as an economic microcosm to be indefinitely multiplied. Its "service" as forerunner related to the *inward arrangement* of the feudal world' (ibid., p. 94; emphasis added).

In other words, the function of the monastery was not so much to illustrate a different form of life as to create pockets of existence in which its content, or its psychological dispositions, had changed. Bahro's contention is that a modern-day Benedictine-style movement would provide the points of light and the conversionary zeal necessary to engineer the changes required by what he conceives to be the profundity of the present crisis. The missionary sense is never far away: 'there should be some initiators (men and women) who make a personal decision, begin by preparing themselves and a project and gather around them a circle of fellow-strivers' (Bahro, 1986, p. 91). The end result, hopes Bahro, would be an overbalancing of the spirit in favour of green reconstruction: 'The accumulation of spiritual forces ... will at a particular point in time which can't be foreseen exceed a threshold size. Such a 'critical mass', once accumulated, then acquires under certain circumstances a transformative influence over the whole society' (ibid., p. 98).

More recently, Bahro made a particularly explicit connection between the changes in consciousness that green community living can bring about, and the idea that these communities are themselves a microcosm of ecotopian society. He is scathing about weekend consciousness-raising encounters which are characterized by their 'accidental and non-committing' character (Bahro, 1994, p. 306), and argues instead that:

> the new subjectivity has to risk itself to everyday life and must concern itself with giving beauty, a ritual framework and a spiritual centre to the daily business of living together ... The real association, that living circle which is initially small, claims at the time to be a 'culture crystal': a whole new society in a nutshell ... The single community can strive to live self-reliantly, so that it can picture to itself the possibility that the whole species could be organised in analogous cells, responsible for *Gaia* – having an appropriate contact with the world of animals, plants and minerals, and with the original elements of earth, water, air and fire.
>
> (Bahro, 1994, p. 306)

This 'double strategy' takes Bahro beyond what I have called here 'lifestyle' modes of social change towards the 'community' strategy that is the subject of the next section. In truth, to the extent that living the community life amounts in any case to a change in lifestyle it is somewhat specious to distinguish between the two.

Bahro's tactics have been roundly criticized by some, not least because they led him into the gold-plated Rolls-Royce world of Bhagwan Shree Rajneesh in California. But the significance of his position is that it takes the spiritual dimension of green politics absolutely seriously. I argued in Chapter 2 that there was a gulf between spirituality (in the guise of deep ecology) and politics in the theory and practice of the green movement, and suggested that the spirituality ought to come to meet the politics. Bahro would reject this approach, saying that if the politics is out of step with the spirit, then the spirit must take precedence over the politics. In this sense, green change might properly involve vacating the corridors of power and occupying the hotly disputed space around spiritual sites such as Stonehenge, or exchanging the pin-striped suit for the Druid's gown. And if the extent of the threat to an established way of life is in direct proportion to the violence of the reaction to it of the forces of law and order, then, judging by police reaction to summer solstice celebrations at Stonehenge (culminating in a Criminal Justice Bill passed by the Conservative Government in Britain in 1994, which criminalized a number of 'New Age' activities) Bahro and his supporters may well have a point.

Communities

A general problem with the strategy of lifestyle change is that it is ultimately divorced from where it wants to go, in that it is not obvious how the individualism on which it is based will convert into the communitarianism that is central to most descriptions of the sustainable society. (This problem is less acute – at least in terms of theory – in Bahro's case, described above, because the change in consciousness that he prescribes is already tied to community living.) It would appear more sensible to subscribe to forms of political action that are already communitarian, and that are therefore both a practice and an anticipation of the advertised goal. In this sense the future is built into the present and the programme is more intellectually convincing and practically coherent.

In this context Robyn Eckersley has argued that 'The revolutionary subject is ... the active, responsible person-in-community, *homo communitas*, if you like' (Eckersley, 1987, p. 19). She goes on to suggest, in a vein referred to above, that this is because 'Perhaps the ultimate principle of ecopraxis is the need to maintain consistency between means and ends' (ibid., p. 21). Consequently, 'The most revolutionary structures are seen to be those that foster the development of self-help, community responsibility and free activity and are consistent with the ecotopian ideal of a loose federation of regions and communes' (ibid., p. 22).

Community strategies might be an improvement on lifestyle strategies, then, because they are already a practice of the future in a more complete sense than that allowed by changes in individual behaviour patterns. They are more clearly an alternative to existing norms and practices, and, to the extent that they work, they show that it is possible to live differently – even sustainably. Rudolf Bahro has expressed it as follows:

> To bring it down to the basic concept, we must build up areas liberated from the industrial system. That means, liberated from nuclear weapons and from supermarkets. What we are talking about is a new social formation and a different civilisation.
>
> (Bahro, 1986, p. 29)

Obviously not just any communities will do. It is not enough to say that 'a major priority for both reds and greens is the campaign to win for communities greater control over their environment' (Weston, 1986, p. 160), without those communities having a clear idea of how they might operate sustainably. In this context, the kinds of communities that represent ecological lifestyles are rural self-sufficiency farms, city farms, some workers' co-operatives, some kinds of squat throughout the cities of Europe, and, more concretely (in Britain), the Centre for Alternative

Technology (CAT) at Machynlleth in Wales and the Findhorn community in Scotland: 'The solution, for both Bahro and Findhornians, is to initiate spiritual reconstruction in alternative communities' (Seel, 1999, pp. 262–3). In 1991 David Pepper published the results of a series of interviews with more than eighty commune members from twelve communes in England, Scotland and Wales (Pepper, 1991). Using a measure of 'greenness' revolving around ecologically sound practices such as the sharing of resources, recycling, cutting energy use, and so on, Pepper comes to the conclusion that

> communards [those studied, at least] have a world view that is indeed radically and overwhelmingly green. This view translates rather patchily into individual and group practice, but it is probably true that communes can provide an institutional context which encourages ecologically sound practices.
>
> (Pepper, 1991, p. 156)

The Schwarzes have observed that 'these ventures operate outside and potentially in opposition to, the prevailing culture' (1987, p. 73), and with that they may have put their finger on the necessary defining characteristic of any strategy that hopes to bring about radical change. In the section on parliamentary change, it was suggested that initiatives in and around the legislature were too easily absorbed, and thus neutralized, by their context. Initiatives that live 'outside' the prevailing culture and its diversionary channels have a much brighter chance of remaining oppositional and therefore of bringing about radical change.

However, even this needs to be qualified because 'to be outside' and 'to be oppositional' are not the same thing, and the difference is crucial in terms of understanding the options for green political strategy. This is because it can be argued that the dominant set of modes and practices needs an opposition against which to define itself and with respect to which to judge itself. In this sense the polarity that opposition sets up helps to sustain and reproduce that which it opposes. One can see this phenomenon in operation at the Centre for Alternative Technology in Wales. At the outset the community at the Centre intended to be 'outside' the prevailing culture, independent of the National Electricity Grid and living a daily life organized around radically democratic and sustainable principles: 'low-tech methods, reduced or simplified methods of consumption, job-rotation, personal growth, priority to collective resources, blurring the distinction of work/non-work, a strong emphasis on community life, and "living the technology" ' (Harper, n.d., p. 4). But, as the same member of the community put it, 'Gradually the bloom faded. I watched it happen in myself. A combination of hard experience, exhaustion, human frailty, pressures of family life, a desire to be acceptable to ordinary humanity, ageing ... turned me into a reluctant moderate' (ibid., p. 2). One CAT member in Pepper's commune study argued that the Quarry (the Centre is built around an old slate quarry) was now a way for people 'already into social change to renew their batteries. But it's not a way to change society. I'd like the green movement to promote communes, but it's more important for it to get political power' (Pepper, 1991, p. 181).

This journey towards moderation must be the story of a thousand alternative communities that have found that opposition ends up at incorporation. Now the CAT processes thousands of visitors a year who come from all over the world and pay money to look in on an experiment that, by virtue of the visitors themselves, is shown to have lapsed. Peter Harper writes, 'Sadly, but inevitably, I see a time of Revisionism ahead ... The Quarry will become more efficient, harmonious, consistent, respectable, and boring. It will be a successful institution, not a community' (n.d., p. 6). The Centre is now a successful institution – that which was decolonized has been recolonized, and we are left to celebrate 'the Quarry's arrival as a respectable and integral part of British society' (ibid., p. 7). Pepper's study suggests that this pattern is not unique to the CAT:

> Perhaps the greatest potential barrier to communes acting as agents for radical rather than reformist social change towards an Ecotopian society is the process whereby they become absorbed into conventional society, that culture to which they have previously run counter.
>
> (Pepper, 1991, p. 204)

Pepper theorizes this, in conclusion, as a three-stage process: an attempt to bypass the system; then using it; then becoming part of it (Pepper, 1991, p. 205). Of course, it might be argued that the respectability produced by becoming part of the system is precisely the Centre's strongest card in the context of persuading visitors to go home and practise the kind of lifestyle change described above. Some might even be so taken by the lifestyle of the community's members that they go and set up their own communities – and if this were to happen to sufficient people (although there is no evidence that it has) it would amount to justification of the strategy of change by example. The CAT's respectability, it is suggested, makes it a likely source of inspiration in that it is recognizably similar to 'our' society: they have telephones and a restaurant, they care about being warm, and they are surrounded by technology, some of it makeshift but some of it extremely complex (if 'alternative'). The members' daily lives do not appear to revolve around long periods of meditation, shamanistic rituals or talking to lettuces, and so the day visitor is less likely to dismiss the community as irrelevant to her or his own experience. I am sure this is true, but one is still confronted with the distinction between environmental and fully green change. The CAT's success will lie in raising an environmental consciousness rather than in providing a 'liberated zone' (in Rudolf Bahro's evocative phrase) of sustainable living, and this is the distinction Harper was pointing to in describing the Centre as a 'successful institution' rather than a 'community'. Most community initiatives, then, oppose the prevailing culture rather than live outside it. Just what 'living outside' means, and how far it is even possible, will be discussed shortly, but it seems clear that part of the reason why community initiatives have not brought about the 'fundamental shift' that Jonathon Porritt mentioned at the beginning of the chapter is because their opposition is easily neutralized and, indeed, turns out to be necessary for the very survival and reproduction of that which it opposes.

What I have called community strategies are arguably an improvement on lifestyle change because they make more ready connections between present practice and future aspirations. However, besides easy neutralization, such strategies depend too heavily (like their lifestyle counterparts) on change by example. They may indeed show us that sustainable styles of life are possible, but as agents for political change they rely entirely on their seductive capacity. The problem is that people refuse to be seduced: rather than producing radical changes in consciousness, sustainable communities perform the role of the surrogate good conscience, and we can go at the weekend to see it operating. Respondents in Pepper's (admittedly restricted) survey were generally downbeat regarding communes forming a vanguard for social change:

> Over six out of ten of our interviewees thought that communes are not important in leading us to a green society, and do not constitute a significant part of the blueprint for survival. Less than three in ten thought that they might be significant, and under one in ten was prepared to be enthusiastic and unconditional in supporting the idea.
>
> (Pepper, 1991, p. 180)

If confrontation appears to result so easily in co-option, then perhaps circumvention is another way forward for the green movement. I have suggested that the principal advantage of community strategies for change is that they anticipate the hoped-for green future, particularly its decentralized communitarian aspects. In this context an interesting practice has recently reappeared, which depends not upon setting up entirely integral communities, but upon allowing communities of work and exchange to 'emerge' through creating a system of what is most generally referred to as 'local money' (Greco, 1994).

Such systems are by no means new and they have usually appeared when local economies stagnate owing to the flight of capital or the underutilization of local skills and resources. The results of such a situation are familiar:

> When local unemployment rises, for whatever reason, people lose their incomes and have less money in their pockets. They spend less money with local traders, who in turn have less money in their pockets, then the whole local economy takes a downturn and becomes sluggish. Unemployed people sit at home while shopkeepers watch half-empty shops. The economic activity which should be the life spring of an economy begins to dry up.
>
> (Dauncey, 1988, p. 51)

The aim of a local money system is therefore both to return a measure of control of currency to the community and to put dormant skills and resources back into circulation. This happens, in theory, because local currencies 'can be spent only within the limited area of the community ... [they] can be created locally in accordance with the needs of the local economy, and ... [they] encourage local people to patronize one another rather than buying from outside the community' (Greco, 1994, p. 46). The results seem sometimes to have been spectacular:

> In the town of Wörgl, Austria, there stands a bridge whose plaque commemorates the fact that it was built by debt-free, locally created money. This was just a small part of a significant experiment that transformed towns and whole areas out of poverty within three months and into prosperity within one year, at a time when there was widespread unemployment in the national economy.
>
> (Weston in Ekins, 1986, p. 199)

This particular experiment took place between about 1929 and 1934 and, significantly, was ended when 200 Austrian mayors met and decided to follow Wörgl's example, whereupon the Austrian National Bank began a long legal battle to have the scheme outlawed. They eventually succeeded and the system was wound up.

One of the best-known contemporary examples of a local money scheme was the Local Employment and Trade System (LETSystem) which ran in the town of Courtenay on Canada's Vancouver Island between 1983 and 1989, and which was the inspiration for 'hundreds of active LETS systems in various stages of development in many countries' (Greco, 1994, p. 88). The general principles of the Courtenay system were as follows:

> A number of people who live locally and who want to trade together get together, agree to the LETSystem rules, and give themselves account numbers. Each person then makes out two lists, one of 'wants' and another of 'offers', with prices attached (following normal market prices). A joint list is made up and circulated to everyone. Then the members look down the list, phone whoever has what they want, and start trading ... The limits of one-to-one barter are eliminated, as you can now trade with the people in the system as a whole: barter is now a collective proposition.
>
> (Dauncey, 1988, p. 52)

No money changes hands because there is no actual 'money' – credits and debits are recorded on a computer and the Green dollars in which LETSystem users trade never get beyond being intangible bits of information. If I sell a car for, say, 2000 Green dollars, then the computer credits me with those dollars, which I can then use within – and only within – the system. The money thus remains inside the system-community and provides the incentive for people to advertise, sell and buy skills and resources. Shopkeepers may decide to sell their goods wholly or partly in Green dollars, and so benefit from the newly generated buying power of LETSystem users.

This is not the place to go into the details of local money experiments and the problems that can come with them: hoarding, inflation, tax liability, social security implications, defaulting on debits by leaving the 'community', and so on. Likewise, I have mentioned only two of the more obvious advantages of such a system in a run-down local economy: money stays local and incentive is provided to exercise skills that might otherwise remain dormant. LETSystem users have reported other benefits, such as simplicity, the personal nature of transactions, and the building of self-confidence that comes with supplying others with goods and services they require.

My intention here has simply been to show how local money schemes might be considered as one potential strategy for green change – a 'community' strategy in my typology in that they anticipate the decentralized communitarian nature of the sustainable society. At the same time though, the Austrian National Bank's reaction to the Wörgl experiment described above might be taken as a sign of the potentially subversive nature of local money schemes. They appear to be less easily co-opted than other examples of community change, and in this respect have characteristics that might well qualify them as a part-strategy for the possible agents of change discussed further below.

Direct action

As far as individual actors in the green movement are concerned, of course, all the approaches to green change discussed above can be combined. Any one person could be a member of a green party as well as a buyer of Ecover washing-up liquid. S/he might also live in a community which was trying to turn the world green by example. More recently, in Britain at least, s/he might also have been one of the many thousands of people battling it out – sometimes violently, sometimes not – with building contractors intent on carrying out the government's road-building programme, or the rather smaller – but still effective – number uprooting genetically modified crops in the government's designated test fields. Direct action to halt what protestors see as environmental degradation has become an increasingly prominent feature of the political scene in recent years, and it is carried out by an apparently disparate collection of people, ranging from middle-class 'Nimbys' through to New Age travellers. Disillusionment with mainstream political parties (including the Green Party) and the agendas they promote has given rise to a form of do-it-yourself politics: groups of (mostly) young people organize around a squat, a sound system, a drug, a piece of land, and try to live a self-reliant life:

> Perhaps because of the very feeling of isolation a growing number of what can only be described as 'tribes' have been popping up quietly all over the country ... Although they all have different identities and aims, when it comes to their motivation, these groups all speak with one voice. They talk about a resurgence of the free-spirit movement ... a quiet dignity that refuses to be caught up in the fast-track of winners and losers, fashions and fads ... Who knows when this spirit began to speed up from a tricklet to a wave but certainly in the past few recession-hit years, a network of the skint but proud has slowly been falling into place.
>
> (Pod,1994, p. 7)

The politics of these groups varies, but a number are moved by concerns that motivate the wider green movement – such as opposition to the road-building programme (Seel, 1997; North, 1998). Rather than (or sometimes, in the case of more traditional protestors, as well as) lobbying their Members of Parliament or joining a mainstream pressure group, activists choose to oppose the roads through direct action. This usually takes the form of a continuing presence at the site in question (if possible) and non-violent (normally) resistance to contractors when they appear for work. Some celebrated battles between contractors and protestors took place in this context in the south of England in the summer of 1994, and opposition to one motorway in particular, gave rise to perhaps the best-known 'tribe' of all – the Dongas. One member of the Dongas explains how her opposition to the motorway constitutes part of a world-view which is recognizably green: 'we've gone back to the essence of what life is all about, living with the land rather than destroying it. We've learned to appreciate the basic things like the warmth of a fire and the natural world around us' (*Pod*, 1994, p. 20). She also shares the decentralist impulse that informs much green political design: 'Looking on the outside, I think everything has become too centralised. A few bods in London controlling areas they've never seen. Local areas should be controlled by local communities' (ibid., p. 20).

In international terms the best-known direct action environmental group is undoubtedly Earth First!, about whom Derek Wall has recently written in fascinating detail (1999). Earth First! was founded in 1980 by a group of activists in the United States of America concerned that timid campaigning was doing too little too late to save the planet. From the outset, Earth First! recommended direct action (or what they call 'monkeywrenching', after their techniques for disabling bulldozers and other heavy machinery) as a strategy for opposing industrialism and preserving wilderness. Their activities have drawn criticism from both inside and outside the green movement, and they are variously accused of valuing animals and trees above human beings, of endangering human life, and of getting the rest of the movement a bad name.

Monkeywrenching is not unprincipled, however. Dave Foreman – an erstwhile central figure in Earth First! – and Bill Haywood compiled a *Field Guide to Monkeywrenching* (1989), in which the principles of sabotage and its political effectiveness are explained and discussed. Above all, Foreman writes that monkeywrenching is non-violent in respect of persons. Earth First! received adverse publicity during its campaign to spike trees with long nails to prevent them being cut down, because of the possibility of injury to loggers from their own saws. The *Field Guide* consequently carefully explains that nails should be driven in high enough up the tree to prevent loggers' access. The intention is to damage industrial saws in the mill rather than injure the loggers themselves (Foreman and Haywood, 1989, pp. 1–17).

The political intentions of Earth First! sabotage are to increase the operating costs of environmentally destructive businesses, to raise public awareness regarding environmental despoliation, and (interestingly) to increase the respectability of more mainstream environmentalists (Foreman and Haywood, 1989, pp. 21–3). As Derek Wall remarks,

> Environmental pressure groups may be able to frame their demands so as to mobilise financial support or maintain letter-writing campaigns, but seem far less effective in transforming public opinion in a more fundamental way or in promoting the growth of green agency.
>
> (Wall, 1999, p. 191)

Judging the practical effectiveness of direct action is a hazardous business: it is extremely difficult to trace effect back to cause with any degree of certainty. Earth First!'s intentions, outlined above, might be taken as the yardstick by which any direct action group's success should be measured, and I think it would be hard to deny success in these terms to the various groups engaged in the road-building opposition described earlier. One report estimated that the Department of Transport was losing £20,000 per day at the height of the protest, and certainly the protest highlighted the road-building programme in a public and dramatic way. In terms of respectability, one can imagine Friends of the Earth (for example) gaining in credibility when placed alongside the Dongas tribe.

On the other hand, direct action protests seem not be connected to a wider movement strategy, and thus run the risk of 'serial evaporation'. As Ben Seel has remarked in connection with the Pollok Free State campaign in Scotland (1994–6),

> the core group was not greatly concerned with questions of how different parts of a wider green movement would co-ordinate, nor with the more difficult questions of coalitions with other social movements or the potential role of a political party.
>
> (Seel, 1997, pp. 134–5)

Similarly, the tactical and strategic differences between types of protest can bring about counter-productive conflict. Commenting on the Solsbury Hill protest, Peter North writes that

On one side were the Dongas, living by their deep ecological values and representing back to society a vision of an alternative; and on the other, S[ave] O[ur] S[olsbury] attempting to mobilise resources to convince the authorities to change their mind and stop building the road.

(North, 1998, p. 20)

He continues,

While debates were at first generally amicable, conflict grew over time as the Dongas attempted to create their own temporary liberated space on the hill, bringing unfavourable publicity and conflict with the landowners which SOS felt mitigated [sic] against their claims for legality and respectability.

(ibid., p. 21)

In each of these cases the road or motorway was still completed, even if a little behind schedule. Direct action supporters would no doubt see this as a case of 'lose a battle, win the war', and they could now point to successive Conservative and Labour ('New' Labour, that is) governments cutting back road-building programmes as evidence of their longer term success (Doherty, 1999, pp. 284–5). Cynics, though, will say that this has more to do with pressure from Members of Parliament in the South of England worried about losing their seats in the next general election than with protestors risking their lives by lying down in front of bulldozers.

Class

Sometimes greens speak as though a simple 'change of consciousness' is enough to bring about radical shifts in social and political life. Arnold Toynbee, cited approvingly by Jonathon Porritt, writes:

The present threat to mankind's survival can be removed only by a revolutionary change of heart in individual human beings. This change of heart must be inspired by religion in order to generate the will power needed for putting arduous new ideals into practice.

(Porritt, 1984a, p. 211)

Generally speaking, this kind of sentiment is accompanied by an exhortation to education as a necessary preface to conversion. However, as David Pepper has rightly observed, 'people will not change their values just through being "taught" different ones' (Pepper, 1984, p. 224). Pepper goes on: 'What, then, is the real way forward, if it is not to be solely or even largely through education? It must be through seeking *reform at the material base of society, concurrent with educational change*' (ibid., p. 224; emphasis in the original). Quite – but how?

The answer to this question might just turn on initially side-stepping it and asking instead: *Who* is best placed to bring about social change? A central characteristic of green political theory is that it has never consistently asked that question, principally because the answer is held to be obvious: everyone. The general political-ecological position that the environmental crisis will eventually be suffered by everybody on the planet, and that therefore the ideology's appeal is universal, has been perceived as a source of strength for the green movement. What could be better, from the point of view of pressing an idea, than to be able to claim that failure to embrace it might result in a global catastrophe that would leave no one untouched? From the present point of view this may be the movement's basic strategic political error because the universalist appeal is, properly speaking, Utopian. It is simply untrue to say that, given present conditions, it is in everybody's interest to bring about a sustainable and egalitarian society. A significant and influential proportion of society, for example, has a material interest in prolonging the environmental crisis because there is money to be made from managing it. It is Utopian to consider these people to be a part of the engine for profound social change.

Perhaps the most sophisticated expression of the universalist approach comes from Rudolf Bahro:

> If proceeding from these assumptions we are seeking a hegemonic project and want to keep to the level of the overall interest of humanity – which is what Marx had in mind with the world-historic mission of the proletariat – we must go beyond Marx's own concept and direct ourselves to a more general subject than the Western working-class of today. Like the utopian socialists and communists who Marx sought to dispense with, we must once again take the species interest as our fundamental point of reference.
>
> (Bahro, 1982, p. 65)

Bahro's point here, couched in language expressive of his Marxist background, is that the social subject to which we must look in order to bring about change is not this or that social class but the whole human race. Again, he writes that 'From all appearances ... the organising factors which can bring the alternative forces together and give them a social co-ordination (as must be desired) will in future not be any particular class interest, but rather a long-term human interest' (Bahro, 1982, p. 115). As I pointed out earlier, he can argue this because it appears transparent that the threatened environmental crisis will not discriminate between classes – the catastrophe, if it is to come, will be visited upon everybody. While this may be true in the long run, it is not necessarily the best point from which to plan immediate political strategy.

In many respects, for instance, one can already see that environmental degradation is not suffered by everyone equally. Organic foods as an alternative to chemical-dosed products, for example, are widely available in principle but their relative expense prevents them being accessible to all. It is not simply a question of education, then, but of money too. Similarly, if one considers the built environment, money makes available green spaces into which to retreat, and satisfying the primal call of the wilderness is an option presently open only to a very few.

More generally, it is simply not in the immediate interests of everybody to usher in a sustainable society. *The Limits to Growth* report remarks that

> The majority of the world's people are concerned with matters that affect only family or friends over a short period of time. Others look farther ahead in time or over a larger area – a city or a nation. Only a very few people have a global perspective that extends far into the future.
>
> (Meadows *et al.*, 1974, p. 19)

This captures the problem of persuasion with which the green movement is confronted. Somehow people are required to begin to think in global terms and with respect to events that might or might not occur generations hence. 'Only a very few people' think like that, and they are precisely the people who already live in sustainable communities, refuse to use chemical pesticides in the garden, and flush the toilet only when they really have to. If these people constitute a vanguard, it is hard at present to see how they are going to drag large numbers of people with them. In the light of this, class theory has it that radical greens must abandon their Utopian, universalistic strategy, and instead identify and organize a group of people in society whose immediate interests lie in living the dark-green life, with all that that implies.

With respect to everything that has been said so far about green strategies for political change, it is interesting to look at the critique that Marx made of the Utopian socialists of the early nineteenth century (without jumping to the conclusion that this endorses everything Marx had to say or comprises an embryonic Marxist critique of ecologism as a whole). This is what he said of them:

They want to improve the condition of every member of society, even that of the most favoured. Hence they habitually appeal to society at large, without distinction of class; nay, by preference, to the ruling class. For how can people, when once they understand their system, fail to see in it the best possible plan of the best possible state of society? Hence they reject all political, and especially revolutionary action; they wish to attain their ends by peaceful means, and endeavour, by small experiments, necessarily doomed to failure, and by the force of example, to pave the way for the new social gospel.

(from *The Manifesto of the Communist Party* [1848], in Feuer, 1976, p. 79)

Word for word, these comments literally describe most present green, as well as Utopian socialist, approaches to political change. Marx makes two principal criticisms here, each of which contributes to his characterization of the type of socialism to which he refers as 'Utopian'. First, that Utopian socialism's appeal was counter-productive: it was objectively impossible to expect all classes to usher in socialism. Second, that its strategy of change through 'small experiments' and 'force of example' was an unfounded attempt to change *people* without changing the *conditions* in which they lived and worked.

Both of these criticisms of Utopian political strategy are relevant to the contemporary green movement. The 'small experimental' nature of much of the movement's practice was made clear above. From the CAT in Wales, through any number of pesticide-free vegetable plots, to the New Age community at Findhorn, Scotland, the practice of much green politics takes the form of a series of 'small experiments'. Marx, of course, made clear his recognition of the political value of the Utopian socialists' enterprises for calling into question the accepted truths of early nineteenth-century European society, and any critique of green Utopianism must do the same for the initiatives mentioned above.

It is well known that Marx's solution to the problem posed by the false universal appeal of the Utopian socialists was to recommend the identification and formation of a class in society (given the right historical conditions) whose prime interest lay in changing that society. This is how he put it in his *Toward a Critique of Hegel's Philosophy of Right* of 1844:

Where is there, then, a *real* possibility of emancipation in Germany? This is our reply. A class must be formed which has *radical chains*, a class in civil society which is not a class of civil society, a class which is the dissolution of all classes, a sphere of society which has a universal character because its sufferings are universal, and which does not claim a *particular redress* because the wrong which is done to it is not a *particular wrong*, but *wrong in general*. There must be formed a sphere of society which claims no traditional status but only a human status, a sphere which is not opposed to particular consequences but is totally opposed to the assumptions of the German political system, a sphere which finally cannot emancipate itself without therefore emancipating all those other spheres, which is, in short, a *total loss* of humanity and which can only redeem itself by a *total redemption of humanity*.

(in Bottomore and Rubel, 1984, p. 190; emphasis in original)

According to Marx, then, the basic characteristics of the 'sphere of society' (or 'class') capable of bringing about profound social change were as follows: first, it had to have 'radical chains', such that, second, its emancipation would involve the general emancipation of humanity; and third, it had to be opposed not just to the 'particular consequences' of a political system but to its general 'assumptions'. For Marx, of course, this class with a universal historical mission was the proletariat. Of course, the proletariat has not proved to be the class that Marx thought it was: its claims were not so radical that it questioned the assumptions of the political system, and its emancipation (while anyway only partial and material) has not led to the emancipation of humanity.

We are left, then, with a critique of Utopian (in Marx's rather specialized sense) political strategies, and how he considers it possible to transcend them. I shall discuss what might be the implications for the green movement of Marx's critique of Utopian socialism a little further on, but first one or two words need to be said about the style of his project, and the difficulties anyone might have adapting it. There is considerable scepticism today among intellectuals on the left with respect not only to the faith that used to be placed in the working class as an agent for social change, but also to the whole notion of 'agents' of this type.

On what might very loosely be termed a post-modern reading, the search for a historical agent on which to found political change and which, moreover, is charged with saving not only itself but humanity as a whole is a universalistic project unwarranted by what we know of the world and how we know it. From this perspective, the universalizing project can only end in violence as its aims and intentions are necessarily frustrated, and as it seeks to recuperate itself by force. As Zygmunt Bauman has written: 'The typically post-modern view of the world is, in principle, one of an unlimited number of models of order, each one generated by a relatively autonomous set of practices' (Bauman, 1987, p. 4), and,

> If, from the modern point of view relativism of knowledge was a problem to be struggled against and eventually overcome in theory and in practice, from the post-modern point of view relativity of knowledge (that is, its 'embeddedness' in its own communally supporting tradition) is a lasting feature of the world.
>
> (Bauman, 1987, p. 4)

It is this relativity that disqualifies the search for totalizing truth or universalizing political ambitions.

Marx, of course, worked in a period that operated on different assumptions and in which, 'Like the knowledge they produce, intellectuals are not bound by localized, communal traditions. They are, together with their knowledge, extra-territorial' (Bauman, 1987, p. 5). Hence, without the merest hint of self-conscious embarrassment, Marx is able to posit a class that will bring about 'the total redemption of humanity'. His framework is clearly modern as opposed to post-modern, and he fulfils (to employ the metaphors that comprise the felicitous title of Bauman's book) the intellectual's legislator rather than interpreter role. It seems that from a post-modern perspective any search for an agent for social change will be characterized as unwarranted (and ultimately violent) legislation, as is made clear in Bauman's sardonic observation: 'the present-day general intellectuals (or rather, the part of this category still faithful to the traditional, legislative definition of their role) are in Alvin Gouldner's famous phrase "shopping for an historical agent" again' (Bauman, 1987, p. 177).

The reason for this short detour into post-modernity is that its critique of totalizing political aspirations must be taken seriously. In many respects, indeed, the green strategies for change that I described earlier respond to post-modern celebrations of difference, diversity, foundationlessness and humility. The point might be made, though, that this has changed nothing: in Porritt's phrase already quoted, it 'has not brought about the kind of fundamental shift that one might have expected'. The second point I would make is that it would be foolish and unwarranted for class theorists to make any universalistic claims for any agent they might identify. Whoever they think most likely to promote fundamental changes in society cannot be seen as paving the way for the salvation of humanity. Their project takes seriously Marx's criticism of Utopian socialism and uses it to expose the Utopian nature of current green strategies for social change, and identifies a group of people whose immediate concerns connect with the movement's ultimate aims. In this sense it is claimed that it would be useful for the movement to take seriously the identification of an agent for green change, but class theorists of such change ought to go no further than that.

We have already established that green ideologues are typically averse to class theories of politics because they believe them divisively to undermine the green universal appeal. There has, though, been some discussion of the general issue of agents for change in green literature. Two suggestions can briefly be followed up: that of the middle class as the instigators of change, and the potentially central role of the 'new social movements', such as feminism, the peace movement, gays and so on.

Jonathon Porritt presents a classic formulation of the first position:

> one must of course acknowledge that the post-industrial revolution is likely to be pioneered by middle-class people. The reasons are simple: such people not only have more chance of working out where their own genuine self-interest lies, but they also have the flexibility and security to act upon such insights.
>
> (Porritt, 1984a, p. 116)

Much depends here on just what one understands by 'pioneer'. If Porritt means simply the questioning of current social and political practices and the presentation of alternatives, then the middle class clearly has a central role to play. Indeed, there is plenty of sociological evidence to show that the environmental movement is preponderantly a middle-class affair. Just why this is the case is hotly disputed, but the debate suggests that throwing one's eggs prematurely in the middle-class basket could be a mistake. The general position combines two suggestions: first, that rises in post-war living standards have shifted political goals (for some) away from material concerns and towards 'quality of life' issues (Inglehart, 1977); and second, that a new middle class of non-marketized professionals (educationalists, health workers, etc.) have occupations that are conducive to the generation and pursuing of green values.

Luke Martell, though (for example) has doubts regarding the long-term position of this middle class in radical green politics on the grounds that 'it is difficult to see a basis for economic interest in middle-class concern for the environment' (1994, p. 130). He points out that

> [R]adical environmentalism argues for slowing down growth and rates of consumption. A comfortable group, but which sees itself to be materially disadvantaged relative to otherwise comparable groups, would not be likely to perceive cuts in growth as in its interest.
>
> (Martell, 1994, p. 130)

This kind of observation renders Porritt's faith in the middle class somewhat problematic – particularly when placed alongside his working hypothesis of self-interest: 'I do not believe that the majority of people will change until they believe it is in their own interests to do so ... A reinterpretation of enlightened self-interest is therefore the key to any radical transformation' (Porritt, 1984a, p. 117). One of Porritt's earlier remarks endorses Martell's worries on this score as far as the middle class is concerned:

> one thing is clear: even if we continue to think in terms of working class and middle class, it is not the latter that has the most to worry about in terms of the current crisis. It is the middle classes that have the flexibility to weather traumatic shifts in social and economic patterns; by and large, they are not the ones to suffer most from mindless jobs, dangerous working conditions, a filthy polluted environment, shattered communities, the exploitation of mass culture, the inhumanity of bureaucrats and the mendacity of politicians.
>
> (Porritt, 1984a, p. 116)

On this reading, and taking into account Porritt's self-interest thesis, it is the working class and not the middle class whose interest lies in shifting away from present social practices. Porritt's conclusion in favour of the latter class, despite his own evidence, can be explained only by inserting him into the liberal tradition to which he belongs, and which has always proclaimed the middle classes as the agents of change.

It is this, too, that leads him to make optimistic remarks about 'the role of small businesses' under the general heading 'the agents of change' (Porritt, 1984a, p. 139). He goes on: 'In the kind of long-term economy that we envisage, small businesses would not just be a useful adjunct to the world of corporate big business: they would be the mainstay of all economic activity' (Porritt, 1984a, p. 139). The problem with the notion of small businesses as agents of change is that their success, and even survival, depends on their producing and reproducing the products and values demanded by the system within which they operate. In the name of efficiency, such businesses may 'have to' cut the work-force, deunionize it, hire temporary labour with no security, and provide poor conditions of work. There is no guarantee whatsoever that small businesses, far from acting as agents for social change, will not rather be vehicles for the reproduction of the system that they seek to overcome. Indeed, in the absence of any strategy for disengaging from the system, the latter is far more likely to be the case.

Beyond the middle class, one sometimes reads that the 'new social movements' represent new forms of political activity that anticipate new forms of society. Fritjof Capra, for example, writes of a 'winning majority' of 'environmentalists, feminists, ethnic minorities etc.', and then that 'the new coalitions should be able to turn the paradigm shift into political reality' (Capra, 1983, p. 465). More explicitly Murray Bookchin refers to 'the new classes' and argues that they are 'united more by cultural ties than economic ones: ethnics, women, counter-cultural people, environmentalists, the aged, the déclassé, unemployables or unemployed, the "ghetto" people' (Bookchin, 1986, p. 152).

Similarly Jürgen Habermas, who is of course not a representative of the green movement itself, has theorized a 'new politics' centring on 'the peace movement, the anti-nuclear and environmental movement, minority liberation movements, the movement for alternative lifestyles, the tax protest movement, religious fundamentalist protest groups and, finally, the women's movement' (Roderick, 1986, p. 136). Habermas goes on to make an important distinction that helps us to make some sense of the social pot-pourri offered up by himself, Capra and Bookchin. He argues that not all of these groups have the same emancipatory potential, and suggests that we distinguish between those that seek 'particularistic' change and 'those that seek fundamental change from a universalistic viewpoint' (Roderick, 1986, p. 136). This ought to remind us of the quotation from Marx cited earlier in which he argued that the source of social change must be found in 'a sphere which is not opposed to particular consequences but is totally opposed to the assumptions of the German political system'. Roderick continues:

> For Habermas, at the present time only the women's movement belongs to this latter category to the extent that it seeks not only a formal equality, but also a fundamental change in the social structure and in real concrete life situation.
>
> (Roderick, 1986, p. 136)

This is a very important observation, particularly in the context of the most typical critique of social movements as agents for social change: i.e. that they have no common interest and therefore cannot act coherently. As Boris Frankel has written, for example, 'women, environmentalists, peace activists, gays, etc., do not have a ready formed identity as a social movement' (1987, p. 235). This is undoubtedly true, but with reference to Habermas' distinction it is hardly important. The crucial project would not be to manufacture an identity between heterogeneous groups, but to identify that group (or those groups) whose project most profoundly questions the presuppositions on which present social practices depend. Only such a group can already be in a sufficiently 'disengaged' position to resist the attempts at colonization by the system that it seeks to overcome, and even then, of course, success is by no means guaranteed. I shall pick up the suggestion that women might constitute such a vanguard shortly.

The point of all this is to suggest that a possible strategy for the green movement would be to identify and foment a group in society that is not only relatively 'disengaged' from it, but that also is already inclined towards the foundations of sustainable living. This will be the agent for radical green change, and in the spirit of experiment I can now sketch what it might look like, beginning with a cursory green materialist analysis of the situation that is producing it.

The green movement will certainly want to argue that the production process is threatened by a shortage of material – that is precisely the point of its founding its ideology in the concept of a finite Earth. If this is correct, then production itself will become ever more expensive (even allowing for temporary technological substitutes/solutions), and the capital required for investment in the process will become ever harder to find. There are two likely responses to this: first, the reduction of the costs of production in ways that will compensate for the increased cost of scarce materials; and second, the encouragement of increased consumption to generate more capital. A serious green materialist analysis would of course need extensive empirical work to back up its own claims.

The point in our context, though, is that the first strategy may come into conflict with the second and generate social tensions (and a social class) that cannot be satisfied within the current scheme of production and consumption. For instance, one of the ways in which the costs of production in the metropolitan countries can be reduced is by employing cheaper labour in other parts of the world. This, naturally, has the effect of increasing unemployment in the metropolitan countries. In turn, the number of people who are marginalized from the second response referred to above – that of encouraging increased consumption – increases. From their perspective, the system is characterized by its failure to fulfil the expectations it generates.

This characteristic is, of course, not new to the general history of the present mode of production, but greens might argue that what is new to our particular period is that the external limits imposed by the Earth circumscribe that system's room for manoeuvre. There is less and less space within which *both* to produce *and* to fulfil the expectations of consumption that the system generates. In other words, it might be argued from a radical green perspective that the external limits imposed on the production process by the Earth itself are beginning to shape a class that is more or less permanently marginalized from the process of consumption. From this point of view it is *the distance from the process of consumption and the degree of permanence of this isolation that currently determine the capacity of any given group in society for radical green social change.*

One (but only one) obvious group in contemporary society fits such a description and has been advanced (particularly by André Gorz) as an agent for change – the unemployed. The demands of this class are potentially radical: it will not seek higher wages, for it has no employment; it will not seek better working conditions, because it has none to begin with; it will not ask for longer holidays, because it is permanently on holiday (at least while not working in the underground economy); and it will not strike, because it has no labour to withdraw. Lastly, because its problems are both caused by the present unsustainable economic system and insoluble within it, it would not press for a change in the ownership of the means of production, but would see that its interests lie in pressing for a change in the means of production themselves, towards a system that is sustainable.

In Marx's terms this class has 'radical chains' and is, as he went on to say, 'a class in civil society which is not a class of civil society'. In other words, it is a class whose daily life sets it apart from all other classes of society. It is a class that does not buy anything and therefore calls into question the production process that fills the shop windows. In this sense, it is a class that is opposed not just to the 'particular consequences' of this particular system, but to its general 'assumptions'. It is therefore so sufficiently 'disengaged' that it might hope to surmount the problems of colonization and recolonization that we saw dogging the parliamentary, lifestyle and community strategies for change.

At this stage we should recall the general thesis (a thesis that, once again, includes the unemployed but does not exclusively relate to them) that it is 'the distance from the process of consumption and the degree of permanence of this isolation that currently determine the capacity of any given group in society for radical green social change', and report the echoes of this thought that have already appeared in the supporting literature. Rudolf Bahro, for instance, has written that

> More and more people are either excluded, marginalised, dismissed, or directly motivated to drop out, with either all or part of their energies. This gives rise by necessity to a strategy ... that combines two elements: a gradually spreading refusal and a deliberate *obstruction*. This is not meant as a new discovery, I simply want to draw attention to what is necessary and deliberate in it.
>
> (Bahro, 1982, p. 154; emphasis in original)

Bahro's notion of people 'dropping out' is the analogue of Marx's class that is 'in' civil society without being 'of' it, and this might be a defining characteristic of any group that hopes to be successful in challenging accepted norms and practices. Joe Weston seems to be pointing towards something similar when he argues that 'It is here, among the disenfranchised, that campaigning social environmentalism has its future' (Weston, 1986, p. 154).

Another clear expression of this type of thinking comes, as I have already suggested, from André Gorz. In *Paths to Paradise* (1985) he wrote: 'the mass of disaffected non-workers is the *possible* social subject of the struggle for work-sharing, generalised reduction of work-time, gradual abolition of waged work by the expansion of autoproduction, and for a living income for all' (p. 35). Gorz's recognition of the need for a social subject for political action and his identification of a 'post-industrial proletariat of the unemployed, occasionally employed, short-term or part-time workers, who neither can nor want to identify themselves with their job or their place in the production process' (Gorz, 1994, p. 73) as such a subject square with the general model described above. Frankel goes on to explain the reasons behind Gorz's position:

> In not identifying with the production of waste, destruction and meaningless work to fill in time, the 'non-class of neoproletarians' are the only ones, Gorz believes, who will break through the 'accumulation ethic' of 'productivism' and bring into being the post-industrial society.
>
> (Frankel, 1987, p. 211)

This emphasizes the point that the radicalization of political consciousness can in principle occur in anyone, but that radical political change can be brought about only by those whose lived experience already demands it of them and makes it possible. Gorz stresses that this lived experience is already one of segregation, not so much in opposition to present forms of living, as alongside and parallel to them:

> Segregation of people for whom there is no permanent, full-time work is the common characteristic ... How authoritarian this segregation will be depends on the political form and traditions of individual regimes: apartheid, gulags, compulsory paramilitary service; shanty-towns and North-American style urban ghettos, crowding together people who are mostly unemployed; or gangs of unemployed youth, subsidised eternal students and endless apprenticeships, temporary, holiday and seasonal workers etc.

In every case, the unemployed are *socially marginalised*, even when they are the majority (as in South Africa or some North American cities). They are deemed to be socially inferior and inadequate and effectively denied all social participation and activity. They remain outcasts and objects of resentment, begrudged whatever charity society grants them.

(Gorz, 1985, p. 36)

In this respect, Gorz's 'neo-proletariat' does not 'identify the capitalist class as the dominant class to be overthrown' (Frankel, 1987, p. 212), but is marginalized even from that socialistic form of thinking. This is a class not in opposition, but in exclusion.

Nor should we be led to think that this class exists only in the metropolitan countries. In a speech in Caracas in 1981, Rudolf Bahro referred to what Arnold Toynbee called 'the external proletariat' and translated it, in general terms, into those who 'are not yet "really subsumed"', i.e. the majority of the population who are marginalised to varying degrees and in varying ways' (1982, p. 129). He continued:

it may well be worthwhile to investigate the connection between the immediate interests of the marginalised sections (and these are growing now also in the metropolises, if on a different scale) and the general interest of a humanity which has reached the earth's limits with its industrial capitalist expansion.

(Bahro, 1982, p. 129)

Bahro is here pointing towards a social subject with similar characteristics to those that I have described (marginalization from the process of production and consumption), but situates it in the so-called Third World. This serves to emphasize the international character of the crisis and the shared interests of the 'metropolitan' and 'peripheral' marginalized, and provides greens with an instance of, and practice for, its slogan: 'act locally think globally'. Such a perspective also begins to give concrete content to Jeremy Seabrook's suggestion that 'the most urgent task is to show how and why the poor would be the chief beneficiaries of Green politics' (Seabrook, 1988, p. 166). That is certainly not the way green politics is usually conceived and I agree with Seabrook that, in the long run,

Nothing could be more damaging to the Green cause than the perception that it is supported by privileged people who have enough for their own needs, and are now eager to limit the access of the poor to those benefits of industrial society which they themselves enjoy.

(Seabrook, 1988, p. 166)

Some progress is being made in this respect, and the connections between poverty and environmental degradation are powerfully expressed by the environmental justice movement in the United States. As Andrew Szasz has written, 'Toxic victims are, typically, poor or working people of modest means. Their environmental problems are inseparable from their economic condition. People are more likely to live near polluted industrial sites if they live in financially strapped communities' (Szasz, 1994, p. 151). In the context for the search for a group coalescing around an issue which has broad social and political implications, it is interesting to read that the hazardous waste movement 'increasingly defines its environmental mission in terms of a larger critique of society ... [I]t even envisions a future in which grass-roots environmentalism spearheads the reconstitution of a broad social justice movement' (Szasz, 1994, p. 166).

Returning to Gorz, Boris Frankel makes three principal criticisms of his position, all of which can be only summarily addressed in the space available here. The first is the observation that 'High unemployment rates, temporary work and marginalized existences have characterized earlier generations and not just the new "neoproletariat"' (Frankel, 1987, p. 212). This may be true, but I have already indicated that from a green perspective these negative aspects are due not solely to the demands of capital accumulation, but also to the likely increasing costs of production caused by maximizing unsustainable extraction in the context of a finite Earth. In other words, it has always been possible for capitalism and 'actually existing socialism' to promise employment and unmarginalized existences within their current systems. If the green analysis of the consequences of our operating in a finite context is correct, then this promise no longer holds. Gorz's 'post-industrial proletariat' thus differs from the industrial proletariat in being – in principle – less open to co-option and colonization than its traditional counterpart.

This point also bears on Frankel's second criticism of Gorz, which is that 'many of the "neo-proletariat" ... do feel guilty about being unemployed, do still identify with waste consumption and the work ethic, and are not mainly oriented to an alternative vision of autonomous free time' (Frankel, 1987, p. 212). In other words, Frankel feels that marginalization from the process of consumption does not necessarily involve rejection of the entire political and economic system: it might just as easily result in an increased desire to become a part of it.

This appears to be a persuasive point, but I think that two responses might be made to it. First, there is the actual and objective existence of a number of people (drawn generally from what are traditionally defined as the middle classes) who have voluntarily decided on non-participation in consumption. Their particular lifestyles vary, but the common factor is a willingness (indeed, a desire) to live with less, or, as radical greens would have it, to 'live lightly on the earth'. This, though, is a small proportion of the general population, and its effect in terms of socio-political change can only be minimal, or 'small experimental', as Marx might have it.

Much more numerous and important are the tens of millions (in Western Europe alone) whose marginalization from the process of consumption might be argued to be structural and therefore insoluble within the current scheme of things. From a green perspective, it is structural because the limits imposed by the Earth on the production process and the accumulation of capital make it impossible for this marginalized class ever to have access to the system's material benefits. Rudolf Bahro has observed that 'So far in history the subordinate classes have essentially always wanted, in the last instance, what the privileged classes already possessed. Their habits are governed by what is in the shop windows which they press their noses against' (1982, p. 49). The point is that radical greens could make the marginalized class aware that this habit has no future, and that its interests lie in a different form of society rather than immersion in the present one. This provides the beginnings of an answer to Martell's objection (similar to Frankel's) that '[T]he problem with Gorz's analysis is that the exclusion of the unemployed from production and consumption is just as likely to make them more committed than anyone else to accumulation. Material values may well be uppermost in their minds' (Martell, 1994, p. 193). The 'may' suggests that the issue is not decided, and to the extent that argument might have anything to do with the outcome, green arguments concerning limitations on capital accumulation have some potential. Gorz's 'post-industrial proletariat' need not subscribe to current practices of production and consumption, but a precondition for it not doing so is an understanding that such practices actually reproduce, rather than alleviate, its marginalization. It is this recognition that Frankel's second criticism of Gorz misses.

His third criticism is that 'Gorz has exaggerated the number of people suffering from "neo-proletarian" symptoms' (Frankel, 1987, p. 213). The thinking here is that there are simply not enough 'post-industrial proletarians' to effect any radical social change. Much depends here on how we are to define membership of the class in the first place: confining it to the officially unemployed is the easiest way of assigning it a minority status. The number can be increased significantly by including all those in temporary or seasonal employment, and those who have found work in 'advanced industrial countries' over the past few years by accepting low wages, poor conditions and geographical displacement. The point of doing this is to illustrate that unemployment is only one form of marginalization from the process of consumption, and that this latter is the crucial general characteristic of any social group likely to bring about political change. In this context Gorz himself writes that:

> [E]stimates that this group is likely to make up 50 per cent of the active population in the 1990s are beginning to seem realistic: in West Germany as in France, more than half the workers newly started in recent years are employed in precarious or part-time jobs. Workers who are employed in this way already constitute more than a third of the wage-earning population. Together with the unemployed, that makes a 'post-industrial proletariat' of 40 to 50 per cent in Great Britain, and in the United States as much as 45–50 per cent.
>
> (Gorz, 1994, p. 73)

Again, if the maximization of production remains the goal of most societies, and if the radical green analysis of a resulting deepening crisis of sustainability is at all correct, then the number of people marginalized from consumption can only, in the long term, increase. These are some possible preliminary responses to Frankel's third criticism of the 'post-industrial proletariat' thesis.

Throughout this section I have been talking about marginalization in the context of the formal processes of production and consumption. This approach is criticized by ecofeminists – on whom I will have more to say in Chapter 5 – for its lack of attention to the crucial sphere of reproduction. In the hands of materialist ecofeminists this criticism turns into a fully-fledged theory of gendered political agency which has women at the forefront of change. Ariel Salleh, for example, remarks that

> The Green movement must use a materialist analysis. This accords beautifully with an ecofeminist premise for women's historical agency, because on an international scale, undertaking 65 per cent of the world's work for 5 per cent of its pay, effectively are 'the proletariat' … women as an economic underclass are astonishingly well placed to bring about the social changes requisite for ecological revolution.
>
> (Salleh, 1997, p. 6)

Marginalized in this way from the formal processes of production and consumption, women also – and critically, for materialist ecofeminists – occupy a critical space in the reproductive process, a space that makes them ideal candidates for bringing about green political objectives. From a materialist ecofeminist point of view, 'humans come to know nature through their bodies and ... make sense of that experience' (Salleh, 1997, p. 38). Women's 'coming to know' is a specific sort, mediated through pregnancy, childbirth and suckling. Women experience a 'continuity with nature' that men currently lack and it is this that makes 'Woman' the 'biological and social mediator of Nature for men' (ibid., p. 49). 'Could women, still invisible as the global majority, actually be the missing agents of History, and therefore Nature, in our troubled times?', asks Salleh. For her, the answer is clearly yes.

Materialist ecofeminism has much to recommend it: its insights into the role and consequences of reproduction are absolutely critical, and any green materialism that ignores this will do so at its peril. It is, though, important to strike a balance between production and reproduction. Focus on the latter has the inevitable consequence of putting women in the vanguard of green change, and while this may be desirable for all sorts of reasons, it is not a consequence that can be derived from a fully-fledged materialist analysis – one that takes full account of production as well as reproduction. Taking account of production brings marginalized men as well as women into the frame, something which materialist ecofeminism cannot do directly, despite Salleh's remark that 'Under certain circumstances, a man can also feed a child at the breast' (Salleh, 1997, p. 37). I stress that it is important that men be brought back into the frame, not just because otherwise the poor things will feel left out, but because a green materialism demands their presence. The slogan for a green materialism might therefore be 'production *and* reproduction' rather than either one or the other.

However one looks at it, though, difficulties with class-based or gender-based strategies for green change remain. Even assuming that the class has been formed or that the gender is conscious of itself as a historical agent, one is left with the problem of how it is going to act. Is it, for example, envisaged as some sort of revolutionary political subject? If so, then the class is confronted with a series of classic problems: the stability of current political systems (in the West at least), the issue of revolutionary organization, and (particularly difficult for non-violent greens) waging the revolutionary struggle.

If, on the other hand, reformist strategies are chosen and the class operates through pressure groups or a parliamentary party, then all of the dilemmas and difficulties referred to in the first part of this chapter resurface: 'How far should compromise be taken?', 'How should elections be contested?', 'Is election a realistic possibility anyway?' Intermediate strategies do present themselves, such as building up green communities through the local money schemes described earlier (perhaps focused on unemployment centres), but all thoughts of green class action seem vitiated by the fact that no unified sense of such a class is presently in sight.

Conclusion

Discussion of any aspect of green politics is always dogged by the necessity to distinguish between its dark-green and light-green, or environmental, manifestations. The issue of green social change is no exception. From a light-green point of view, for instance, the reflections which took place under the heading 'class' will probably seem superfluous. It appears self-evident that a parliamentary presence, or pressure through the lobby system, can bring about a cleaner, more sustainable environment. It appears self-evident that we can lead more environment-friendly lives by buying the right things and refusing to buy the wrong ones. It also appears self-evident that sustainable communities are vital as sources of inspiration for the rest of us to live more lightly on the Earth.

But from ecologism's point of view all of these strategies must be measured in terms of the radical green critique of present practices developed in Chapter 3, and the kind of life it is suggested we need to lead to overcome them. Bringing about that kind of sustainable society is an infinitely more difficult task than simply putting environmentalism on the political agenda. So far, that is what the strategies adopted have done, and taking radical green politics seriously – rather than some attenuated environmentalist version of it – might involve a move beyond those strategies.

5   Ecologism and other ideologies

We now have the fundamentals of ecologism in place. We have discussed its critique of contemporary society, we have outlined its proposals for an ecologically sound society, and we have assessed its approach to bringing such a society about. I have claimed that ecologism is a new political ideology, worthy of attention in the new millennium alongside other more familiar ones such as liberalism, conservatism and socialism. If this is correct, then it is only natural to want to compare and contrast this new ideology with those which it seeks to challenge. This is what I propose to do in the present chapter. In so doing, it is my intention to deepen our understanding of what marks ecologism off from those other ideologies. I regard attempts by liberals, conservatives and socialists to appropriate ecological thought for themselves to be chimerical, for as I pointed out in the Introduction, ecologism is as different from each of them as they are from each other. The examination carried out in this chapter should drive home this point.

In principle, the list of ideologies with which ecologism could be compared and contrasted is a long one. In choosing to devote attention to just four of them I might be accused of pruning that long list unduly. There are two reasons for doing so, however. The first is that I wanted to give each of these four ideologies a run for its money. Where broad comparisons have been carried out (for example, Hay, 1988; Martell, 1994, Ch. 5; Garner, 1996, Ch. 3) the range of coverage has been bought at the cost of making it rather thin, with typically a page or two devoted to each ideology. Particularly recently, and particularly in the cases of the four ideologies I deal with here, some very interesting comparative work has been done, and it is simply not possible to do this work justice in a short space.

Second, the ideologies I have chosen for assessment might legitimately be regarded as lying at the roots of those I have left out. This is to say that liberalism, conservatism and socialism are widely held to be the most fundamental ideologies of the modern era, and other less fundamental ones can often be read through them (although never wholly reducible to them). I hope, therefore, to have provided an indirect service to those who would want to contrast ecologism with nationalism or with fascism, for example, although I am acutely aware of the breadth I have nevertheless sacrificed. Feminism might not generally be held to be in the same league as liberalism, conservatism and socialism (although I am not so sure myself), but the justification for including a detailed discussion of it here is that it has influenced the development of ecologism in a way unmatched by any other ideology with the possible exception of socialism. This influence has also, I think, been reciprocal.

For no particular reason, the ideologies with which I compare and contrast ecologism are in the following order: liberalism, conservatism, socialism and feminism.

Liberalism

Ten years ago, Mark Sagoff asked whether environmentalists could be liberals (Sagoff, 1988, pp. 146–70). At the time, the question appeared rather esoteric in that the interesting ideological and theoretical relationships seemed to be between environmentalism (or, as I want to call it here, ecologism) and socialism, or environmentalism and feminism, rather than between environmentalism and liberalism. It is now clear that Sagoff was more perceptive than most of the rest of us, not because ecosocialism and ecofeminism are not interesting – they are – but because the increasing dominance of the liberal world-view in academic and political life has necessarily brought the environmental and liberal agendas into close contact, with the result that some of the most intellectually interesting (if politically questionable) work in environmental political theory is being done in this area.

So Robyn Eckersley was able to write in 1992 that

> Although some emancipatory theorists, such as John Rodman, have noted and discussed these byways in liberal thought [that is, potential compatibilities between liberalism and radical ecology], the general tendency has been to look to other political traditions for the ideals and principles that would underpin an ecologically sustainable *post-liberal* society.
>
> (Eckersley, 1992, pp. 23–4)

Since then a number of theorists – Hayward (1995), Eckersley herself (1996), Wissenburg (1998a), B. Barry (1999) and Miller (1999), for example – have sought to demonstrate compatibility between liberal and environmental themes or, more strongly, to show how the ecological political project can be expressed more or less completely in the liberal idiom.

My own view is that the answer to the compatibility question depends entirely on one's terms of reference: environmentalism and liberalism are compatible, but ecologism and liberalism are not. So even if it is true to say that political ecology 'draws on' liberalism, Martell is wrong to jump to the conclusion that this 'shows that green political theory does not stand alone as a new political theory' (Martell, 1994, p. 141). The tensions between liberalism and ecologism are by now well rehearsed. Martell himself points out that

> there is a lot in liberal political theory that runs counter to radical ecology. Individualism, the pursuit of private gain, limited government and market freedom are contradicted by radical ecology commitments to the resolution of environmental problems as a collective good and to intervention and restrictions on economic and personal freedoms to deal with them.
>
> (Martell, 1994, p. 141)

The issue of liberty is crucial here. As Wissenburg says, 'in no respect can liberal democracy and environmental concerns be so much at odds as where liberty is concerned' (Wissenburg, 1998a, p. 33), and while it would be wrong to regard political ecology as just a series of personal and social prohibitions, there is no doubt that ecologism's stress on 'limits' of all sorts amounts to the potential curtailment of certain taken-for-granted freedoms, particularly in the realms of production, consumption and mobility. It will not be enough for liberals to be told that these restrictions will be offset by hoped-for improvements in the quality of life: liberty is central to the liberal prospectus, and liberals will regard threats to it with great suspicion.

Liberals resist being told what to think as well as what to do. More technically, they regard their felt *preferences* as an accurate indicator of their *interests*, and they will say that attempts by the state to influence tastes and preferences are generally unwarranted. Likewise, liberals do not typically welcome suggestions that people do not know what is in their own best interest. So, 'From a liberal perspective, the objection to denying the equation of people's interests with what they think or say they are is that this appears at the same time to be denying basic respect for people's autonomy' (Hayward, 1995, p. 203). The problem from a political-ecological point of view is that this autonomy may clash with ecological objectives: 'Liberal democracy is totally incompatible with attempts to dictate people's tastes and preferences, yet we may reasonably assume that preferences are one of the determining factors of sustainability' (Wissenburg, 1998a, p. 7). Far from regarding people's preferences as sacrosanct, political ecologists seek to influence them all the time, and if we add to this the various potential restrictions on liberty referred to above, then the tensions between liberalism and ecologism become palpable.

Often, autonomy for liberals is understood to mean the freedom to develop and pursue one's own moral goals in life. From this point of view, 'Liberalism is the political theory that holds that many conflicting and even incommensurable conceptions of the good may be fully compatible with free, autonomous, and rational action' (Sagoff, 1988, pp. 150–1), and so, 'The liberal state does not dictate the moral goals its citizens are to achieve; it simply referees the means they use to satisfy their own preferences' (ibid., p. 151). It will be clear from Chapter 2 that political ecologists have a quite distinctive view regarding our moral relationship with the non-human natural world, and this is a view that they will feel bound to encourage the rest of us to endorse. This gives rise, though, to another potential tension between liberalism and ecologism – and to the question from Mark Sagoff that heads this section: 'If the laws and policies supported by the environmental lobby are not neutral among ethical, aesthetic and religious ideals but express a moral conception of people's appropriate relation to nature, can environmentalists be liberals?' (ibid., p. 150).

There are two reasons why Sagoff thinks they can, the first of which has been adopted by many people who would like to press for compatibility between liberalism and ecologism (e.g. B. Barry, 1995, pp. 145–51). This first reason turns on the common distinction in liberal theory between the structure of institutions and the social policies that emerge from them (Sagoff, 1988, p. 166). Sagoff suggests that while liberals must be neutral in respect of the former (that is, that the institutions be fair between the individuals who participate in them), there is nothing to prevent them having decided views on social policy – even views that are based upon 'particular ethical, cultural, or aesthetic convictions' (ibid.). Convictions of this sort, of course, amount to convictions regarding the nature of the Good Life about which liberals are traditionally supposed to be neutral. Sagoff squares the circle by making the distinction between institutions and policy and arguing that liberal neutrality applies only to the former and not necessarily to the latter. So Sagoff's 'liberal environmentalist' will argue for neutrality only at the level of institutions, while remaining perfectly free to advance and defend Good Life-type views about the proper relationship between human beings and the non-human natural world.

Sagoff's second reason for believing that environmentalists can be liberals is based on liberalism's 'tolerance for competing views' (Sagoff, 1988, p. 167), and its endorsement of institutions 'in which individuals and groups may argue for the policies they favor and may advocate various conceptions of the good' (Sagoff, 1988, p. 167). It is a short step from here to the conclusion that anyone with a conception of the good they wish to advance would be well advised to endorse the liberal project because only in a liberal political environment is there the guarantee of being able to advance it. It is an even shorter step to the conclusion that this advice applies to environmentalists too, or at least to those environmentalists whose political prospectus is driven by a view of the good. We might even say that, by this point, Sagoff wants to say not only that environmentalists *can* be liberals, but that they *should* be liberals.

This second argument, though, merely confirms what we knew already: that liberalism tolerates competing conceptions of the Good Life. What political ecologists will want to know, in addition, is whether liberalism will bring about their objectives. No political system can offer such guarantees, of course, but liberalism's thoroughgoing focus on the *means* rather than the *ends* of political association makes it even less compatible than some other political ideologies with an end-orientated conception of political and social life such as ecologism. So while it is true that 'Liberal social policy cannot be inferred from liberal political theory' (Sagoff, 1988, p. 166) – i.e. that liberal political theory's neutrality as regards institutions should not be taken to entail morality-free social policy – political ecologists are likely to support institutions and policies that endorse *their* view of what morality should be, rather than 'merely' neutral ones.

Nor may it be so easy for a putative green liberalism to avoid nailing its colours to the mast as far as a moral conception of people's relationship with non-human nature is concerned. As Marcel Wissenburg surveys the likely future relationship between liberalism and ecologism, he writes that,

> We may also expect the introduction of the notion of limits to growth and resources, and with it that of sustainability, to lead to questions of a substantive normative nature. A sustainable society need not be one big Yellowstone Park – we can imagine a worldwide version of Holland stuffed with cows, grain and greenhouses, or even a global Manhattan without the Park to be as sustainable and for many among us as pleasant as the first. Hence a greener liberalism

will have to define more clearly what kind of sustainability, what kind of world, it aims for.

(Wissenburg, 1998a, p. 81)

If Wissenburg is right about this – and I believe he is – then this 'greener liberalism' will be obliged to develop a moral conception of our relationship with the non-human natural world as a necessary step on the road to deciding what kind of world we want to hand on to future generations. On this reading, environmental sustainability *by definition* raises questions regarding the Good Life, and so if liberalism is to have a 'take' on environmental sustainability then it must also have a definitive moral conception of 'people's appropriate relation to nature' (in Sagoff's words, 1988, p. 150). If this is a pill that liberalism cannot swallow – as I suspect it cannot – then this may be where liberalism and ecologism finally part company.

The history of liberal thought gives some succour to those who seek compatibilities between liberalism and radical ecology. Marcel Wissenburg, among others, has identified two types of liberal legacy, one centred on the work of John Locke and the other on John Stuart Mill and Jeremy Bentham (Wissenburg, 1998a, pp. 74–6). The former type, according to most commentators, is broadly inimical to the modern ecological project, while the latter has resources that can be enlisted in favour of some aspects of it. In Lockean times, writes Wissenburg, 'Nature had two roles to play in liberal thought: physically, it was an inexhaustible source of resources; intellectually, it was the incarnation of the laws of nature over which humankind had triumphed, which it had transcended' (Wissenburg, 1998a, p. 74). It will be clear by now that this view of the 'role' of nature is roundly rejected by contemporary political ecologists: the limits to growth thesis suggests that nature's resources are not boundless, and the idea that human beings can 'triumph' over the laws of nature is the hubris that political ecologists blame – in part – for environmental problems surrounding issues such as genetically modified foods (discussion of the possibility of a more ecologically-friendly reading of Locke can be found at Hayward, 1994, pp. 130–6, and Dobson, 1998, pp. 144–8).

Similarly, Wissenburg refers to 'the crucial role of reason' in classical liberalism (Wissenburg, 1998a, p. 74). The idea, or category, of reason, is central to liberalism since the view that all human beings possess reason (even if they do not always use it), constitutes 'the beginning of arguments for the political equality and influence of citizens, for the individual as the source of all political authority, for the priority of private over state interests' (ibid.). The explosive nature of this idea in the late seventeenth century should not be underestimated. But inclusion and exclusion are two sides of the same coin, and just as possessors of reason were drawn into the charmed circle, so those beings lacking it were left outside. As Wissenburg puts it: 'Classical liberalism recognizes only one essential distinction in nature: the line dividing reasonable and unreasonable beings' (Wissenburg, 1998a, p. 75). This is an essential and enduring distinction in one type of liberalism that legitimizes discrimina-tory treatment between humans and other animals.

The second type of liberalism – that developed through the work of Mill, Bentham and their followers – tells a different story, however. As Bentham famously said, 'The question is not, Can they *reason?* nor, Can they *talk?* but, Can they *suffer?*' (Bentham, 1960: ch. 17, sec. 1). This new category of 'sentience' clearly broadens the community of beings entitled to moral consideration – broadens it sufficiently, indeed, to include some non-human animals. We saw all this in Chapter 2, and we also saw that the game of defining the 'X' in the question 'What faculty, X, must beings possess to be entitled to moral considerability?' can be played intermina-bly. For classical liberalism, 'X' is reason, and this gives one kind of answer to the question. For Bentham (and utilitarians in general), 'X' is sentience, and this gives another kind of answer. Ecocentrics will answer the 'X' question in different ways again; Robyn Eckersley, as we saw (p. 42), refers to the 'characteristic of self-reproduction or self-renewal' (Eckersley, 1992, p. 60). This broadens the community of 'moral patients' beyond anything to be found even in Mill and Bentham, and provides circumstantial evidence that, however hard they try, liberals will not find much in their historical legacy to satisfy ecocentrics.

On the other hand, the idea of *rights* is inseparable from liberalism, and this idea can be – and has been – enlisted in favour of environmental objectives. This appropriation can take the form of piggy-backing such objectives on specifically *human* rights. Tim Hayward points out that the idea of a 'right to ... an environment of a quality that permits a life of dignity and well-being' was mooted as early as 1972 at the Stockholm UN Conference on the Human Environment. From an environmental point of view, though, there are problems with such a rights strategy. In the first place, as Hayward observes, the problem with the idea of a 'right to an adequate environment' for political ecologists is that 'it does not really go beyond the view that the environment is just a resource which humans have a right to use for their own benefit' (Hayward, 1995, p. 144). Second, the 'limits to growth' thesis suggests that 'natural ecosystems have a limited carrying capacity which simply cannot support all the demands of a growing human population, and so cannot necessarily support all the rights they might want to claim either' (ibid., pp. 144–5).

This second objection points to the need to limit population growth. Such a policy may itself have distinctly non-liberal implications (see Wissenburg, 1998b), but Hayward refers to evidence that suggests that affluence is an effective contraceptive, and he also suggests (along with many others, e.g. B. Barry, 1999) that women's emancipation is the key to reduced birth rates. What should be noted, though, is that the 'affluence' solution both falls foul of the limits to growth thesis, and is also the cause of the type of environmental problem associated with wealthy societies. Likewise, the 'emancipation' solution comes from *feminism* not from *liberalism*, so we are perhaps entitled to conclude that liberalism – on its own – lacks the intellectual resources for dealing with the problems associated with piggy-backing environmental objectives on human rights.

Another way in which liberal rights-talk can make 'green' sense is in the context of animal rights. A flavour of this move has already been given in Chapter 2, and there is no need to go over the same ground again. Suffice to say that assuming some animals can be regarded as rights-holders (Feinberg, 1981), then rights-claims can, in principle, be as politically useful for those animals as they are for human beings. This begs the question, of course, of whether rights-claims *are* politically useful, even when social and economic rights are added to the political rights normally associated with the liberal project. Ted Benton, for one, has deployed a Marxist critique of such rights in the context of animals, and he suggests that the discourse of rights will always come up against the practice of exploitation:

> rights are unlikely to be effective in practice unless those who have the power to abuse them are already benevolently disposed to their bearers ... Where humans gain their livelihood from a practice which presupposes a 'reification' of animals, or gain pleasure from sports which involve systematic animal suffering, it seems unlikely that a rational argument that this treatment is unjust to the animals concerned would be sufficient to make the humans concerned change their ways.
>
> (Benton, 1993, p. 94)

The crucial thing, he concludes, is to take into account 'the socio-economic and cultural positions and formations of the human agents concerned' (ibid.).

One final and very promising area in which rights have been deployed in the name of environmental objectives is in the context of future generations. It might not be immediately apparent how the rights of future generations and environmental sustainability are connected, but once we realize that 'the environment' is one of the things we hand on to future generations, and if we accept that future generations have a right to a sustainable and satisfying environment, then future generation rights and environmental sustainability can be seen to be intimately linked. As Hayward astutely points out: 'In talking about rights of future generations, one is already addressing matters of environmental concern' (Hayward, 1994, p. 142).

In this context, as in many others, the work of the most influential (liberal) theorist of modern times, John Rawls, has proved remarkably fecund. Rawls it was who, in his *A Theory of Justice*, developed a 'savings principle' (Rawls, 1973, p. 287), whereby present generations are enjoined to save for future ones. Much turns on just what form this 'saving' is to take, of course, but if it is understood to include environmental goods and services (understood in the broadest sense), then this liberal theory of justice, at least, looks compatible with environmental objectives. Recently, Marcel Wissenburg has argued that this is true of *all* liberal theories of justice: 'liberals in general need to include a savings principle in their respective theories of justice – and ... (some form of) obligations to future generations is a *conditio sine qua non* of any liberal theory of justice' (Wissenburg, 1998a, p. 134). Once again, the *nature* of these obligations is crucial, but Wissenburg believes it entirely compatible with a conditional view of liberal rights that these obligations take the form of what he calls the 'restraint principle':

> no goods shall be destroyed unless unavoidable and unless they are replaced by perfectly identical goods; if that is physically impossible, they should be replaced by equivalent goods resembling the original as closely as possible; and that if this is also impossible, a proper compensation should be provided.
>
> (Wissenburg, 1998a, p. 123)

From an environmental point of view this looks very promising. Yet – as ever – the devil is in the detail: what, precisely, does 'unless unavoidable' mean? Carnivores and vegetarians, for example, will have different answers to this question. More broadly still, the 'unless unavoidable' proviso takes us back full circle to an earlier point: that the idea of environmental sustainability enjoins us, by definition, to have a definitive moral conception of 'people's appropriate relation to nature' – precisely the kind of conception, though, that liberalism eschews.

The liberal language of rights, then, can be deployed in the service of environmental objectives, but not with conclusive success. My own view is that the intentions of ecologism need the idea of *responsibilities* to be added to those of rights because, as Hayward remarks, this

> seems to capture the key ecological intuition that it is necessary to change our basic attitude to the world from one which considers 'what we can get out of it' to one which considers 'what we can and must do for it'.
>
> (Hayward, 1994, p. 163)

Whether animals or future generation human beings have rights or not, their peculiar vulnerability to our actions 'demands' a responsible attitude of care and concern (Goodin, 1985). Normally, rights and duties are seen as reciprocal – 'rights exist if and only if corresponding duties exist' (Hayward, 1994, p. 169) – and ecologism's contribution to this debate lies in severing the connection between rights and duties.

In sum there will always be tensions, to say the least, between liberalism and ecologism. To the oft-remarked differences of opinion over autonomy and individualism we must add ecologism's insistence on a definitive view of the proper moral relationship between human beings and the non-human natural world – a bridge too far for liberalism. We must acknowledge the uses to which rights-talk can be put for environmental ends, but also temper this with the recognition that such talk can never fully express the nature of the relationship between human beings and 'nature' that ecologism seeks to establish. Finally, liberalism is firmly located in a tradition of thought and practice that distinguishes sharply between the human and 'natural' realms, both descriptively and prescriptively. Ecologism, by contrast, insists that we are human *animals*, with all the implications that this brings in its train.

Conservatism

In the context of modern political thought, one of ecologism's signal and novel contributions is the idea that our *natural* condition affects and constrains our *political* condition. This is to say that – following on from the last remark in the previous section – our condition as human *animals* constrains us in ways similar to those experienced by all animals. There are differences, of course. Human animals are able to construct plans for life and strategies for realizing them in ways that most, if not all, animals are incapable of doing. It is this capacity for autonomous thought and action on which liberal thought focuses, as we saw in the previous section, and this view of the human condition dominates contemporary politics.

Political ecologists do not reject this view entirely, but they do recommend that it be tempered by a hard-headed look at our natural
circumstances. The lesson of the limits to growth thesis, as we saw in
Chapter 3, is that human beings – like any other animal – have to
consume natural resources, and that given that these resources are
limited, human projects such as open-ended economic growth are
impossible to sustain. In this regard, ecologism taps into a tradition that is
closer to the conservative than the liberal sensibility. Thomas Malthus,
for example, famous for his *An Essay on the Principle of Population* (1792),
is widely regarded as contributing to the conservative tradition – largely
because of his belief in 'the limits to social progress imposed by man's
place in nature' (Wells, 1982, p. 2).

The intellectual history of the past two hundred years is littered with
thinkers who have questioned the idea of progress as understood by
modernity, but ecologism's reluctance to endorse modernity's notion of
progress is not based on 'some view of the cyclic growth and degeneration
of civilizations', nor on 'objections based on a philosophical and
epistemological opposition to the notion of a "scientific" history' (as in
rejections of the Marxist notion of progress), but on a 'particular vision of
man's relationship to the physical and biological world: what could be
called "the ecological viewpoint" ' (Wells, 1982, p. 3). This viewpoint is
animated by the fundamentally conservative thought that 'the basic
political question – "what should be done?" – depends on an account of
what *can* be done' (ibid., p. 15).

In ecologism, this account of what can be done turns on an understanding of human beings' place in nature. Moreover, the guiding idea of
political ecology is that this is an *ecological* place rather than an
evolutionary place, with all the implications that this entails. Most
particularly, the ecological view talks of 'climax states' of relative stability,
while the evolutionists' motif is that of 'progress'. Malthus's ecological
view was superseded by that of Darwin and Wallace, whose ideas were
grasped with alacrity by progressive thinkers such as Marx, who

> welcomed the new biological outlook and the support it gave to an
> evolutionary and by implication, progressive – view of human
> society. The idea of general, and perhaps unlimited, progress so
> strongly attacked by Malthus had been restored as a dominant theme
> in social and political theory.
>
> (Wells, 1982, p. 12)

With the restoration of the ecological idea in politics, battle with the
evolutionary view of political progress has once again been joined.

Luke Martell has summarized the connections between radical green and conservative thinking in the following way:

> Some greens urge humans to be more humble and accommodating before nature, adapting to its laws and rhythms and putting less emphasis on exercising control over their environment and manipulating it to their own advantage. They are often sceptical and critical of Enlightenment ideas about the capacity of human rationality and the commitment to progress and innovation.
>
> (Martell, 1994, p. 140)

These are all recognizably conservative notions, and each one amounts to useful ammunition for those who would claim that ecologism and conservatism are fundamentally similar ideologies.

So similar, indeed, that a sustained attempt has been made by John Gray, sometime supporter of Thatcherite liberal conservatism but now an advocate of a social democratic conservatism, to appropriate political ecology for the conservative cause (Gray, 1993b). Gray urges us to reject 'the self-image of the Greens as inheritors of the radical protest movements of earlier times, and as making common cause with contemporary radical movements, such as feminism and anti-colonialism' (ibid., p. 124). On the contrary, 'Far from having a natural home on the Left, concern for the integrity of the common environment, human as well as ecological, is most in harmony with the outlook of traditional conservatism of the British and European varieties' (ibid.), and,

> Many of the central conceptions of traditional conservatism have a natural congruence with Green concerns: the Burkean idea of the social contract, not as agreement among anonymous ephemeral individuals, but as a compact between the generations of the living, the dead and those yet unborn; Tory scepticism about progress, and awareness of its ironies and illusions; conservative resistance to untried novelty and large-scale social experiments; and, perhaps most especially, the traditional conservative tenet that individual flourishing can occur only in the context of forms of common life.
>
> (Gray, 1993b, p. 124)

To these similarities, Gray adds the observation that 'both Greens and conservatives consider risk-aversion the path of prudence when new technologies, or new social practices, have consequences that are large and unpredictable, and, most especially, when they [sic] are unquantifiable but potentially catastrophic risks associated with intervention' (Gray,

1993b, p. 137). This is the Greens' 'precautionary principle' for decision-making in all but name – widely advocated in recent debates regarding the experimental planting of genetically modified crops, and supported by many political conservatives.

The evidence for congruence between radical political ecology and conservatism, then, seems strong, but there are a number of areas where the relationship is severely strained, and others still where it cannot be said to exist at all. We can begin with Gray's 'traditional conservative tenet that individual flourishing can occur only in the context of forms of common life' (Gray, 1993b, p. 124), and that this is an idea shared by 'Green theory' (ibid., p. 136). But just what is this 'common life', and is it the same for political ecologists and for conservatives? From a conservative point of view, Gray says that people's 'deepest need is a home, a network of common practices and inherited traditions that confers on them the blessing of a settled identity' (ibid., p. 125). The common life of which he speaks is therefore defined in primarily *historical* and *cultural* terms, as expressed through *tradition*. There are indeed radical greens for whom culture and history are very important. Some of the resistance to road-building programmes, for instance, is based on a belief in the cultural significance of features of the land which are destroyed by building contractors. My own view, though, is that valuing 'nature' in the currency of 'culture' in this way is precisely what distances *conservative* defences of nature from *political-ecological* ones. The political ecologist sees value in nature in itself, and if this value derives from history at all, it is *natural* history that counts, and not *human* history in the form of tradition and culture.

This is as much as to say that the 'common life' of which radical greens speak is an ontological and moral one that crosses species boundaries. It is important for Gray that common cultural, conservative forms

> cannot be created anew for each generation. We are not like the butterfly, whose generations are unknown to each other; we are a familial and historical species, for whom the past must have authority (that of memory) if we are to have identity.
>
> (Gray, 1993b, p. 124)

But the moral and ontological common life of political ecologists *can* be created anew for each generation through the intellectual effort of grounding inter-species responsibility in a thoroughgoing naturalism that recognizes the implications of our being human *animals*.

So the ecocentrism of radical greenery sets it apart from conservatism just as it sets it apart from all other modern political ideologies. The only time Gray mentions anthropocentrism, the *bête noire* of the political ecologist, is in the following context: 'Green theory is an invaluable corrective of the Whiggish, anthropocentric, technological optimism by which all the modernist political religions are animated' (Gray, 1993b, p. 175). There is no evidence adduced, though, to suggest that traditional conservatism is anything other than as irredeemably anthropocentric as other political ideologies. Where conservative defences of the non-human natural world exist they are usually rooted in romanticism rather than in an appreciation of the independent moral standing of non-humans that animates much radical green thought.

The second point at which we should interrogate Gray's agenda is on the apparently unassailable point regarding intergenerational relations. It is true that conservatism, unlike any other political ideology with the exception of contemporary liberalism, talks of 'a compact between the generations of the living, the dead and those yet unborn' (Gray, 1993b, p. 124), and that intergenerational responsibility is a crucial feature of the political-ecological agenda. Edmund Burke, the 'father of British conservatism' whom Gray paraphrases here, puts it like this:

> one of the first and most leading principles on which the common-wealth and the laws are consecrated, is lest the temporary possessors and life-renters in it, unmindful of what they have received from their ancestors, or of what is due to their posterity, should act as if they were the entire masters; that they should not think it amongst their rights to cut off the entail, or commit waste on the inheritance, by destroying at their pleasure the whole original fabric of their society; hazarding to leave to those who come after them, a ruin instead of an habitation – and teaching these successors as little to respect their contrivances as they had themselves respected the institutions of their forefathers. By this unprincipled facility of changing the state as often, and as much, and in as many ways as there are floating fancies or fashions, the whole chain and continuity of the commonwealth would be broken. No one generation could link with the other. Men would become little better than the flies of a summer.
>
> (Burke, 1790/1982, pp. 192–3)

What is striking about these remarks is that the generations in which Burke is most interested are past generations – those from whom we inherit what we have and to whom we owe some obligation of preservation. The green view of intergenerational obligation is rather different to this. Most obviously, the generations that usually interest political ecologists are *future* generations. One thing the present generation can be sure of, they say, is that our actions will affect the conditions under which future people live their lives, and this generates a responsibility for us of which other political ideologies have no conception. Conservatism is interested in the conserving and preserving *of the past*; ecologism is interested in conserving and preserving *for the future*. Herein lies a signal difference between the conservative and ecological political imaginations. (Political ecologists might do well to bear in mind, though, Burke's aphoristic warning that 'People will not look forward to posterity, who never look backward to their forefathers'; Burke, 1790/1982, p. 119.)

The third difference between conservatism and ecologism is rooted in disputes about the nature and relevance of 'imperfection'. It is a conservative commonplace that human beings are irredeemably flawed in their nature, and that political aspirations should reflect this. This is to say that political projects aimed at perfecting society will founder on the rock of unalterable human shortcomings and weaknesses. In this regard, political aspirations need to be drawn up within well-defined limits. As we have seen, the language of limits is the language of ecologism as well as of conservatism:

> The earth is finite. Growth of anything physical, including the human population and its cars, buildings and smokestacks, cannot continue forever … The limits to growth are limits to the ability of the planetary *sources* to provide those streams of materials and energy, and limits to the ability of the planetary *sinks* to absorb the pollution and waste.
>
> (Meadows *et al.*, 1992, pp. 8–9)

Gray refers to sentiments of this sort as evidence of an anti-Utopian sensibility that is common to both conservatism and ecologism (Gray, 1993b, p. 127). Burkean conservatism and political ecology (as I have been describing it) seem to be as one in their opposition to the hubristic carelessness expressed in Utopian talk of 'indefinite malleability'. The anti-Utopian's principal target, says Krishan Kumar, is hubris (Kumar, 1987, p. 103), and so is the political ecologist's. If Utopians uncompromisingly believe that '[T]here are no fundamental barriers or obstacles to man's earthly perfection [and that] scarcity can be overcome' (Kumar, 1991, p. 29), then the gap between Utopians and political ecologists is as wide as it can be: scarcity is the most basic and unalterable feature of the human condition as far as political ecologists are concerned (for a full and entertaining analysis of the relationship between Utopianism and political ecology, see de Geus, 1999). So, Utopianism demands malleability and political ecology's interpretation of the human condition denies its possibility. Does this apparent opposition to Utopianism imply a deep congruence between conservatism and ecologism?

I think not. The crucial and relevant distinction here is between malleability of the human *condition* and the malleability of human *nature*. It is perfectly possible to believe that the human condition is fixed, while human nature is not, and this is indeed what political ecologists believe. Political ecologists do not possess the 'pessimistic and determinist view of human nature' which is common to conservatives and anti-Utopians (Kumar, 1987, p. 100), and nor do they believe in 'original sin' (ibid.), if by this we mean unredeemable sin. Tim Hayward believes that 'one cannot reasonably assume that people are generally motivated to do other than what they take to be in their own interest' (Hayward, 1998, p. 7), and proceeds to build his own environmental political theory on the foundations of a reinterpretation of human self-interest that will include respect for '(at least some significant classes of) nonhuman beings' (ibid., p. 118). What makes this an environmental political theory rather than an ecological one is its basis in *human* self-interest, but political ecologists will also refuse the belief that self-interest itself is the only credible, or possible, human motivation. So while political ecologists believe that there are (more or less) fixed limits to production, consumption and waste, they have a Utopian sense of what is possible within those limits. Unlike conservatives, radical greens believe that human beings are capable of transformation; that they can, if they wish, abandon the acquisitive, instrumental and use-related relationship with the natural environment that dominates the modern imagination.

Acutely, John Gray observes that what he calls green conservatism is an instance of an

> ancient paradox, with which the modern world abounds in examples, that conservatives cannot help becoming radicals, when current practice embodies the hubristic and careless projects of recent gen-erations, or has been distorted by technological innovations whose consequences for human well-being have not been weighed.
>
> (Gray, 1993b, p. 128)

In the current environmental climate conservatives may well find themselves opposed to much of the *status quo*, but radical conservatives are not the same as radical greens, and on at least the three counts discussed above the gap between the conservative and radical green agenda as far as the environment is concerned is wide and deep.

Socialism

In the context of socialism and the largely successful assault launched on it by the right over the past twenty years, the last thing socialism needed, so the argument goes, was a challenge to its hegemony towards the left-hand end of the political spectrum. Early responses to the environmental movement from the socialist left were certainly hostile and often focused on its middle-class nature, either so as to illustrate its marginal relevance to the working class in particular and thus to socialism in general, or, more aggressively, to cast it in the role of a positive distraction from the fundamental battles still to be fought between capital and labour. Either way, the nascent green movement was generally presented as a blip on the screen of radical politics, which would, probably, soon disappear and which, certainly, had nothing to say to the left that was worth listening to.

In the pages that follow I shall set out what I consider to be the principal socialist criticisms of green politics, and then show the ways in which socialists sensitive to the ecological position have reinterpreted their own tradition so as to accommodate it. The debate between ecologism and socialism continues to be acrimonious at times and often there is no debate at all. Jonathon Porritt and Nicholas Winner, for example, refer to David Pepper's presentation of the green movement as 'deeply conservative' and 'reactionary' and as 'just so much angry sputtering from worn-out ideologues who have long since lost touch with the real world' (1988, p. 256). Sandy Irvine and Alec Ponton pointedly characterize socialism as 'fair shares in extinction' (1988, p. 142). Elsewhere, though, and particularly in the work of Raymond Williams (n.d.), Boris Frankel (1987), James O'Connor (1996), Peter Dickens (1992) and Ted Benton (1993 and 1996) great strides have been taken (on the socialist side at least) to come to terms with the green perspective without abandoning original socialist impulses. Others, such as Joe Weston (1986), David Harvey (1993) and David Pepper (1993a and 1993b), have remained more or less unreconstructed after their engagement with green thought. This is not to say that they do not take ecological problems seriously – they most certainly do – but the favoured strategy of 'unreconstructionists' is to subsume the ecological point in a socialist framework, leaving the latter much as it was at the outset. Witness David Harvey who calls, first, for a 'creative rather than a destructive tension' between socialist and ecological politics, but then rather gives the game away by looking for a 'distinctively "ecological" angle to progressive socialist politics' (Harvey, 1993, p. 4). It is with these varied contributions that this section of the chapter is in part engaged.

The first area of contention between ecologism and socialism is over the source of the ills of contemporary society. Socialists identify capitalism as that source, while political ecologists are much more likely to refer to 'industrialism'. We know by now that one of the reasons the green movement considers itself to be 'beyond left and right' is because it believes this traditional spectrum of opposition to be inscribed in a more fundamental context of agreement: a 'super-ideology' called 'industrialism'. Greens 'stress the similarities between capitalist and socialist countries' (Porritt and Winner, 1988, p. 256) in that they are both held to believe that the needs of their respective populations are best satisfied by maximizing economic growth. The equating of capitalism with socialism engendered by the identification of 'industrialism' is the aspect of green thinking most often attacked by its socialist critics, and Joe Weston's 'It is time that greens accepted that it is capitalism rather than industrialism *per se* which is at the heart of the problems they address' (1986, p. 5) is a typical refrain.

Socialists make remarks like this, in the first place, not because they don't agree with ecologists that environmental decay is upon us but because they argue that it is capitalism's use of industry to produce for profit and not for need, rather than 'industry' itself, that causes the problems. 'Capitalism,' writes David Pepper, 'is about the accumulation of capital through producing commodities.' The capitalist dynamic involves periodic crises of overproduction which are resolved 'by creating new wants, and by extending the system globally to new consumers in new markets'. This dynamic of production and consumption means that '[C]apitalism *must*, inherently if not constantly and explicitly, degrade and destroy that part of its means of production that comes from "nature" ' (Pepper, 1993a, p. 430). This is as much as to say that capitalism is a precondition for the politics of ecology: 'world capitalism itself has created the conditions for an ecological socialist movement' (O'Connor, 1991, p. 5).

James O'Connor also famously argues, like Marx, that capitalism may be digging its own grave, but for reasons that have as much to do with a contradiction between the forces/relations of production and the *conditions* of production as with the time-honoured Marxist contradiction between the forces and relations of production themselves. O'Connor calls this the 'second contradiction' of capitalism, according to which 'the combined power of capitalist production relations and productive forces self-destruct by impairing or destroying rather than reproducing their own conditions' (O'Connor, 1996, p. 206). Examples of such impairment, says O'Connor, are global warming, acid rain, salinization, and pesticide poisoning, all of which, he avers, threaten profit-making. This second contradiction, like the first, gives rise to opposition, not this time in the form of the labour movement, but in the form of the new social movements which harbour the potential for transcending the contradictions that give rise to them. The 'second contradiction' thesis has given rise to a great deal of comment, particularly in the journal *Capitalism, Nature, Socialism* (and see Benton, 1996, Part 3, for an extended discussion), and in our context it illustrates the yawning gap between greens, who argue that industrialism is the root of environmental degradation, and ecological Marxists, who affirm that capitalism is both the cause of the environmental crisis and the horizon that needs to be transcended if we are to deal with it.

Radical greens will probably accept that a fundamental break with capitalism is indeed a necessary condition for restoring environmental integrity but they do not see it as a sufficient condition, particularly when they point to former communist countries which had some of the worst environmental records in the entire world. Socialists respond by pointing out that none of these countries were socialist in the sense they want to ascribe to the word (Miliband, 1994), and that this is because they have developed the same 'form of demand for material goods' as the capitalist nations, in competition with them. In this sense 'capitalism permeates the whole globe' (Weston, 1986, p. 4). As Bahro wrote:

> We have precisely learned that the Russian revolution did not manage to break with the *capitalist horizon of development of productive forces*. We have seen how right round the globe it is one and the same technology that has triumphed.
>
> (Bahro, 1982, p. 131)

In this way socialists side-step the green invitation to consider the environmental problems suffered by socialist countries and to draw the conclusion that there is little to choose between socialist and capitalist management of industry (from the environment's point of view). They then suggest that a truly socialist society would produce for need and not for profit, and that consideration of the environment would be integral to policy formation because the 'traditional humanist concerns of socialism' inevitably involve consideration of human/non-human nature interaction (Pepper, 1993a, p 438).

However, in one important respect (from a socialist point of view) the issue is not over what a socialist society might or might not do, but that the green refusal to recognize capitalism as the root of the problem renders ecology incapable of fighting its battles in the right places. If from an environmental perspective the socialist view of capitalism is correct, then ecologism's best way forward is to confront the capitalist manifestation of industrialism rather than the many-headed hydra, industrialism itself.

Joe Weston reminds us that this would involve the restatement of traditional socialist principles and practices, on the basis that 'what we find is that behind virtually all environmental problems, both physical and social, is poverty' (1986, p. 4). Pepper makes a similar point: '[A]s the 1992 Earth Summit in Rio showed, the most fundamental issues in global environmental politics revolve around social justice, wealth distribution and ownership and control of the means of production, particularly land' (1993a, p. 429). Many socialists will then analyse phenomena like deforestation from just this point of view – the fundamental problem is much more one of inequitable land distribution (which produces the slash-and-burn farmers) and structural poverty (which produces periodic but highly damaging jungle gold rushes), than it is one of an insatiable and environmentally insensitive desire to eat hamburgers. From this point of view, environmentalist (or even ecologist) strategies will be found wanting: Weston suggests that

> Saving hedgerows does not confront capitalism in the same way as do issues relating to poverty; poverty is, after all, of crucial importance to capitalism and has to be maintained in order to preserve the balance of power in market relationships.
>
> (Weston, 1986, p. 156)

Poverty, then, is at the root of most environmental problems and a far-reaching redistribution of wealth is the solution. Crucially, an attack on poverty would constitute an attack on capitalism, and would therefore be a blow against the root cause of environmental decay.

The green question now might be: Why should a redistribution of wealth bring about improvements in the environment? Much evidently turns on just what 'environment' one is talking about, and it is a socialist strategy with respect to ecologism to accuse it of too narrow a definition of the term. It is probably true that radical redistributions of wealth would improve the sanitation, housing and food of millions of dispossessed poor both here and in the so-called Third World, and that this would constitute a significant improvement in their environment. But it is hard to see how a redistribution of wealth on its own would address green warnings about the unsustainability of present industrial practices. One can perfectly well imagine a world in which incomes between and within countries were more or less the same, but which still subscribed to the view that there were no limits to industrial growth. Indeed, this is precisely the world that the dominant themes of socialism have advertised since its inception, and is the reason why greens are wary of attacks on capitalism that have no ecological content. In this sense, Weston talks past the green movement rather than to it when he says:

> The problems with which most people are now faced are not related to 'nature' at all: they are related to poverty and the transfer of wealth and resources from the poor to an already wealthy minority of the Earth's population.
>
> (Weston, 1986, p. 14)

My own view is that the 'justice' and 'environment' agendas are related in the way that the circles in Venn diagrams are related. That is to say, there are areas of common concern but it is a mistake to regard them as wholly and completely mapping on to one another. The powerful 'environmental justice' movement in the United States is often deployed as evidence that the environmental and justice movements can sing from the same hymn sheet, but a close examination of the US movement's aspirations shows that it is more concerned with human justice than with environmental protection. Malcolm Dowie, for example, has written that 'The central concern of the new movement is human health' (Dowie, 1995, p. 127), and while there is obviously a link between a healthy environment and human health, concern for the latter will not cover all the objectives of political ecologists. Similarly, Laura Pulido has noted Pezzoli's important observation that 'communities engaged in what appear to be environmentally related struggles at times may not be committed to an environmental agenda' (Pulido, 1996, p. 16). This needs to be taken into account by those who argue that the environmental and justice movements are as one (the issue of the relationship between justice and the environment is addressed in detail in Dobson, 1998 and 1999).

A second point of disagreement between socialists and political ecologists concerns 'the environment' itself. It transpired above that Joe Weston's argument that a redistribution of wealth would help solve environmental problems was based upon an interpretation of 'environment' not usually associated with the green movement. In his opinion, greens have policed the word into meaning 'nature': 'the prime concern of the greens is indeed ecology and "nature", which means that other, far more immediate environmental problems are neglected' (Weston, 1986, p. 2). In this context it is indulgent and irresponsible for the green movement to concentrate its 'not inconsiderable resources upon protecting hedgerows, butterflies and bunny rabbits' (ibid., p. 12) while the day-to-day built environments of large numbers of people are in such urgent need of reconstruction.

Sections of the green movement appear to have taken this kind of criticism on board – witness the Friends of the Earth's 'Cities for People' campaign – but there is still a sense in which Weston's critique speaks past the movement rather than to it. Greens have a very good reason for referring so often to the biospherical environment: they are concerned for its survival as a long-term supporter of human and non-human life. From this perspective (eco)socialists are right to ask greens to reassess their understanding of 'the environment', but wrong to ask them to focus on inner-city environments if the recipes for them are not placed in the context of the search for a sustainable society.

Socialists (and others) will argue, in any case, that there is no such thing as 'nature' unmediated by human beings, and therefore no great difference between the urban environment and the environment created by farmed land or deforestation: social relations and the capitalist mode of production that underpins them 'produce' the environment. Green exhortations to 'protect' or 'conserve' the environment betray the unfounded impression that there is an 'untouched' nature alongside the bits already corrupted by human beings, and it is this untouched nature that receives the movement's greatest attention. Pepper writes that '[T]here is not a self-contained "humanity" counterposed to and ever battling with a self-contained "non-human" world' but rather each is 'part of a unity that is composed of "contradictory" opposites' Pepper, 1993a, p. 440), and that the ecocentric view regarding our supposed alienation from nature is internally self-contradictory since it 'rests on a *dualistic* conception of the human–nature relationship: a conception it is supposed to reject' (ibid., p. 443).

Again, I think that this speaks past the radical green point rather than to it. Both Marxism and deep ecology are types of monism, of course, but all monists separate out parts of the common substance for different purposes. It is no contradiction to hold a monist view regarding the nature of things and simultaneously distinguish between human and non-human nature (indeed Pepper himself continually does so). Even Spinoza, perhaps the most thoroughgoing monist of them all, allows for two 'attributes' (thought and extension) of a single 'substance' (Spinoza, 1677/1955). Marxists will make the distinction within *their* monism in order, then, to theorize the dialectical relation between the social and 'natural' (nearly always, for socialists, in inverted commas) worlds. Deep ecologists will distinguish within *their* monism, for example, so as to talk of the ethical relationship which should hold between human and non-human nature.

Socialists, in any case, will argue that an awareness of the social construction of the environment would have three effects: first, it would lead to a healthy widening of green activity; second, it would promote an understanding of the capitalist roots of environmental decay – both in the countryside and in the cities; and third, it would improve the chances of the green movement obtaining a mass following.

This last point needs some explanation. Joe Weston argues that the green movement as presently constituted is an expression of the ennui of a particular section of the middle class – the professional, educated section. Green politics is 'an attempt to protect the values – rather than simply the economic privilege – of a social group which rejects the market-orientated politics of capitalism and the materialistic analysis made of it by Marxists' (Weston, 1986, p. 27). These values are reflected, partly, in the 'green' definitions of the environment most often advanced by the movement, referred to above. To the extent that this is 'a political perspective which is specific to a particular social group' (ibid., p. 28) and, moreover, a social group that is of limited size, no mass movement can be formed around it. On this reading ecologism will not progress beyond its minority, subordinate status until it speaks to the kinds of environmental problems suffered by masses of people, and 'that means developing ways to conceptualise and represent ecological issues in ways that speak to the aspirations of the working class movement' (Harvey, 1993, p. 48). This it will never do, suggests Weston, unless it breaks out of its middle-class laager and recognizes that 'rather than conserving the environment in which most people now live, the inner city and the shanty town need destroying' (Weston, 1986, pp. 14–15).

A third faultline between socialists and political ecologists can be found in disputes over the issue of 'limits to growth'. Indeed, the most instructive test to carry out on would-be green socialists is to see how far they have accepted the fundamental green position that there are material limits to productive growth. Some have done so completely and in the process would appear significantly to have reassessed the content of their socialism. Rudolf Bahro, for example, commented when he was still a socialist that he found it 'quite atrocious that there are Marxists who contest the finite scope of the earth's exploitable crust' (1982, p. 60). We now know that Bahro's dwelling on thoughts like this led him to abandon socialism entirely. Not so Joe Weston and Raymond Williams, but they would probably nevertheless agree with the following remarks:

> I do not believe that anyone can read the extensive literature on the ecology crisis without concluding that its impact will oblige us to make changes in production and consumption of a kind, and on a scale, which will entail a break with the lifestyles and expectations that have become habitual in industrialized countries.
>
> (Ryle, 1988, p. 6)

Joe Weston certainly agrees, up to a point: 'it must be stressed that this rejection of green politics does not mean that we now believe that natural resources are infinite' (Weston, 1986, p. 4) and adds that the left can learn from the Greens to call the project of 'perpetual industrial expansion' into question (ibid., p. 5). Raymond Williams, too, accepts the ecological position with respect to 'the central problem of this whole mode and version of production: an effective infinity of expansion in a physically finite world' (Williams, 1986, p. 214) and suggests that 'the orthodox abstraction of indefinitely expanded production – its version of "growth" – has to be considered again, from the beginning' (ibid., p. 215).

Others, though, such as David Pepper, find this sort of thing hard to swallow: Pepper is concerned 'not to abandon humanism by over-pandering to green assumptions about the "natural" limits to the transformation of nature' (Pepper, 1993a, p. 434). David Harvey, too, believes that the idea of natural limits is too simplistic and insufficiently dialectical. He suggests that

> if we view 'natural resources' in the rather traditional geographical manner, as 'cultural, technological and economic appraisals of elements residing in nature and mobilised for particular social ends' ... then 'ecoscarcity' means that we have not the will, wit or capacity to change our social goals, cultural modes, our technological mixes, or our form of economy and that we are powerless to modify 'nature' according to human requirements.
>
> (Harvey, 1993, p. 39)

Harvey's intention here is to damn political ecologists for their (imputed) belief that human beings are powerless in the face of a hostile natural world characterized by scarcity. Yet the intention is subverted upon the realization that political ecology is actually all about doing what Harvey claims political ecologists think is impossible. Political ecologists *do* think we have the 'will, wit and capacity to change our social goals, cultural modes', etc. They even think that we have the power to 'modify "nature" according to human requirements' – the question is really over 'How much?', and a significant part of the answer is given, for political ecologists, by the fact that our actions take place under the sign of scarcity. This, in the end, is the 'brute fact' (for political ecologists) which Marxist critics seek to defuse through deployment of the sense of a *dialectical* relationship between human beings and the 'natural' world.

The reconsiderations of socialists like Williams seem to involve them in reconsidering socialism itself. Williams writes that 'any socialist should recognise the certainty that many of the resources at their present levels of use are going to run out' (Williams, n.d., p. 15), and that consequently socialists should rethink their traditional belief that the relief of poverty requires 'production, and more production' (ibid., p. 6). But then it turns out that this is not a traditional socialist belief after all, for Williams suggests that: 'We have to build on the socialist argument that productive growth, as such, is not the abolition of poverty' (ibid., p. 15). Williams seems to be saying both that socialism does hold the belief that the relief of poverty requires more production and, then, that it does not.

Of course, socialists have always argued for an equitable distribution of what is produced and in this sense Williams is consistent, but socialism has no dominant tradition of production itself being called into question, and this is what Williams is hinting at here. Certainly the now-defunct British journal *Marxism Today*, for example, would consider his position to be heretical: 'the question of reindustrialisation and growth distinguishes the Ecology Party, and green politics generally, quite sharply from the Left' (quoted in Porritt, 1984b, p. 25). Similarly Frank Richards restates the classic left position when he writes that 'The number of people which can be supported by an area of land is not given by nature, but by the sort of society in which they are organised' (1989, p. 21).

Raymond Williams, then, appears above to be rereading socialism, and when he refers to 'the pressure point on the whole existing capitalist mode of production' as 'the problem of resources' (n.d., p. 16) he leaves us in no doubt. We will not find this kind of analysis of the weaknesses of capitalism in any of the dominant sources of socialist thought. To this degree, acceptance of the green position that there are limits to productive growth can have considerable repercussions with respect to the content of the socialism espoused by socialists.

One of the repercussions that stands out is a rethinking of the socialist tradition itself in the sense of a stressing of some aspects of it at the expense of others. Not surprisingly, it is decentralist, non-bureaucratic, non-productivist socialism to which writers like Williams most often refer, and the Utopian socialists and William Morris are those usually resurrected as evidence for its existence (even by David Pepper: 1993a, pp. 431, 447, 449). Thus, Rudolf Bahro suggested that 'we shall scarcely come up against any elements that have not already emerged in the writings of one or other of the old socialists, including of course the utopians' (Bahro, 1982, p. 126). By 1994 he was saying: 'If pushed hard I couldn't deny that I am a utopian socialist because so many of the elements of utopian socialism appear in my commune perspective' (Bahro, 1994, p. 235). Martin Ryle echoes this sentiment: 'utopian socialism would seem to be an obvious point of convergence between greens and socialists' (1988, p. 21), while Robin Cook of the Labour Party is more specific: 'the future of socialism may lie more with William Morris than with Herbert Morrison' (Gould, 1988, p. 163), as is Raymond Williams: 'The writer who began to unite these diverse traditions, in British social thought, was William Morris' (n.d., p. 9).

From the other side, Jonathon Porritt accepts such genealogies too: 'My own personal points of familiarity and very close connection with the Left come from the early libertarian traditions, William Morris and so on, and from the anarchist tradition of left politics', and he adds a significant point: 'I think that form of decentralised socialism is something that has had a pretty rough time in socialist politics during the course of this century' (1984b, p. 25).

What emerges from these exchanges is evidence for the selective way in which both socialists and ecologists refer to the socialist tradition. Usually, Porritt does not make the distinctions he makes above. He is keen to dissociate ecologism from socialism because he sees the latter as part of the old order, and so usually refers to it in its bureaucratic, productivist guise. To the extent that there is a decentralist tradition within socialism this is a disingenuous move, but it would be equally disingenuous for socialists to respond to the ecologists' challenge by arguing (suddenly) that William Morris is what real socialism is all about.

Sometimes socialists bend over too far backwards in their search for compatible characters. When David Pepper refers for example to a 'Kropotkin–Godwin–Owen' tradition (in Weston, 1986, p. 120), one wonders whether we're talking about socialism at all any more. At the very most there is only one socialist among those three, and, although Pepper does cover himself by positing an 'anarchist rather than centralist' form of socialism (ibid., p.115), the adjective 'anarchist' has the effect of divesting socialism of much of the resonance usually attributed to it. But there is little to be gained from semantics. The important point is that claims for a convergence between socialism and ecology rest on the resurrection of a subordinate tradition within socialism. To this extent the question of whether or not socialism and political ecology are compatible cannot be answered without first asking: 'What kind of socialism?', and in the end the answer will turn on whether the Utopian/William Morris tradition argues for a sustainable society in anything like a modern green sense (Lee, 1989).

In conclusion, some socialists, under pressure from greens, will reassess the traditional goals of production and indiscriminate growth, they will seek to rescue subordinate strains in their political tradition and they may ponder the role of the working class in future political transformations. Greens themselves need to listen to the socialist critique and to think harder about the relationship between capitalism and environmental degradation, about just what 'the environment' is, and about the potential for social change implicit in the identification of a social subject. In the end, Martin Ryle is probably right to identify political ecology and socialism as engaged on a 'converging critique': they both see capitalism as wasteful of resources in terms of production and consumption, and they both criticize it for its inegalitarian outcomes (1988, p. 48).

Feminism

Within feminism generally there is a discussion as to the best way for feminists to proceed: whether to seek equality with men on terms largely offered by men, or whether to focus on the differences between men and women and to seek to re-evaluate upwards the currently suppressed (supposed) characteristics of women. Beyond this distinction, some ecofeminists see ecofeminism as an opportunity to refuse the choice it implies and to opt, instead, for a refigured politics that goes beyond dualism. To the extent that ecofeminists subscribe to the 'difference' strategy, they do so not with a view to liberating women only but also with a view to encouraging men to adopt 'womanly' ways of thinking and acting, thus promoting healthier relationships between people in general, and also between people (but especially men) and the environment. In what follows I shall take 'difference' ecofeminism to be the discussion's centre of gravity, and develop the 'deconstructive' version through a critique of it.

'Difference' ecofeminism seems to be built around three principal sets of thoughts. In the first place, such ecofeminists usually argue for the existence of values and ways of behaving that are primarily female in the sense of more fundamentally possessed by or exhibited by women rather than men. These characteristics may be 'socially' or 'biologically' produced, and considerable importance can be attached to deciding which view is adopted. First, to the extent that ecofeminists would like to see men taking on these characteristics, they have to believe it is possible for them to do so. In other words, they cannot argue that it is necessary to be a woman to have such characteristics, although they might suggest that men cannot know what they are unless they listen to women telling them. Second, the belief that characteristics are biologically rooted is open to the charge of essentialism, and thereby to the accusation that such characteristics are unalterably attached to one or the other gender. If we then argue that some characteristics are undesirable, then the gender that has them is stuck with them: any possibility of 'progress' is undone. Associated with this belief is the idea that female values have, historically, been undervalued by patriarchy and that it is the 'difference' ecofeminist's task to argue for their positive re-evaluation. Of course, if there are female values and ways of behaving then there are also male values and ways of behaving. In asking that female traits be re-evaluated upwards, these ecofeminists do not necessarily demand that male traits be policed out of existence – rather they are likely to seek a balance of the two.

The second idea is that the domination of nature is related to the domination of women, and that the structures of domination and the reasons for it are similar in both cases: 'The identity and destiny of women and nature are merged', write Andrée Collard and Joyce Contrucci (1988, p. 137). The third idea – related to and tying up the first two – is that women are closer than men to nature and are therefore potentially in the vanguard as far as developing sustainable ways of relating to the environment is concerned – '[E]cofeminists argue that women have a unique standpoint from which to address the ecological crisis' (Mellor, 1992b, p. 236). I shall expand on these three notions and show how some feminists have balked at the ecofeminist programme – and particularly the first point (in its essentialist form, at least) – because of what they believe to be its reactionary implications. In some ('deconstructive') hands this has led to a re(de)fining of ecofeminism; Valerie Plumwood, for example, argues that what is common to all 'ecological feminisms' is no more than a rejection of the belief in the 'inferiority of the sphere of women and of nature' (1993, p. 33). It is what one does next, having rejected this belief, that distinguishes 'difference' and 'deconstructive' feminism.

With respect to values and behaviour, Ynestra King writes that 'We [i.e. women] learn early to observe, attend and nurture' (1983, p. 12) and Stephanie Leland refers to 'feminine impulses' such as 'belonging, relationship and letting be' (1983, p. 71). These are the kinds of characteristics (sometimes referred to, as I have already remarked, as constitutive of the 'feminine principle') usually ascribed to women by ecofeminists, and, although Valerie Plumwood rightly suggests that the devaluation of male modes of thought and behaviour does not necessarily entail the affirmation of female traits, my impression is that 'difference' ecofeminists usually do make such affirmations.

In support of her position, Plumwood writes: 'What seems to be involved here is often not so much an affirmation of feminine connected-ness with and closeness to nature as distrust and rejection of the masculine character model of disconnectedness from and domination of the natural order' (1988, p. 19). But this appears to be contradicted by, for example, Judith Plant's assertion that 'Women's values, centred around life-giving, must be revalued, elevated from their once subordinate role' (n.d., p. 7), and by Hazel Henderson's advocacy of reassessment:

Eco-feminism ... values motherhood and the raising and parenting of children and the maintaining of comfortable habitats and cohesive communities as the most highly productive work of society – rather than the most de-valued, as under patriarchal values and economics where the tasks are ignored and unpaid.

(Henderson, 1983, p. 207)

It is certainly the case that male values – for example, discrimination, domination and hierarchy (Leland, 1983, pp. 68–9), and 'a disregard for the housekeeping requirements of nature' (Freer, 1983, p. 132) – are seen as positively harmful if pursued to the exclusion of other values. In this context Jean Freer scathingly characterizes the space programme as an exercise in which 'Plastic bags full of men's urine were sent to circulate endlessly in the cosmos', and then asks, 'How can they claim to be caring?' (Freer, 1983, p. 132). Ynestra King concludes:

We see the devastation of the earth and her beings by the corporate warriors, and the threat of nuclear annihilation by the military warriors as feminist concerns. It is the same masculinist mentality which would deny us our right to our own bodies and our own sexuality, and which depends on multiple systems of dominance and state power to have its way.

(King, 1983, p. 10)

There are several difficulties – apart from political-strategic ones – associated with the assertion of female values and the desire to upgrade them. Valerie Plumwood points out (1988, p. 21) that to begin with there is the notorious problem of identifying female traits in the first place: we could only know what a representative sample of 'female' women would look like if we already had some idea of what female traits were, but then the traits would be announced *a priori*, as it were, rather than deduced through observation. Isn't it also true to say that some men exhibit 'female' characteristics and some women 'male' characteristics, in which case such characteristics are not founded in gender as such but in, for example, socialization working on gender?

Next, there is a series of what might be considered negative traits such as subservience associated with women by women (including, of course, a large number of feminists). If we are to use woman as the yardstick for valued characteristics, we are left with no room to judge with respect to what we might suspect to be negative traits in what is regarded as typically female behaviour. We can regard subservience as negative only if we value its opposite positively and this will mean valuing positively a characteristic normally associated with men. In other words, how are we to decide which are positive and which are negative forms of thought or behaviour? We may not want to say that all female characteristics are positive and neither do we want to argue, it seems, that all male traits are negative. But the generalized assertion that female traits are positive allows us no discriminatory purchase.

A related way of approaching this question might be to ask: 'Given that both male and female characteristics have been developed under patriarchy, what gives us the grounds for suggesting that either form is worthwhile?' The separatist feminist might say that what ecofeminists refer to as healthy traits are as tainted with patriarchy as unhealthy ones, and that the only way to find out what genuine female characteristics are like (if they exist at all) would be to disengage from patriarchy as far as possible, and to let such traits 'emerge'. As Mary Mellor points out: 'Feminists have long argued that until women have control over their own fertility, sexuality and economic circumstances, we will never know what women "really" want or are' (1992b, p. 237).

'Difference' ecofeminists do not usually adopt this strategy: they simply identify some traits that they argue most women already have, they value them positively, and then suggest that both we (all of us) and therefore the planet would be better off if we adopted such traits:

> Initially it seems obvious that the ecofeminist and peace argument is grounded on accepting a special feminine connectedness with nature or with peaceful characteristics, and then asserting this as a rival ideal of the human (or as part of such an ideal).
>
> (Plumwood, 1988, p. 22)

Plumwood's refusal of the 'obvious' is what sets her and others (see, for example, King, 1989) on the road to 'deconstructive' ecofeminism. She argues against the idea of accepting the feminine and rejecting the masculine (her terms) and goes instead for rejecting them both – most recently in a sophisticated argument locating her feminist strategy within a general attack on dualistic thinking (Plumwood, 1993). There she argues that:

> Women have faced an unacceptable choice within patriarchy with respect to their ancient identity as nature. They either accept it (naturalism) or reject it (and endorse the dominant mastery model). Attention to the dualistic problematic shows a way of resolving this dilemma. Women must be treated as just as fully human and as fully part of human culture as men. But both men and women must chal-

lenge the dualised conception of human identity and develop an alternative culture which fully recognises *human* identity as continuous with, not alien from, nature.

(Plumwood, 1993, p. 36)

In an earlier form this was presented as a 'degendered' model for the human which

> presupposes that selection of characteristics is made on the basis of independent criteria of worth. Criteria selected will often be associated with one gender rather than another, and perhaps may turn out to resemble more closely the characteristic feminine rather than the characteristic masculine traits. But they're degendered in the sense that they won't be selected because of their connection with one gender rather than the other, but on the basis of independent considerations.
>
> (Plumwood, 1988, p. 23)

This project would be hard to complete (what would such 'independent considerations' look like? What would it mean to be 'fully human'?) and its implications cannot be followed through here. Suffice to say that Plumwood's feminism

> would represent women's willingness to move to a further stage in their relations with nature, beyond that of powerless inclusion in nature, beyond that of reaction against their old exclusion from culture, and towards an active, deliberate and reflective positioning of themselves *with* nature against a destructive and dualising form of culture.
>
> (Plumwood, 1993, p. 39; emphasis in original)

My principal interest in Plumwood's position here is that it enables us to mark her off from what I understand to be a pair of basic 'difference' ecofeminist principles: that character traits can be identified as either male or female, and that the female ones are those that most obviously need presently to be reasserted, both for our sake and for the planet's. Plumwood herself distances her position from this sort of ecofeminism by referring to her project as a 'critical ecological feminism' (see for example, Plumwood, 1993, p. 39). This renaming of positions within or around the ecofeminist project is often a sign of unhappiness with the 'difference' feminist position: Mary Mellor (for example) describes hers as a 'feminist green politics' (1992a, p. 238) rather than an ecofeminism.

It is specific to both ecofeminisms to which I refer here that their advocates see them as good not only for women but also for the non-human natural world. Ecofeminists identify a relationship between the subjection of nature by men and the subjection of women by men. The nature of this link can take two forms: weak and strong. In the weak case, patriarchy is seen as producing and reproducing its domination across a whole range of areas and anything that comes under its gaze will be subjected to it. The link between women and nature in this case is simply that they are two objects for patriarchal domination, without the subjection of one necessarily helping to produce and reproduce the subjection of the other. Thus, Christine Thomas quotes Rosemary Radford Reuther: 'Women must see that there can be no liberation for them and no solution to the ecological crisis within a society whose fundamental model of relationships tends to be one of domination' (Thomas, 1983, p. 162).

Judith Plant makes a similar point: 'we are helping to create an aware-ness of domination at all levels' (Plant, n.d., p. 4), and then continues with a thought that gives a flavour of the strong link sometimes identified between women and nature in the sense of their common subjection: 'Once we understand the historical connections between women and nature and their subsequent oppression, we cannot help but take a stand on war against nature' (ibid.). This latter comment points to connections between the exploitation of women and of nature that go beyond their merely being subject to the generalized gaze of patriarchy.

Plant is suggesting that historical study of their exploitation leads to the conclusion that patriarchy has posited a particular identity between the two that produces and reproduces their common subjection. In this sense, argue the ecofeminists, the struggle for women's liberation must be a struggle for nature as well and, likewise, the despoiling of nature should not be viewed as separate from the exploitation of women. Both have their roots in patriarchy: 'We believe that a culture against nature is a culture against women' (King, 1983, p. 11).

Those who suggest a strong link argue that patriarchy confers similar characteristics on nature and on women and then systematically devalues them. Thus both are seen as irrational, uncertain, hard to control. Janet Biehl writes:

> In Western culture, men have traditionally justified their domination of women by conceptualising them as 'closer to nature' than them-selves. Women have been ideologically dehumanised and deration-alised by men; called more chaotic, more mysterious in motivation, more emotional, more moist, even more polluted.
>
> (Biehl, 1988, p. 12)

Just when this began to occur is a matter of dispute among ecofeminists. Basically the debate is between two groups – 'those who locate the problem for both women and nature in their place as part of a set of dualisms which have their origin in classical philosophy and which can be traced through a complex history to the present' and those who would rather refer to 'the rise of mechanistic science during the Enlightenment and pre-Enlightenment period' (Plumwood, 1986, p. 121). Indeed, because the first group finds no necessary relationship between the subjection of women and that of nature it is perhaps wrong to refer to them as ecofeminists.

We have already identified the ambiguous relationship that the green movement as a whole has with Enlightenment traditions, and it is entirely consistent that some ecofeminists should see a link between the Baconian impulse to dominate nature and the subjection of women – especially once similar characteristics have been conferred on both. The modern scientific project, which has its roots in Francis Bacon, is held to be a universalizing project of reduction, fragmentation and violent control. 'Difference' ecofeminists will counter this project with the feminine principles of diversity, holism, interconnectedness and non-violence. 'Deconstructive' ecofeminists will argue that the Enlightenment further rigidified a set of dualisms that were in place long before the Enlightenment period began, and which need to be transcended rather than re-evaluated. The problem with the 'difference' position in this context is that its adherents tend to paint too rosy a picture of the pre-Enlightenment period. Organicism may have given way to mechanicism, but the organicists still found reason to persecute witches. It seems that what can be said is that the mechanicist view of nature reinforced the subjection of women, but that this subjection has its roots somewhere else.

Indeed, as Janet Biehl has counterfactually suggested: 'Societies have existed that ... could revere nature (such as ancient Egypt) and yet this "reverence" did not inhibit the development of full-blown patricentric hierarchy' (1988, p. 13). To this extent men do not need an array of thoughts justifying the subjection of nature in order to dominate women, although it seems likely that such thoughts have been used since the seventeenth century to reinforce that domination. In this way, ecofeminists who link the subjection of women and of nature cannot provide fundamental reasons for the fact of the domination of women by men, but they can point to the way in which, now, women and nature are held to possess similar characteristics and that these characteristics 'just happen' to be undervalued.

In linking the subjection of women and nature (Merchant, 1990), ecofeminists point out that the intellectual structures justifying both are the same. 'Difference' ecofeminists go on to suggest that preventing further destruction of the environment will involve being more 'in tune' with the non-human natural world, that women are habitually closer to nature than men, and that therefore women are best placed to provide role models for environmentally sensitive behaviour.

For some ecofeminists, the basis of this closeness to nature is biology: 'Because of the reproductive cycle it is much harder for women to escape a sense of connection with the natural world', says Elizabeth Dodson Gray (in Plumwood, 1986, p. 125), and Hazel Henderson remarks that 'Biologically, most women in the world do still vividly experience their embeddedness in Nature, and can harbour few illusions concerning their freedom and separatedness from the cycles of birth and death' (1983, p. 207). Maori women bury their afterbirth in the earth as a symbolic representation of the connectedness of women as life-givers and the Earth as the source and fount of all life. Others, sympathetic to the link between ecology and feminism but not wishing to swallow biological essentialism, will suggest that women's lived experiences give them a head start as far as acquiring an ecological sensibility is concerned:

> [T]o the extent that women's lives have been lived in ways which are less directly oppositional to nature than those of men, and have involved different and less oppositional practices, qualities of care and kinds of selfhood, an ecological feminist position could and should privilege some of the experiences and practices of women over those of men as a source of change *without being committed to any form of naturalism.*
>
> (Plumwood, 1993, p. 35; my emphasis)

This view is broadly endorsed by Ariel Salleh, who writes that

> so far as political action is concerned, it does not matter whether sexed differences are ontological fact or historical accident. The case for women as historical actors in a time of environmental crisis rests not on universal essences but on how the majority of women actually work and think now.
>
> (Salleh, 1997, p. 6)

Mary Mellor refers to this as 'materialist ecofeminism', the importance of which is that 'it does not rest on psychological of biologically essentialist explanations' (Mellor, 1997, p. 169). Instead, 'Women's identification with the "natural" is not evidence of some timeless unchanging essence, but of the material exploitation of women's work, often without reward' (ibid., p. 189). According to Mellor's version of materialist ecofeminism, women have a special relationship with what she calls 'biological' and 'ecological' time. She defines these as follows: 'Ecological time is the pace of ecological sustainability for non-human nature. Biological time represents the life-cycle and pace of bodily replenishment for human beings' (ibid., p. 189). In the biological realm, women undertake usually unacknowledged work related to the reproduction of human life, and in the ecological realm – and particularly in subsistence societies – they are often responsible for nurturing life from the land and for ensuring its sustainability. For these two *material* reasons, women have a unique standpoint as far as the non-human natural world is concerned, and are exploited in quite specific ways. In particular, women's 'embodiedness and embeddedness' is both the source of a new kind of politics – one which recognizes the unavoidability and crucial nature of being 'encumbered' – and the origins of men's domination over them. As Mellor puts it, women's work in the reproductive and ecologically productive spheres has left 'social space and time largely in the hands of men' (ibid., p. 189). They have used this to quite particular effect, to develop a politics and a practice of 'autonomy' which is only possible so long as someone else is doing the 'heteronomous' work involved in reproducing life itself.

> The hallmark of modern capitalist patriarchy is its 'autonomy' in biological and ecological terms ... Western 'man' is young, fit, ambitious, mobile and unencumbered by obligations. This is not the world that most women know. Their world is circumscribed by obligated labour performed on the basis of duty, love, violence or fear of loss of economic support.
>
> (Mellor, 1997, p. 189)

This evidently bears upon the green movement's general aspiration to have us living more lightly on the Earth. As we saw in Chapter 2, deep ecologists argue for a change of consciousness with respect to our dealings with the non-human natural world. Warwick Fox wants a shift in priorities such that those who interfere with the environment should have to justify doing so, rather than having the onus of justification rest on the environment's defenders. A precondition for this, he argues, is an awareness of the 'soft' boundaries between ourselves and the non-human natural world. I pointed out at the time that in this connection deep ecologists are presented with a formidable problem of persuasion – most people simply do not think like that and it is hard to see how they ever will.

Some ecofeminists, though, suggest that there are already millions of people thinking like that, or at least potentially on the brink of doing so – women themselves. On this reading, women's closeness to nature puts them in the green political vanguard, in touch with a world that Judith Plant describes and that many members of the green movement would like to see resurrected – a world in which 'rituals were carried out by miners: offerings to the gods of the soil and the subterranean world, ceremonial sacrifices, sexual abstinence and fasting were conducted and observed before violating what was considered to be the sacred earth' (n.d., p. 3).

One problem that ecofeminism needs to confront in the context of the wider aims of the green movement is the reconciliation of the demand for positive evaluation of the activity of childbirth, and the need to reduce population levels. Of course, there is no need for such an evaluation to imply a large number of actual births, but a culture that held childbirth in high esteem might find it hard to legitimize population control policies. But again, in the properly functioning sustainable society, people would learn to reach and maintain sustainable reproductive rates, much as members of a number of communities (particularly in Africa and Latin America) already do.

'Difference' ecofeminism, in particular, has not been without its critics and Janet Biehl, for one, believes that the linking of women with nature and the subsequent subordination of both is precisely the reason why it is dangerous to try to use the link for emancipatory purposes:

> [W]hen ecofeminists root women's personality traits in reproductive and sexual biology, they tend to give acceptance to those male-created images that define women as primarily biological beings ... [this] is to deliver women over to the male stereotypes that root women's character structure entirely in their biological being.
>
> (Biehl, 1993, p. 55)

Plumwood, too, makes it absolutely clear why this sort of ecofeminism is seen in some quarters of the feminist movement as reactionary: 'The concept of nature ... has been and remains a major tool in the armoury of conservatives intent on keeping women in their place', and

> Given this background, it is not surprising that many feminists regard with some suspicion a recent view, expressed by a growing number of

writers in the ecofeminist camp, that there may be something to be said in favour of feminine connectedness with nature.

(Plumwood, 1988, p. 16; and see also 1993, p. 20)

In similar vein, Mary Mellor makes the useful distinction between feminism and feminine values: 'Even where male green thinkers claim that a commitment to feminism is at the centre of their politics, this often slides into a discussion of *feminine values*' (Mellor, 1992b, p. 245), and while it ought to be pointed out that the evidence in this chapter suggests that there are plenty of female writers who do the same thing, Mellor's general point is well taken: '[T]o espouse a feminine principle without addressing the power relations between men and women is to espouse an ecofeminine rather than an ecofeminist position' (Mellor, 1992b, p. 246).

Janet Biehl's critique is principally aimed at deep ecologists, whom she sees as engaged on a project that will guarantee the domination of women by men, but her remarks are equally applicable to 'difference' ecofeminism. Women should not be asked, she writes, to 'think like a mountain' – in the context of women's struggle for selfhood, autonomy and acceptance as rational beings, this amounts to 'a blatant slap in the face' (Biehl, 1988, p. 14). She parodies deep ecologists (and 'difference' ecofeminists) who claim that 'male' values and characteristics are worthless: 'Never mind becoming rational; never mind the self; look where it got men, after all; women were better-off than men all along without that tiresome individuality' (Biehl, 1988, p. 13).

The deep-ecological attempt to encourage us to virtues of modesty, passivity and humility with respect to the natural world (and to other human beings), it is argued, can only backfire in the context of women's liberation. From this point of view, the women's movement has precisely been about undoing modesty and humility (and refusing to bear a child every ten or twelve months) because these characteristics have worked in favour of patriarchy. In the context of patriarchy (i.e. now), women cannot afford to follow the deep-ecological programme, and to the degree that ecofeminism subscribes to deep-ecological parameters it does women no favours either: 'it is precisely humility, with its passive and receptive obedience to men, that women are trying to escape today' (Biehl, 1988, p. 14).

These worries seem well founded, in that at one level ecofeminism amounts to asking people in general to adopt 'female' ways of relating to the world in the knowledge that women are more likely to do so than men. If this happens, and if such ways of relating to the world and their devaluation are indeed part of the reason for women's subordination to men, then women's position can only get worse. 'Difference' ecofeminism therefore proposes a dangerous strategy (a strategy that Plumwood calls 'uncritical reversal'; Plumwood, 1993, p. 31) – to use ideas that have already been turned against women in the belief that, if they are taken up and lived by everyone, then a general improvement in both the human and non-human condition will result. If they are not taken up, then women will have 'sacrificed themselves to the environment', and this is a price some feminists are clearly not prepared to pay: '[In] the absence of a feminist perspective ... there is a danger that green politics will not even produce a de-gendered proclamation of the "feminine principle" but an overt or covert celebration of the masculine' (Mellor, 1992b, p. 249).

'Deconstructive' ecofeminism, on the other hand, is left with problems of its own. The refusal to choose between the masculine and the feminine has the happy consequence of avoiding the pitfalls associated with basing a transformative politics on the latter, but it leaves the future (arguably) too open-ended. In place of either a masculine or a feminine rationality, Plumwood argues for an ecological rationality that 'recognises and accommodates the denied relationships of dependency and enables us to acknowledge our debt to the sustaining others of the earth' (Plumwood, 1993, p. 196). But what does this mean, and how will it be brought about? Until further work is done, the space beyond dualism is occupied by a fog of indeterminacy – liberating and simultaneously frustrating for its lack of signposts.

Conclusion

I said at the beginning of this chapter that the evidence produced in it should deepen our understanding of the distinctiveness of ecologism as a political ideology. I think it has. Ecologism cannot be 'reduced' to any of the ideologies discussed here, with the faintly possible exception of feminism, and none of these ideologies can be said successfully to have appropriated ecologism for itself. Unlike any other ideology, ecologism is concerned in a foundational way with the relationship between human beings and their natural environment. More specifically, the two principal and distinguishing themes of ecologism, its belief in the limits to material growth and its opposition to anthropocentrism, are nowhere to be found in liberalism, conservatism and socialism – and they are nuanced in ecofeminism, where anthropocentrism is replaced by androcentrism, for example. Our conclusion must be that ecologism is an ideology in its own right, partly because it offers a coherent (if not unassailable) critique of contemporary society and a prescription for improvement, and partly because this critique and prescription differ fundamentally from those offered by other modern political ideologies.

Conclusion

We have established the differences between ecologism and other major political ideologies, and the incompatibility between what I have called environmentalism and ecologism is now clear. Ecologism seeks radically to call into question a whole series of political, economic and social practices in a way that environmentalism does not. Ecologism envisages a post-industrial future that is quite distinct from that with which we are most generally acquainted. While most post-industrial futures revolve around high-growth, high-technology, expanding services, greater leisure, and satisfaction conceived in material terms, ecologism's post-industrial society questions growth and technology, and suggests that the Good Life will involve more work and fewer material objects. Fundamentally, ecologism takes seriously the universal condition of the finitude of the planet and asks what kinds of political, economic and social practices are (a) possible and (b) desirable within that framework. Environmentalism, typically, does no such thing.

In terms of human relationships with the non-human natural world, ecologism asks that the onus of justification be shifted from those who counsel as little inference as possible with the non-human natural world to those who believe that interference is essentially non-problematic. Environmentalists will usually be concerned about intervention only as far as it might affect human beings; ecologists will argue that the strong anthropocentrism that this betrays is far more a part of our current problems than a solution to them.

Practical considerations of limits to growth and ethical concerns about the non-human natural world combine to produce, in ecologism, a political ideology in its own right. We can call it an ideology (in the functional sense) because it has, first, a description of the political and social world – a pair of green spectacles – which helps us to find our way around it. It also has a programme for political change and, crucially, it has a picture of the kind of society that ecologists think we ought to inhabit – loosely described as the 'sustainable society'. Because the descriptive and prescriptive elements in the political-ecological programme cannot be accommodated within other political ideologies (such as socialism) without substantially changing them, we are surely entitled to set ecologism alongside such ideologies, competing with them in the late twentieth-century political market-place. In contrast, I maintain that the various sorts of environmentalism (conservation, pollution control, waste recycling, etc.) can be slotted with relative ease into more well-known ideological paradigms, and that the way these issues have been readily taken up right across the political spectrum shows this co-option at work.

But what of the relationship between ecologism and environmentalism? One obvious answer is to see ecologism as the Utopian picture that all political movements need if they are to operate effectively. On this reading, green politics has a reformist as well as a radical wing, with the latter acting as a kind of puritan policeman, calling the reformists to order when they stray too far off line during their 'march through the institutions'. This is as much as to say that questions about whether or not the dark-green picture as I have described it in this book is realizable are to miss the point. Indeed, its Utopianism, with the vision and committed creativity that it can generate, is, on this reading, ecologism's strongest card.

More positively still, the Utopian vision provides the indispensable fundamentalist well of inspiration from which green activists, even the most reformist and respectable, need continually to draw. Green reformers need a radically alternative picture of post-industrial society, they need deep-ecological visionaries, they need the phantom studies of the sustainable society, and they need, paradoxically, occasionally to be brought down to earth and to be reminded about limits to growth. Dark-green politics remind reformists of where they want to go even if they don't really think they can get there. On this view there is what we might call a 'constructive tension' between ecologism and environmentalism.

But is it so obvious that the tension is constructive? There are those who will argue that radical green ideas are wholly counterproductive in that they 'are beginning to lead the environmental movement toward self-defeating strategies, preventing society from making the reforms it so desperately needs' (Lewis, 1992, p. 2). This is an increasingly popular view among commentators on environmental politics – even among those more sympathetic to its intentions than Lewis. Tim Hayward (1995, 1998) and John Barry (1999) both endorse it in rather different ways, for example. Hayward refers to the 'two dogmas' of ecologism, a belief in intrinsic value and a critique of anthropocentrism (1998, Chs 2 and 3; I discussed Hayward's position on anthropocentrism in Chapter 2), signalling with the word 'dogma' his sense that these foundation stones of green political thought are unexamined and are, in the longer run, a hindrance to the acceptability of environmental politics. Hayward argues that widely held green understandings of these terms are conceptually incoherent *as well as* politically counterproductive. His belief is that an 'enlightened self-interest' is the best way forward, since it is more conceptually coherent than biocentrism or ecocentrism, and because it accords better with basic human motivations.

Similarly, John Barry rejects deep ecology as foundational for green politics for the pragmatic reason that it will not secure widespread support (J. Barry, 1999, pp. 26 and 42). He argues instead for the cultivating of an 'ecological virtue', based on a critical attitude to anthropocentrism, and a stewardship 'ethics of use', which would be practised by green citizens: 'the practice of the "ecological virtues" is constitutive of this green conception of citizenship' (ibid., p. 65). I shall suggest some possible radical green responses to these remarks later in the chapter.

From Lewis's point of view eco-radicalism threatens the environment by 'fuelling the anti-environment countermovement' (Lewis, 1992, p. 6), and he makes it his business, therefore, to dismantle what he sees as the four postulates of 'radical environmentalism' as well as its informing 'underlying belief': 'that economic growth is by definition unsustainable' (ibid., p. 3). The four postulates are:

> that 'primal' (or 'primitive') peoples exemplify how we can live in harmony with nature (and with each other); that thoroughgoing decentralization, leading to local autarky, is necessary for social and ecological health; that technological advance, if not scientific prog-ress itself, is inherently harmful and dehumanizing; and that the capitalist market system is inescapably destructive and wasteful.
>
> (Lewis, 1992, p. 3)

Lewis considers all these views to be wrong-headed (ibid., p. 9), and he rejects the eco-radical attack on economic growth by arguing that growth in *value* is perfectly compatible with long-term sustainability: '[W]hile the global economy certainly cannot grow indefinitely in *volume* by pouring out an ever mounting cavalcade of consumer disposables, it *can* continue to expand in *value* by producing better goods and services ever more efficiently' (ibid., p. 10; emphasis in original).

Radical greens might respond to the 'four postulate' criticism by saying that they do not recognize themselves in its composite picture. Lewis appears to have caricatured a caricature of an extreme wing of one sort of West Coast North American environmentalism, and generically dubbed the outcome 'eco-radicalism'. While there is truth in every cartoon, there is plenty of imagination too, and I hope that the rest of this present book provides evidence for the undue selectivity of Lewis's artwork. If – as I suspect – Lewis has got the target wrong, then the success of his attack must be equivocal. Radical greens might also say that his knock-down argument regarding economic growth is curious in that it concedes to radical greens just what they want: a recognition that present rates of economic growth *by volume* are unsustainable. I can imagine no green arguing that growth in terms of value is unsustainable (although I can imagine some pretty fierce arguments over how to determine value in the first place).

As far as the strategic question is concerned, radical greens might suggest that their radicalism, far from turning people off green politics altogether, makes eco-moderates seem more respectable than they already are, thereby smoothing their path through the corridors of power. I pointed out in Chapter 4, indeed, that this was a guiding theme of Earth First!'s direct action programme:

> the actions of monkeywrenchers invariably enhance the status and bargaining position of more 'reasonable' opponents. Industry considers moderate environmentalists to be radical until they get a taste of real radical activism. Suddenly the soft-sell of the Sierra Club and other white-shirt-and-tie eco-bureaucrats becomes much more attractive and worthy of serious negotiation. These moderate environmentalists must condemn monkeywrenching so as to preserve their own image, but they should take full advantage of the credence it lends to their approach.
>
> (Foreman and Haywood, 1989, p. 22)

There are those who will argue, in any case, that Lewis is making a fuss over nothing: that radical green politics is so much in the shadow of its reformist cousin that it is virtually invisible. Ironically, this could be the result of the explosion in the political popularity of environmental issues during the late 1980s. It might seem curious to suggest that radical green politics is the victim of reformist success but, from a point of view that has it that the tension between environmentalism and ecologism is destructive rather than constructive, that may be what has happened. The green movement has spent years trying to get the environment on to the political agenda, and the major political parties have so artfully stitched a green stripe into their respective flags that there seems to be no need for a specifically green (much less *radically* green) politics any longer. As Anna Bramwell has put it: 'What is usable in the Green critique has largely been subsumed by the political system' (Bramwell, 1994, p. 206). On this reading, radical green politics has disappeared behind brighter lights and louder voices, and the call for radical social, political and economic change is muted – if not silent.

Radical greens are evidently in an uncomfortable position. On the one hand they have a message to give, and on the other hand they are confronted by a public and culture that they think prevent them from giving it. So they turn reformist in certain public forums either because they think that to be radically green would be to marginalize themselves, or because the discussions in those forums (particularly in television and radio) are weighted towards what already interests the public (polluted rivers, dying seals) rather than what might interest them if they got the chance to hear about it. There is nothing new in all this; it is the typical dilemma of any radical form of politics, and it can produce a burdensome form of political schizophrenia. In this context, Jonathon Porritt once described how being both director of Friends of the Earth and an individual member of the Green Party (in Dodds, 1988, p. 201) pulled him in different directions at the same time.

It works like this: there is a desire to popularize green politics, to 'get the message across', and there is a desire to make sure that the green message is radical rather than merely reformist. But the rub appears to be that in order to get any message across at all it has to be reformist and not radical. Porritt refers, for example, to FoE's highly successful campaign to encourage producers to phase out the use of chlorofluorocarbons in aerosols. He noted that by the end of 1989 only some 5 or 10 per cent of aerosols would use CFCs, compared with nearly three-quarters just a year or so earlier. This, as he writes, is 'All good stuff – a small, incremental step towards a safer environment'. Then he asks: 'But does it actually bring us anywhere nearer sustainability?' (in Dodds, 1988, pp. 200–1). And, of course, this is the point – eradicating CFCs from aerosols is a respectable green achievement, but is it a radical one?

Porritt himself observes:

> Various deep Greens (including members of the Green Party) were quick to castigate Friends of the Earth for not campaigning against aerosols in general, inasmuch as they are indisputably unnecessary, wasteful and far from environmentally benign even if they don't use CFCs. Such critics suggested (and who can blame them?) that by campaigning for CFC-free aerosols, we were in fact condoning, if not positively promoting, self-indulgence, vanity, and wholly unsustainable patterns of consumption.
>
> (in Dodds, 1988, p. 201)

This catches the dilemma in all its radicality; if, as the final phrases suggest, environmental campaigns can contribute to unsustainability, then light-green and dark-green politics are in conflict rather than in concert – the notion of 'constructive tension' is called into question. In other words, it is not simply a semantic question about whether or not environmentalism and ecologism are the same thing and, if not, how different they are, but a question that has political-strategic implications. If radical and reformist greens pull in different directions, then this is serious indeed, because the classic defence of the political schizophrenic is that, even if the two positions are in different places, at least they are on the same track. Put differently the light-green will argue that light-green education can lead to dark-green radicalization, that the normal course of things is for the former to evolve into the latter: 'On balance I believe that more good will be done than harm if one sees such an approach as part of a transitional strategy', writes Porritt (in Dodds, 1988, p. 199).

Porritt might even begrudgingly suggest that anything is better than nothing, even if no evolution takes place at all: 'After all, confronted with the choice between green yuppies or naturally nasty yuppies, between mindful green consumers or relatively mindless, old-style consumers, it's your proverbial Hobson's choice' (in Dodds, 1988, p. 199). In these senses radical greens can happily defend the occasional reformist posture because they might thereby green the odd yuppy and improve the Body Shop's annual turnover. But what will the radical side of the green schizophrenic make of all this? Is environmentalist popularity bought at the cost of more radical, mostly private convictions?

A central strategic issue to be confronted by the green movement, then, is whether light-green politics (environmentalism) makes dark-green politics (ecologism) more or less likely. Roughly speaking, it will be held to be more likely if it is believed that both forms of politics are heading in the same direction, even though one might lag slightly behind the other. It will be held to be less likely if it is believed that these forms of politics work more substantially against, rather than with, each other. In this latter case, the conclusion will not be to encourage people to see environmentalism as a 'transitional strategy' for ecologism, but to argue that it is no transitional strategy at all.

There are, of course, arguments for and against both positions, and there are a number of ways of articulating the former (and, it seems, increasingly popular) 'convergence thesis'. The general theme running through these various articulations is that the *policy outcomes* of radical and reformist programmes are very similar, even if the *reasons and values* underlying them are different. Very broadly speaking, the policy intention of both reformists and radicals is to protect the environment. Radical greens have long argued that this objective cannot be achieved so long as economic growth remains the *leitmotif* of industrial and industrializing societies, and so long as our attitude towards environmental protection is guided by anthropocentric lights. The 'first wave' attack on the limits to growth view came from resource cornucopians such as Herman Kahn and Julian Simon who simply argued (and still do) that there is more than enough to go round, more or less for ever: '[We]e now have in our hands ... the technology to feed, clothe, and supply energy to an ever-growing population for the next 7 billion years' (Simon, in Myers and Simon, 1994, p. 65).

These arguments are still put, but they have been buttressed (or in some cases supplanted) by a much more sophisticated 'second wave' response to the limits to growth position which goes by the name of 'ecological modernization'. In his outstanding book on the politics of pollution, Albert Weale describes how ecological modernizers during the 1980s began to challenge the view that there was 'a zero-sum trade-off between economic prosperity and environmental concern' (Weale, 1992, p. 31). Ecological modernizers put three arguments: first, '[I]f the "costs" of environmental protection are avoided the effect is frequently to save money for present generations at the price of an increased burden for future generations' (ibid., p. 76); second, '[I]nstead of seeing environmental protection as a burden upon the economy the ecological modernist sees it as a potential source for future growth ... a spur to industrial innovation' (ibid., p. 78); and third,

> With the advent of global markets, the standards of product acceptability will be determined by the country with the most stringent pollution control standards. Hence the future development of a post-industrial economy will depend upon its ability to produce high value, high quality products with stringent environmental standards enforced.
>
> (Weale, 1992, p. 77)

This decoupling of economic growth and environmental degradation has the apparent effect of drawing (at least one of) the principal sting(s) at the disposal of radical ecologists. In strategic terms, why bother with radical ecological ideas if we can, as it were, have our cake and eat it? I shall return to this question in a moment, but first another approach to the 'convergence thesis' needs to be canvassed. Ecological modernizers focus their attention on the economic growth equation, or what we might call the 'material' fault line within the pro-environmental caucus. But what about the arguments outlined in Chapter 2 regarding anthropocentrism and biocentrism? Surely it makes a difference to policy whether one adopts an anthropocentric rather than a biocentric stance in respect of environmental protection?

One person who thinks it doesn't is Bryan Norton. That Norton is a 'converger' is in no doubt, and in his search for unity among environmentalists he thinks he knows where to look: 'I have ... tried not to use environmentalists' rhetoric – the explanations they give for what they do – but their actions – the policies they actually pursue – as the fixed points on my map' (1991, p. x). So environmentalists of any persuasion might agree on the founding of a wilderness preserve, but not on *why* it should be preserved. Norton argues that whether it is preserved because the wilderness area is sacred or because of the recreational use to which it is put is immaterial from a policy point of view. He suggests that all the objects of radical ecologists can be achieved from within a broadly anthropocentric perspective:

> introducing the idea that other species have intrinsic value, that humans should be 'fair' to all other species, provides no operationally recognizable constraints on human behaviour that are not already implicit in the generalized, cross-temporal obligations to protect a healthy, complex, and autonomously functioning system for the benefit of future generations of humans.
>
> (Norton, 1991, p. 226)

More particularly, he argues for a form of 'lexical ordering' of priorities: 'productivity values have free play until their pursuit threatens the larger context, at which point limits, to be articulated in the ecological terms of system fragility, constrain choices based on a pure productivity criterion' (Norton, 1991, p. 83). He concludes that

> A hierarchical system of value therefore opens the door to new possibilities for understanding environmental ethics. Environmentalists need not choose between the worldview of anthropocentric economic reductionism and biocentrism. Another possibility is an hierarchically organized and *integrated* system of values.
>
> (Norton, 1991, p. 239)

The attraction of Weale's ecological modernizers and Norton's policy convergers is that they offer us a 'both ... and' solution rather than 'either ... or' ones: *both* economic growth *and* environmental protection, *both* productivity *and* ecosystem preservation. Once again the question arises: If there is anything in these positions, why bother with radical ecology, tactically, strategically or otherwise? Does radical ecology have any 'added value', or is it – in the final analysis – an irritating distraction from the business of having our cake and eating it?

Radical ecologists might begin, of course, by disputing – or at least modulating – some of the arguments put by ecological modernizers and policy convergers. The three arguments put by Weale on behalf of the ecological modernizers are all subject to a degree of interrogation. First, why should hard-headed industrialists worry about future generations? Reasons for doing so will surely come from *outside* the ideology of ecological modernization – and one place they might come from is the camp of radical ecologists (although not only from there, of course). Radical ecology serves the purpose, on this reading, of providing grist for the ecological modernizer's mill.

Second, the view that environmental protection is a potential source of future growth is subject to two caveats. First, this is only securely true in the right environment (as it were): in societies (or groups of them) where 'quality of life' objectives are enshrined in general programmes – as they are (implicitly) in the Preamble and Article 2 (particularly the revised version) of the European Community's original Treaty of Rome (Hildebrand, 1992, pp. 17 and 37). Arguably, the fact that 'environmental amenity is a superior good' (Weale, 1992, p. 76) only becomes policy-relevant when the non-provision of environmental amenity has adverse repercussions for policy-makers. Unfortunately, across vast swathes of the globe policy-makers remain largely untouched by the effects of their folly, and this is no less true of their handling of their environment than it is of other areas of policy.

Second, not all environmental protection measures are functional for growth, and Weale himself points to evidence from the Netherlands which suggests that environmental protection might produce negative growth rates. The Dutch National Environment Policy Plan (NEPP) was published in 1989, and it contained some of the most radical policy proposals for pollution control ever countenanced by a national government. Weale describes the details and implications of the plan in full (Weale, 1992, pp. 125–53), but only one or two aspects of it are relevant to us here. First, large-scale emission reductions were factored into the plan because it was discovered that '*even with the full application of existing end-of-pipe technologies* it would not be possible to prevent a decline in environmental quality in the Netherlands' (ibid., p. 134; emphasis in original). Indeed, in order to meet the environmental objectives laid down in the plan, it was argued at the pre-planning stage that '*volume* and structural changes were needed in the economy' (ibid., p. 135; my emphasis).

This reference to changes in volume lends some succour to radical ecologists because (as I pointed out in Lewis's connection above), it is precisely a reduction in volume for which radical greens argue. The effects on Dutch GNP of implementation of the NEPP were calculated to be a fall of 2.6 per cent if the Netherlands went it alone, and a fall of 0.9 per cent if other countries followed suit (Weale, 1992, p. 135), although Weale points out that these figures do not include any savings that might accrue from implementation (e.g. through energy conservation), nor any competitive benefits that might flow from it.

Significantly the recommendation regarding volume and structure changes 'did not seem an attractive conclusion since it threatened to put the cause of environmental protection on a collision course with economic development, and environmental policy would therefore return to the old zero-sum conflict with other policy objectives' (Weale, 1992, p. 135). At the very least, all this suggests that this aspect of the ecological modernization thesis is up for grabs, in that the decoupling of economic growth and environmental degradation may not be a painless *interruptus*. Indeed, it may not be possible at all, in which case the radical green argument returns to the surface, bloodied but unbowed.

The third ecological modernization argument was that in a world of stringent environmental standards, competitive advantage will be gained by any country whose products meet or exceed such standards. Radical greens might argue that this is only true subject to two limiting conditions. First, the products in question must be those for which 'stringent pollution control standards' are relevant – cars produced in Japan might be a case in point, but cheap plastic toys produced in China are not. Ecological modernization is partly a thesis about the 'standards of product acceptability' (Weale, 1992, p. 77), but environmental concerns are not a factor in determining the acceptability of all products, and they may not – of course – even be the overriding factor determining the acceptability of products such as cars. Ecological modernization's hold, then, over the acceptability of products may be somewhat tenuous.

The second limiting condition in this context is that 'stringent pollution control standards' must be in place for the said competitive advantage to be gained, and (globally) this is not the case for most markets of most goods. Ecological modernizers might argue that it is part of their agenda to ensure this sort of legislation, but one suspects that tough environmental standards are more likely in places where there is already an 'environmental culture'. Once again, it could be argued that such a culture is fostered *beyond* the confines of ecological modernization, and to the extent that radical ecology is a cultural critique it is tempting to suggest that the ecological modernizers need the space carved out by their more radical counterparts.

Finally, ecological modernizers will point to declining energy consumption per unit of GNP as evidence that the link between economic growth and energy consumption has been broken – thereby calling into question an apparent article of faith for radical ecologists (Weale, 1992, p. 25). It is true that this link has been broken in OECD countries over the past twenty years, but radical ecologists might point to three contributing factors, two of which at least may not be easy to reproduce world-wide: 'The decoupling of economic growth from energy consumption was encouraged by high energy prices, faster economic growth of the service sector, and the relocation of energy-intensive industries to developing countries' (World Resources Institute, 1992, p. 145). The two factors hard to reproduce world-wide are the second and third. Not all economies can depend on a burgeoning service sector for their survival because traditional industrial products (ships, bridges and so on) will be continually required, even if not produced in the countries that require them. Second, energy-intensive industries cannot forever be relocated; OECD energy consumption figures have improved at the cost of *displacing* consumption, not (from a global point of view) *reducing* it (World Resources Institute, 1992, pp. 144–5).

Bryan Norton's arguments regarding policy convergence are also subject to critique. In the first place, his 'lexical ordering' seems able to license some pretty fierce despoliation before the 'system fragility' constraint kicks in. At best, radicals might argue, his focus on systems rather than individuals seems tailor-made to justify a certain amount of mayhem to individuals provided system fragility is not thereby endangered. And at worst, the 'free play' of production could go on for a very long time before the 'larger context' was deemed to be under threat. How many 'non-essential' individuals, species and habitats could go under before the possibility of production itself was threatened? The very fact that this question can be so framed without misrepresenting Norton's position is, of course, the principal reason why radical greens will regard his hand extended in friendship with some caution – from their 'in principle' point of view no part of human or non-human nature can be regarded as non-essential.

Convergence theories, then, can take various forms. In some (such as Martin Lewis's), convergence amounts to liquidation of the radical perspective. Lewis and his supporters will claim that radical ecology is just plain wrong, and that the cause of environmental protection is best served by reformist ideas and policies. Other commentators (such as Bryan Norton) will argue that policy outcomes are the same whether based upon radical or reformist values. Circumspection dictates, then, that the line of least resistance is chosen – arguing for environmental protection from within accepted paradigms. Others (such as ecological modernizers) suspect that there is a fundamental flaw in radical ecology regarding the relationship between economic growth and environmental degradation, and that economic growth is actually functional for environmental protection.

I have hinted that one radical green response to these critiques is to confront them head on. Another response might be to accept defeat – temporarily at least – but to claim simultaneously a considerable victory. There was a time when the environment was a fringe interest, an optional extra to be taken up when all other aspects of public policy had been dealt with. The Treaty of Rome of 1957 that established the European Economic Community, for instance, contained no 'explicit reference to the idea of environmental policy or environmental protection' (Hildebrand, 1992, p. 17), and environmental enthusiasts had to rely on creative interpretation of various of the Treaty's articles to further their ambitions. By 1992 and the Maastricht Treaty, though, '[T]he traditional economic growth ethos of the community [had] been "greened" considerably' (ibid., p. 37). Environmental protection, sustainability and environment-respecting growth are all explicitly mentioned in the new Treaty's articles, and the environment has now officially 'acquired full status as a policy falling within the Union's priority objectives' (ibid., p. 37).

The political and economic history of this signal shift in intention is complex – and needs to be buttressed, in any case, by a *cultural* history. The realm of culture is probably where the future of radical ecology lies, for that is where the space is carved out in which new questions regarding the politically possible and the socially desirable are put. Once put, they do not go away and sooner or later 'a culture that is infused with ... a sense of personal, civic and ecological responsibility' (Eckersley, 1992, p. 182) demands a response from professional policy-makers. This cultural arena is the one that sympathetic yet revisionist critics of ecologism such as Hayward, John Barry and Norton forget in their determination to make environmental politics more attractive (as they see it). Barry is surely right to say that

> The centrality of citizenship to green arguments for democracy comes from the belief that the achievement of sustainability will require more than institutional restructuring of contemporary Western lib-eral democracies. Such institutional changes are necessary, but not sufficient, from a green point of view. The green contention is that macro- and micro-level reorganization needs to be supplemented with

changes in general values and practices. In short, institutional change must be complemented by wider cultural-level changes.

(J. Barry, 1999, p. 228)

The question is, where will these changes in general values and practices at the cultural level come from? My view is that they will be produced, if at all, at the promptings of the radical critique advanced by ecologism itself. Radical ecology's role for the twenty-first century is as a condition for the possibility of its reformist cousin. Without radical ecology, the convergence thesis advanced by Norton, the 'ecologising of the Enlightenment' proposed by Hayward (1995), and the cultivation of 'ecological virtue' suggested by John Barry (1999, pp.31–5), would be literally unthinkable. Barry criticizes 'binary' accounts of green politics such as the one given in this book (environmentalism 'versus' ecologism) on the grounds that they are 'a hindrance to the future evolution of green politics' (J. Barry, 1999, p. 4). But he produces a few binary oppositions of his own, such as that between green ideology and green political theory (the latter is regarded as more 'mature'; ibid., p. 6), and between deep ecology and an 'ethic of use' for the environment. Conceptually and strategically Barry's oppositions are, I think, unhelpful. Green political theory cannot do without green ideology and probably would not exist without it, and deep ecology *is* an ethic of use for the environment. The point is that the reformists need the radicals just as the radicals need the reformists. The way ahead is not to try to replace one set of 'truths' with another, but to see that Barry's 'cultural-level changes' require them to work in tandem.

On this reading, reformism is necessary in that it provides us with a green platform, a new consensus on our relationship with our environment, from which we can make the leap to more radically green practices. There are, of course, radical critics, coming from the other direction, who say that reformism may constitute a barrier rather than a platform. It may from a dark-green point of view immunize rather than sensitize, by obscuring the informing principle of green politics: that infinite growth in a finite system is impossible, and that therefore green production and consumption are (in the long term) as unsustainable as present forms of production and consumption. On this reading, environmentalism saps radical energy and pulls up the drawbridge against green change.

Such a perspective suggests that, *pace* Norton (for example), environmentalism and ecologism diverge rather than converge. Jonathon Porritt, for one, appears unsure which line to take. We have seen him 'on balance', above, arguing in favour of the 'transitional strategy' notion, but he is equally aware of the traps it lays, especially in its green consumerist disguise:

> At best, it may mitigate the most immediate symptoms of ecological decline, but the short-term advantages gained in the process are almost certainly outweighed by the simultaneous immunisation of such consumers against reality ... Green consumerism may marginally assist environmentalists in some of their campaigns, but its very effectiveness depends on not attempting to do down or supplant today's industrial order; and on not promoting awareness of its inherent unsustainability.
>
> (in Dodds, 1988, pp. 199–200)

And so we find ourselves back at square one: the radical green demand to call today's industrial order into question. But how to do it? Friends of the Earth was faced with the fact in its CFC campaign that it 'would have made little, if any headway with an anti-aerosol campaign' (ibid., p. 201), even though calling today's industrial order into question would have involved just that. Porritt wants at least as much 'to be out there explaining why the old mechanistic world view of Bacon, Descartes and Newton is now wholly redundant ... as to be arguing the merits of flue gas desulphurisation' (ibid., p. 203). The 'greening' of households, retailing, industry and governments, even of people – however insecure – is the signal achievement of ecologism's first two decades. This is as much as to say that Act One of the green movement's paradise play is over; radical greens will look forward to seeing the curtain lifted on Act Two.

Bibliography

Allaby, M. and Bunyard, P. (1980) *The Politics of Self-Sufficiency* (Oxford: Oxford University Press).

Anderson, F. R. *et al.* (n.d.) *Environmental Protection: Law and Policy* (New York: Little, Brown).

Anderson, V. (1991) *Alternative Economic Indicators* (London: Routledge).

Atkinson, A. (1991) *Principles of Political Ecology* (London: Belhaven Press).

Attfield, R. (1983) *The Ethics of Environmental Concern* (Oxford: Blackwell).

——(1990) 'Deep ecology and intrinsic value', *Cogito*, 4 (1).

Bahro, R. (1982) *Socialism and Survival* (London: Heretic Books).

——(1986) *Building the Green Movement* (London: GMP).

——(1994) *Avoiding Social and Ecological Disaster: The Politics of World Transformation* (Bath: Gateway Books).

Ball, T. and Dagger, R. (1991) *Political Ideologies and the Democratic Ideal* (London: HarperCollins).

Barry, B. (1995) *Justice as Impartiality* (Oxford: Clarendon Press).

——(1999) 'Sustainability and intergenerational justice', in A. Dobson (ed.) *Fairness and Futurity: Essays on Environmental Sustainability and Social Justice* (Oxford: Oxford University Press).

Barry, J. (1994) 'The limits of the shallow and the deep: green politics, philosophy and praxis', *Environmental Politics*, 3 (3).

——(1996) 'Sustainability, political judgement and citizenship: connecting green politics and democracy', in B. Doherty and M. de Geus (eds) *Democracy and Green Political Thought: Sustainability, Rights and Citizenship* (London: Routledge).

——(1999) *Rethinking Green Politics* (London: Sage).

Bauman, Z. (1987) *Legislators and Interpreters* (Oxford: Polity).

Bentham, J. (1960) *The Principles of Morals and Legislation* (Oxford: Blackwell).

Benton, T. (1993) *Natural Relations: Ecology, Animal Rights and Social Justice* (London: Verso).

——(ed.) (1996) *The Greening of Marxism* (New York: Guilford Press).

Biehl, J. (1988) article in *Green Line*, 59 (February).

——(1993) 'Problems in ecofeminism', *Society and Nature*, 2 (1).

Bookchin, M. (1972) *Post-Scarcity Anarchism* (Montreal: Black Rose Books).

——(1982) *The Ecology of Freedom* (Palo Alto: Cheshire Books).

——(1986) *The Modern Crisis* (Philadelphia: New Society).

——(1989) *Remaking Society* (Montreal: Black Rose Books).

——(1991) 'Where I stand now', in M. Bookchin and D. Foreman (eds) *Defending the Earth* (Montreal: Black Rose Books).

——(1995) *Re-Enchanting Humanity: A Defence of the Human Spirit Against Antihumanism, Misanthropy, Mysticism and Primitivism* (London: Cassell).

Bookchin, M. and Foreman, D. (eds) (1991) *Defending the Earth* (Montreal: Black Rose Books).

Bottomore, T. (1982) *Elites and Society* (Harmondsworth: Penguin).

Bottomore, T. and Rubel, M. (1984) *Karl Marx: Selected Writings in Sociology and Social Philosophy* (Harmondsworth: Penguin).

Bramwell, A. (1989) *Ecology in the 20th Century* (New Haven: Yale University Press).

——(1994) *The Fading of the Greens: The Decline of Environmental Politics in the West* (New Haven: Yale University Press).

Brennan, A. (1988) *Thinking about Nature* (London: Routledge).

British Ecology Party Manifesto (1983) (London: Ecology Party).

British Green Party Manifesto (1987) (London: Green Party).

Brundtland, Gro Harlem (1989) 'Economía ecológica', *El País* (Temas de Nuestra Epoca), 30 March, 4.

Brundtland Report (n.d.) *Our Common Future* (London: Earthscan).

Bunyard, P. and Morgan-Grenville, F. (eds) (1987) *The Green Alternative* (London: Methuen).

Burke, E. (1790/1982) *Reflections on the Revolution in France* (Harmondsworth: Penguin).

Caldecott, L. and Leland, S. (eds) (1983) *Reclaim the Earth* (London: The Women's Press).

Capra, F. (1975) *The Tao of Physics* (London: Wildwood House).

——(1983) *The Turning Point* (London: Flamingo).

Carson, R. (1965) *Silent Spring* (Harmondsworth: Penguin).

Collard, A. and Contrucci, J. (1988) *Rape of the Wild* (London: The Women's Press).

Conroy, C. and Litvinoff, P. (eds) (1988) *The Greening of Aid* (London: Earthscan).

Cornford, P. (ed.) (1988) *The Organic Tradition* (Bideford: Green Books).

Daly, H. (1977a) 'The politics of the sustainable society', in D. Pirages (ed.) *The Sustainable Society* (New York: Praeger).

——(1977b) 'The steady-state economy: what, why, and how', in D. Pirages (ed.) *The Sustainable Society* (New York: Praeger).

——(1992) *Steady-State Economics* (2nd edn) (London: Earthscan).

Dauncey, G. (1988) *After the Crash* (Basingstoke: Green Print).

de Geus, M. (1999) *Ecological Utopias: Envisioning the Sustainable Society* (Utrecht: International Books).

Devall, B. (1980) 'The deep ecology movement', *Natural Resources Journal*, 20.

Dickens, P. (1992) *Society and Nature: Towards a Green Social Theory* (New York: Harvester Wheatsheaf).

Dobson, A. (1989) 'Deep ecology', *Cogito*, 3 (1).

——(1990) *Green Political Thought* (London: Routledge).

——(1993a) 'Ecologism', in R. Eatwell and A. Wright (eds) *Contemporary Political Ideologies* (London: Pinter).

——(1993b) 'Critical theory and green politics', in A. Dobson and P. Lucardie (eds) *The Politics of Nature: Explorations in Green Political Theory* (London: Routledge).

——(1994a) 'Environmentalism', in M. Foley (ed.) *Ideas That Shape Politics* (Manchester: Manchester University Press).

——(1994b) 'Ecologism and the relegitimation of socialism', *Radical Philosophy*, 67 (Summer).

——(1996a) 'Democratising green theory: preconditions and principles', in B. Doherty and M. de Geus (eds) *Democracy and Green Political Thought: Sustainability, Rights and Citizenship* (London: Routledge).

——(1996b) 'Representative democracy and the environment', in W. Lafferty and J. Meadowcroft (eds) *Democracy and the Environment: Problems and Prospects* (Cheltenham: Edward Elgar).

——(1998) *Justice and the Environment: Conceptions of Environmental Sustainability and Dimensions of Social Justice* (Oxford: Oxford University Press).

——(ed.) (1999) *Fairness and Futurity: Essays on Environmental Sustainability and Social Justice* (Oxford: Oxford University Press).

Dobson, A. and Lucardie, P. (eds) (1993) *The Politics of Nature: Explorations in Green Political Theory* (London: Routledge).

Dodds, F. (ed.) (1988) *Into the 21st Century* (Basingstoke: Green Print).

Doherty, B. (1999) 'Paving the way: the rise of direct action against road-building and the changing character of British environmentalism', *Political Studies*, 47 (2).

Doherty, B. and de Geus, M. (eds) (1996a) *Democracy and Green Political Thought: Sustainability, Rights and Citizenship* (London: Routledge).

——(1996b) 'Introduction', in B. Doherty and M. de Geus (eds) *Democracy and Green Political Thought: Sustainability, Rights and Citizenship* (London: Routledge).

Donald, J. and Hall, S. (1986) *Politics and Ideology* (Milton Keynes: Open University Press).

Dowie, M. (1995) *Losing Ground: American Environmentalism at the Close of the Twentieth Century* (Cambridge, Mass.: MIT Press).

Dryzek, J. (1987) *Rational Ecology* (Oxford: Blackwell).

——(1990) *Discursive Democracy: Politics, Policy and Political Science* (Cambridge: Cambridge University Press).

——(1997) *The Politics of the Earth: Environmental Discourses* (Oxford: Oxford University Press).

Eatwell, R. and Wright, A. (eds) (1993) *Contemporary Political Ideologies* (Pinter: London).

Eccleshall, R., Geoghegan, V., Jay, R., Kenny, M., Mackenzie, I. and Wilford, R. (1994) *Political Ideologies: An Introduction* (2nd edn) (Hutchinson: London).

Eckersley, R. (1987) 'Green politics: a practice in search of a theory', paper delivered at the Ecopolitics II Conference, University of Tasmania, 22–25 May 1987.

——(1992) *Environmentalism and Political Theory: Toward an Ecocentric Approach* (London: UCL Press).

——(1996) 'Connecting ecology and democracy: the rights discourse revisited', in B. Doherty and M. de Geus (eds) *Democracy and Green Political Thought: Sustainability, Rights and Citizenship* (London: Routledge).

Ekins, P. (ed.) (1986) *The Living Economy* (London: Routledge & Kegan Paul).

Ekins, P. and Max-Neef, M. (1992) *Real-Life Economics: Understanding Wealth Creation* (London: Routledge).

Elkington, J. and Burke, T. (1987) *The Green Capitalists* (London: Victor Gollancz).

Elliot, R. and Gare, A. (eds) (1983) *Environmental Philosophy* (Milton Keynes: Open University Press).

Feinberg, J. (1981) 'The rights of animals and unborn generations', in E. Partridge (ed.) *Responsibilities to Future Generations* (New York: Prometheus Books).

Ferguson, M. (1981) *The Aquarian Conspiracy: Personal and Social Transformation in the 1980s* (London: Paladin).

Feuer, L. (1976) *Marx and Engels: Basic Writings on Politics and Philosophy* (Glasgow: Fontana).

Foley, M. (1994) *Ideas That Shape Politics* (Manchester: Manchester University Press).

Foreman, D. and Haywood, B. (eds) (1989) *Ecodefense: A Field Guide to Monkeywrenching* (2nd edn) (Tucson: Ned Ludd Books).

Foreman, M. (1991) 'Second thoughts of an eco-warrior', in M. Bookchin and D. Foreman, *Defending the Earth* (Montreal: Black Rose Books).

Foster, J. (ed.) 1997) *Valuing Nature? Economics, Ethics and Environment* (London: Routledge).

Fox, W. (1984) 'Deep ecology: a new philosophy of our time?', *The Ecologist*, 14 (5/6).

——(1986a) *Approaching Deep Ecology: A Response to Richard Sylvan's Critique of Deep Ecology* (Tasmania: University of Tasmania).

——(1986b) 'Ways of thinking environmentally', talk given to Fourth National Environmental Education Conference, Australia, September.

——(1990) *Towards a Transpersonal Ecology: Developing New Foundations for Environmentalism* (Boston: Shambhala Press).

Frankel, B. (1987) *The Post-Industrial Utopians* (Oxford: Polity Press).

Frankland, E.G. (1988) 'The role of the Greens in West German parliamentary politics, 1987', *Review of Politics*, Winter.

Freer, J. (1983) 'Gaia: the Earth as our spiritual heritage', in L. Caldecott and S. Leland (eds) *Reclaim the Earth* (London: The Women's Press).

Garner, R. (1996) *Environmental Politics* (Hemel Hempstead: Prentice Hall/Harvester Wheatsheaf).

German Green Party Manifesto (1983) (London: Heretic Books).

Goldsmith, E. (1972) *A Blueprint for Survival* (London: Tom Stacey).

——(1988) *The Great U-Turn: De-Industrializing Society* (Bideford: Green Books).

Goldsmith, E. and Hildyard, N. (1986) *Green Britain or Industrial Wasteland?* (Oxford: Polity Press).

Goodin, R. (1985) *Protecting the Vulnerable: A Reanalysis of Our Social Responsibilities* (Chicago: University of Chicago Press).

——(1992) *Green Political Theory* (Cambridge: Polity Press).

——(1996) 'Enfranchising the Earth, and its alternatives', *Political Studies*, 44 (5).

Goodwin, B. (1987) *Using Political Ideas* (Chichester: John Wiley).

Gorz, A. (1982) *Farewell to the Working-Class* (London: Pluto).

——(1985) *Paths to Paradise/On the Liberation from Work* (London: Pluto).

——(1994) *Capitalism, Socialism, Ecology* (London: Verso).

Gould, P. (1988) *Early Green Politics* (Brighton: Harvester Press).

Gray, J. (1993a) *Beyond the New Right: Markets, Government and the Common Environment* (London: Routledge).

——(1993b) 'An agenda for green conservatism', in J. Gray *Beyond the New Right: Markets, Government and the Common Environment* (London: Routledge).

Greco, T. (Jr) (1994) *New Money for Healthy Communities* (Tucson: Thomas H. Greco).

Green Party (England and Wales) Manifesto for a Sustainable Society(1999) (London: Green Party, http://www.greenparty.org.uk).

Grubb, M., Koch, M., Munson, A., Sullivan, E. and Thornson, K. (1993) *The Earth Summit Agreements: A Guide and Assessment* (London: Earthscan/RIIA).

Hamilton, M. (1987) 'The elements of the concept of ideology', *Political Studies*, 35 (1).

Hampson, N. (1979) *The Enlightenment* (Harmondsworth: Penguin).

Harper, P. (n.d.) 'Life at the Quarry' (unpublished).

Harvey, D. (1993) 'The nature of environment: the dialectics of social and environmental change', *The Socialist Register*.

Hay, T. (1988) 'Ecological values and Western political traditions: from anarchism to fascism', *Politics*, 8 (2).

Hayward, T. (1994) 'The meaning of political ecology', *Radical Philosophy*, 66 (Spring).

——(1995) *Ecological Thought: An Introduction* (Oxford: Polity Press).

——(1997) 'Anthropocentrism: a misunderstood problem', *Environmental Values*, 6 (1).

——(1998) *Political Theory and Ecological Values* (Cambridge: Polity Press).

Heilbroner, R. (1974) *An Inquiry into the Human Prospect* (New York: Harper & Row).

Henderson, H. (1983) 'The warp and the weft: the coming synthesis of ecophilosophy and ecofeminism', in L. Caldecott and S. Leland (eds) *Reclaim the Earth* (London: The Women's Press).

Heywood, A. (1992) *Political Ideologies: An Introduction* (London: Macmillan).

Hildebrand, P. (1992) 'The European Community's environmental policy, 1957 to "1992": from incidental measures to an international regime', *Environmental Politics*, 1 (4).

Hülsberg, W. (1988) *The German Greens* (London: Verso).

Inglehart, R. (1977) *The Silent Revolution: Changing Values and Political Style Among Western Publics* (Princeton: Princeton University Press).

Irvine, S. (1989) *Beyond Green Consumerism* (London: Friends of the Earth).

Irvine, S. and Ponton, A. (1988) *A Green Manifesto: Policies for a Green Future* (London: Macdonald Optima).

Jacobs, M. (1997) 'Environmental valuation, deliberative democracy and public decision-making institutions', in J. Foster (ed.) *Valuing Nature? Economics, Ethics and Environment* (London: Routledge).

——(1999) 'Sustainable development as a contested concept', in A. Dobson (ed.) *Fairness and Futurity: Essays on Environmental Sustainability and Dimensions of Social Justice* (Oxford: Oxford University Press).

Jahn, D. (1994) 'Unifying the Greens in a united Germany', *Environmental Politics*, 3 (2).

Johnson, L. (1991) *A Morally Deep World: An Essay on Moral Significance and Environmental Ethics* (Cambridge: Cambridge University Press).

Kenny, M. (1994) 'Ecologism', in R. Eccleshall, V. Geoghegan, R. Jay, M. Kenny, I. Mackenzie and R. Wilford *Political Ideologies: An Introduction* (2nd edn) (Hutchinson: London).

King, Y. (1983) 'The eco-feminist imperative', in L. Caldecott and S. Leland (eds) *Reclaim the Earth* (London: The Women's Press).

——(1989) 'The ecology of feminism and the feminism of ecology', in J. Plant (ed.) *Healing the Wounds: The Promise of Ecofeminism* (London: Green Press).

Kumar, K. (1987) *Utopia and Anti-Utopia in Modern Times* (Oxford: Basil Blackwell).

——(1991) *Utopianism* (Milton Keynes: Open University Press).

Kumar, S. (ed.) (1984) *The Schumacher Lectures: Volume II* (London: Blond & Briggs).

Lafferty, M. and Meadowcroft, J. (eds) (1996a) *Democracy and the Environment: Problems and Prospects* (Cheltenham: Edward Elgar).

——(1996b) 'Democracy and the environment: congruence and conflict – preliminary reflections', in M. Lafferty and J. Meadowcroft (eds) *Democracy and the Environment: Problems and Prospects* (Cheltenham: Edward Elgar).

Leach, R. (1991) *British Political Ideologies* (New York and London: Philip Allen).

Lee, K. (1989) *Social Philosophy and Ecological Scarcity* (London: Routledge).

Leland, S. (1983) 'Feminism and ecology: theoretical connections', in L. Caldecott and S. Leland (eds) *Reclaim the Earth* (London: The Women's Press).

Leopold, A. (1949) *A Sand County Almanac* (Oxford: Oxford University Press).

Lewis, M. (1992) *Green Delusions: An Environmentalist Critique of Radical Environmentalism* (Durham: Duke University Press).

Light, A. (ed.) (1998) *Social Ecology after Bookchin* (New York and London: Guilford Press).

Lovelock, J. (1979) *Gaia* (Oxford: Oxford University Press).

——(1986) 'Gaia: The World as Living Organism', *New Scientist*, 18 December.

Lutz, W. (ed.) (1994) *The Future Population of the World: What Can We Assume Today?* (London: Earthscan).

McLellan, D. (1986) *Ideology* (Milton Keynes: Open University Press).

Macridis, R. (1992) *Contemporary Political Ideologies: Movements and Regimes* (5th edn) (New York: HarperCollins).

Marien, M. (1977) 'The two visions of post-industrial society', *Futures*, October.

Martell, L. (1994) *Ecology and Society: An Introduction* (Cambridge: Polity Press).

Mathews, F. (1991) *The Ecological Self* (London: Routledge).

——(ed.) (1995) 'Ecology and democracy', *Environmental Politics*, (Special Issue) 4 (4).

Max-Neef, M. (1992) 'Development and human needs', in P. Ekins and M. Max-Neef *Real-Life Economics: Understanding Wealth Creation* (London: Routledge).

Meadows, D., Meadows, D., Randers, J. and Behrens III, W. (1974) *The Limits to Growth* (London: Pan).

Meadows, D., Meadows, D. and Randers, J. (1992) *Beyond The Limits: Global Collapse or a Sustainable Future* (London: Earthscan).

Mellor, M. (1992a) *Breaking the Boundaries: Towards a Feminist Green Socialism* (London: Virago).

——(1992b) 'Green politics: ecofeminist, ecofeminine or ecomasculine?', *Environmental Politics*, 1 (2).

——(1997) *Feminism and Ecology* (Cambridge: Polity Press).

Merchant, C. (1990) *The Death of Nature* (New York: Harper & Row).

Midgley, M. (1983a) *Animals and Why They Matter* (Harmondsworth: Penguin).

——(1983b) 'Duties concerning islands', in R. Elliot and A. Gare (eds) *Environmental Philosophy* (Milton Keynes: Open University Press).

Miliband, R. (1994) 'The plausibility of socialism', *New Left Review*, 206 (July/August).

Mill, J.S. (1859/1972) *Utilitarianism, On Liberty and Representative Government* (London: Dent and Dutton).

Miller, D. (1999) 'Social justice and environmental goods', in A. Dobson (ed.) *Fairness and Futurity: Essays on Environmental Sustainability and Social Justice* (Oxford: Oxford University Press).

Myers, N. (1985) *The Gaia Atlas of Planet Management* (London: Good Books).

Myers, N. and Simon, J. (1994) *Scarcity or Abundance? A Debate on the Environment* (London: Norton).

Naess, A. (1973) 'The shallow and the deep, long-range ecology movement. A summary', *Inquiry*, 16.

——(1984) 'Intuition, intrinsic value and deep ecology', *The Ecologist*, 14 (5/6).

——(1989) *Ecology, Community and Lifestyle* (Cambridge: Cambridge University Press).

North, P. (1998) ' "Save our Solsbury!": the anatomy of an anti-roads protest', *Environmental Politics*, 7 (3).

Norton, B. (1991) *Toward Unity Among Environmentalists* (New York and Oxford: Oxford University Press).

O'Connor, J. (1996) 'The second contradiction of capitalism', in T. Benton (ed.) *Natural Relations: Ecology, Animal Rights and Social Justice* (London: Verso).

Oelschlaeger, M. (1991) *The Idea of Wilderness* (New Haven: Yale University Press).

O'Neill, J. (1993) *Ecology, Policy and Politics: Human Well-Being and the Natural World* (London: Routledge).

Ophuls, W. (1977) 'The politics of a sustainable society', in D. Pirages (ed.) *The Sustainable Society* (New York: Praeger).

Ophuls, W. with Boyan (Jr), A. (1992) *Ecology and the Politics of Scarcity Revisited: The Unraveling of the American Dream* (New York: W.H. Freeman).

O'Riordan, T. (1981) *Environmentalism* (London: Pion).

O'Riordan, T. and Cameron, I. (1994) *Interpreting the Precautionary Principle* (London: Earthscan).

Owen, D. (1980) *What is Ecology?* (Oxford: Oxford University Press).

Paehlke, R. (1988) 'Democracy, bureaucracy and environmentalism', *Environmental Ethics*, 10.

Partridge, E. (ed.) (1981) *Responsibilities to Future Generations* (New York: Prometheus Books).

Pearce, D., Markandya, A. and Barbier, B. (1989) *Blueprint for a Green Economy* (London: Earthscan).

Pepper, D. (1984) *The Roots of Modern Environmentalism* (Beckenham: Croom Helm).

——(1991) *Communes and the Green Vision: Counterculture, Lifestyle and the New Age* (London: Green Print).

——(1993a) 'Anthropocentrism, humanism and eco-socialism: a blueprint for the survival of ecological politics', *Environmental Politics*, 2 (3).

——(1993b) *Eco-Socialism: From Deep Ecology to Social Justice* (London: Routledge).

Pirages, D. (ed.) (1977a) *The Sustainable Society* (New York: Praeger).

——(1977b) 'Introduction: a social design for sustainable growth', in D. Pirages (ed.) *The Sustainable Society* (New York: Praeger).

Plant, J. (n.d.) 'Women and nature', *Green Line*, offprint.

——(ed.) (1989) *Healing the Wounds: The Promise of Ecofeminism* (London: Green Press).

Plumwood, V. (1986) 'Ecofeminism: an overview and discussion of positions and arguments', in 'Women and Philosophy', supplement to *Australasian Journal of Philosophy*, 64 (June).

——(1988) 'Women, humanity and nature', *Radical Philosophy*, Spring.

——(1993) *Feminism and the Mastery of Nature* (London: Routledge).

——(1997) 'Androcentrism and anthropocentrism: parallels and politics', in K. Warren (ed.) *Ecofeminism: Women, Culture, Nature* (Bloomington: Indiana University Press).

Poguntke, T. (1993) 'Goodbye to movement politics', *Environmental Politics*, 2 (3).

Ponting, C. (1991) *A Green History of the World* (Harmondsworth: Penguin).

Porritt, J. (1984a) *Seeing Green* (Oxford: Blackwell).

——(1984b) Interview in *Marxism Today* (March).

Porritt, J. and Winner, D. (1988) *The Coming of the Greens* (London: Fontana).

Pulido, L. (1996) *Environmentalism and Economic Justice* (Tucson: University of Arizona Press).

Rawls, J. (1973) *A Theory of Justice* (Oxford: Oxford University Press).

Redclift, M. (1987) *Sustainable Development* (London: Methuen).

Reed, C. (1988) 'Wild men of the woods', *Guardian*, 13 July.

Regan, T. (1988) *The Case for Animal Rights* (London: Routledge).

Richards, F. (1989) 'Can capitalism go green?', *Living Marxism*, 4 (February).

Riechmann, J. (1997) 'Ecologismo y ambientalismo', *Revista de Libros*, 9 (September).

Roderick, R. (1986) *Habermas and the Foundations of Critical Theory* (London: Macmillan).

Rolston, H. (1983) 'Are values in nature subjective or objective?', in R. Elliot and A. Gare (eds) *Environmental Philosophy* (Milton Keynes: Open University Press).

Rousseau, J.-J. (1762/1968) *The Social Contract* (Harmondsworth: Penguin).

Ryle, M. (1988) *Ecology and Socialism* (London: Radius).

Sagoff, M. (1988) *The Economy of the Earth: Philosophy, Law and the Environment* (Cambridge: Cambridge University Press).

Sale, K. (1984) 'Mother of all: an introduction to bioregionalism', in S. Kumar (ed.) *The Schumacher Lectures: Volume II* (London: Blond & Briggs).

——(1985) *Dwellers in the Land: the Bioregional Vision* (San Francisco: Sierra Club).

Salleh, A. (1984) 'Deeper than deep ecology: the eco-feminist connection', *Environmental Ethics*, 6.

——(1997) *Ecofeminism as Politics: Nature, Marx and the Postmodern* (London: Zed Books).

Saward, M. (1993a) 'Green democracy?' in A. Dobson and P. Lucardie (eds) *The Politics of Nature: Explorations in Green Political Theory* (London: Routledge).

——(1993b) 'Green theory', *Environmental Politics*, 2 (3).

Schumacher, F. (1976) *Small is Beautiful* (London: Sphere).

Schwarz, W. and Schwarz, D. (1987) *Breaking Through* (Bideford: Green Books).

Seabrook, J. (1988) *The Race for Riches* (Basingstoke: Green Print).

Seel, B. (1997) 'Strategies of resistance at the Pollok Free State road protest camp', *Environmental Politics*, 6 (4).

——(1999) 'Strategic identities: strategy, culture and consciousness in the New Age and road protest movements', unpublished Ph.D. thesis, Keele University, UK.

Sessions, G. (ed.) (1994) *Deep Ecology for the 21st Century* (Boston and London: Shambhala Press).

Seymour, J. and Girardet, H. (1987) *Blueprint for a Green Planet* (London: Dorling Kindersley).

Shiva, V. (1988) *Staying Alive* (London: Zed Books).

Simon, J. and Kahn, H. (1984) *The Resourceful Earth: A Response to Global 2000* (Oxford: Blackwell).

Simonon, L. (1983) 'Personal, political and planetary play', in L. Caldecott and S. Leland (eds) *Reclaim the Earth* (London: The Women's Press).

Simons, M. (1988), article in *Green Line*, 64 (July–August).

Singer, P. (1975) *Animal Liberation* (New York: Review Books).

Smith, M. (1998) *Ecologism: Towards Ecological Citizenship* (Buckingham: Open University Press).

Spinoza, B. de (1677/1955) *On the Improvement of Understanding, The Ethics, Correspondence* (New York: Dover).

Spretnak, C. and Capra, F. (1985) *Green Politics* (London: Paladin).

Stoett, P. (1994) 'Cities: to love or to loathe?' *Environmental Politics*, 3 (2).

Strong, D. M. (1988) *Dreamers and Defenders: American Conservationists* (Lincoln: University of Nebraska Press).

Sylvan, R. (1984a) 'A critique of deep ecology' (part one), *Radical Philosophy*, 40.

——(1984b) 'A critique of deep ecology' (part two), *Radical Philosophy*, 41.

Szasz, A. (1994) *Ecopopulism: Toxic Waste and the Movement for Environmental Justice* (Minneapolis: Minnesota University Press).

Thomas, C. (1983) 'Alternative technology: a feminist technology?', in L. Caldecott and S. Leland (eds) *Reclaim the Earth* (London: The Women's Press).

Thompson, J. (1983) 'Preservation of wilderness and the Good Life', in R. Elliot and A. Gare (eds) *Environmental Philosophy* (Milton Keynes: Open University Press).

Tokar, B. (1988) 'Social ecology, deep ecology and the future of green thought', *The Ecologist*, 18 (4/5).

——(1994) *The Green Alternative* (2nd edn) (San Pedro: R. and E. Miles).

Tudge, C. (1996) *The Day Before Yesterday: Five Million Years of Human History* (London: Pimlico).

Vincent, A. (1992) *Modern Political Ideologies* (Oxford: Blackwell).

——(1993) 'The character of ecology', *Environmental Politics*, 2 (2).

Wall, D. (1999) *Earth First! and the Anti-Roads Movement* (London: Routledge).

Ward, B. and Dubos, R. (1972) *Only One Earth: The Care and Maintenance of a Small Planet* (London: André Deutsch).

Warren, K. J. (1987) 'Feminism and ecology: making connections', *Environmental Ethics*, 9.

——(ed.) (1997) *Ecofeminism: Women, Culture, Nature* (Bloomington: Indiana University Press).

Weale, A. (1992) *The New Politics of Pollution* (Manchester: Manchester University Press).

Wells, D. (1982) 'Resurrecting the dismal parson: Malthus, ecology, and political thought', *Political Studies*, 30 (1).

Weston, I. (ed.) (1986) *Red and Green* (London: Pluto).

Williams, R. (n.d.) *Socialism and Ecology* (London: SERA).

——(1986) *Towards 2000* (Harmondsworth: Pelican).

Wissenburg, M. (1998a) *Green Liberalism: The Free and the Green Society* (London: UCL Press).

——(1998b) 'The rapid reproducers paradox: population control and individual procreative rights', *Environmental Politics*, 7 (2).

Witherspoon, S. (1996) 'Democracy, the environment and public opinion in Western Europe', in W. Lafferty and J. Meadowcroft (eds) *Democracy and the Environment: Problems and Prospects* (Cheltenham: Edward Elgar).

World Resources Institute (1992) *World Resources 1992–93: A Guide to the Global Environment* (Oxford: Oxford University Press).

Young, S. (1992) 'The different dimensions of green politics', *Environmental Politics*, 1 (1).

Index

acid rain 180
Adjusted National Product (ANP) 76, 93
Aitken, R. 50
Allaby, M. 85, 101
anarchism 4, 6, 7, 71, 99, 104, 105,
   109, 188
Anderson, V. 76, 93
animal rights 41, 170
anthropocentrism 5, 26, 40, 45, 48,
   51–60, 175, 200, 202, 207–8
Aquinas, T. 92
Atkinson, A. 10
Attfield, R. 41, 43, 45–6
authoritarianism ix, 73, 74, 99, 114–24
'autopoiesis' 42

Bacon, F. 10, 38, 195, 214
Bahro, R. 60, 61, 84, 89, 91, 103, 104,
   108, 110, 129–30, 133, 133–5, 136,
   136, 137, 139, 146–7, 155–6, 157,
   159, 181, 185, 187
Ball, T. xi, 5, 6
Barry, B. 164, 166, 170
Barry, J. ix, 72, 114, 119, 202, 203,
   212–13
Basic Income Scheme 95
Bauman, Z. 149–50
Bell, D. 30
Bentham, J. 168, 169
Benton, T. 170, 179, 181
Bhagwan Shree Rajneesh 135
Biehl, J. 194, 195, 198, 199
biocentrism 28, 208

bioregionalism 72, 99–101, 102–3, 104,
   120
'biospherical egalitarianism' 43, 44, 53
Body Shop, the 131, 132
Bohr, N. 38
Bookchin, M. 24, 40, 52–4, 83, 153
Bottomore, T. 149
Bramwell, A. 23, 31–2, 54, 69, 114,
   127, 204–5
Brundtland, Gro Harlem 90
Bundestag, the 128, 129
Bunyard, P. 19, 25, 36, 45, 47, 68, 78,
   79, 81, 85, 88, 89, 101, 106, 110,
   124, 131
Burke, E. 67, 174, 176

Cameron, J. 67
capitalism 27, 29, 30, 73, 179–80, 181,
   182, 183
Capra, F. 18, 26, 38, 39, 55–6, 57, 127,
   128, 129, 153
Carson, R. 33
Centre for Alternative Technology
   136–7, 137–9, 148
citizenship ix
Club of Rome 63, 65, 67
Collard, A. 190
'communities' 136–42
conservatism ix, 1, 2, 5, 12, 28, 67,
   163, 164, 172–8, 200
consumption 16, 17, 77–89, 132, 154,
   160, 178
Contrucci, J. 190

Cook, R. 187–8

Dagger, R. xi, 5, 6
Daly, H 69, 77, 87, 98, 112
Darwin, C. 31, 173
Dauncey, G. 140
decentralization 23, 97, 103–111, 115, 120, 128, 140, 142, 143, 188
deforestation 76, 184
deep ecology 40–51, 59, 60, 61, 72, 135, 184, 199, 202, 203, 213
De Geus, M. 114, 120, 121, 177
democracy ix, 4, 22, 23–4, 73, 74, 103, 106, 107, 114–24, 128, 137, 165, 212
Descartes, R. 38, 214
Dickens, P. 179
direct action 142–5
diversity 22–3, 40, 102–3
Dobson, A. xi, 2, 13, 31, 37, 41, 62, 118, 120, 122, 123, 168, 183
Dodds, F. 205, 206, 214
Dodson Gray, E. 196
Doherty, B. 114, 120, 121, 145
Donald, J. 4, 7, 12
Dongas, the 143, 144, 145
Dowie, M. 183
Dryzek, J. ix, 118
Dubos, R. 70

Earth First! 51–2, 54, 81, 82, 83, 143–4, 204
Earth Summit, the 70, 182
Eatwell, R. 4, 5
Eccleshall, R. 5
Eckersley, R. 8, 26, 33, 42, 53–4, 72–3, 74, 108, 109, 118, 136, 164, 169, 212
ecocentrism 7, 8, 11, 29, 53, 71, 72, 133, 169, 184, 203
ecofeminism 160, 164, 189–200
ecological modernisation 207–11
ecologism ix, xi, 1–3, 6, 7–8, 13–35, 36, 37, 38, 40, 57, 61, 64, 71,73, 74, 77, 78, 98, 111, 112–13, 146, 147, 162, 163, 164, 165, 166, 167, 172,

173, 174, 175, 177, 178, 179, 185, 200, 201–14
ecology 39–40
Ecology Party (Britain) 13
Ecover 142
Ehrlich, P. 18
Ekins, P. 66, 69, 75, 79, 89–90, 91, 95
energy 87–9
Enlightenment, the 10, 11, 12, 29, 31, 34, 103, 108, 174, 195, 213
'Environmental fascism' 42
'environmental justice' 158, 183
environmental sustainability *see* sustainability
environmental taxation 96
environmentalism xi, 2, 3, 4, 6, 7–8, 13, 14, 17, 32, 33, 34, 40, 64, 162, 164, 165, 166, 167, 201, 202, 204, 206
Epicurus 41
equality 10, 22, 24–5, 27, 80, 103, 115, 168, 182
European Union 109

fascism 1, 6, 164
Feinberg, J. 170
feminism ix, 7, 22, 26, 54, 153, 164, 170, 174, 189–200
Ferguson, M. 133
Feuer, L. 60
Findhorn 133, 137, 148
Fischer, J. 128
Foreman, D. 52, 83, 143–4, 204
Fox, W. 42, 44, 46, 47–9, 50, 51, 58–9, 197
Frankel, B. 97, 103, 105, 106, 107, 108, 109, 110, 112, 153, 156, 157, 158, 159, 160, 179
Freer, J. 191
French Revolution 28, 33, 106
Friedman, M. 95
Friends of the Earth 113, 132, 184, 205
future generations 123, 170–1, 172, 176–7, 208

GM foods 132, 175

Gaia 43, 135
Galtung, J. 89, 90
Garner, R. 163
Girardet, H. 130–1
global warming 180
Godwin, W. 188
Goldsmith, E. 27, 71, 78, 81, 83, 84,
    85, 86, 101, 103–4, 105, 109, 113
Goodin, R. ix, 37, 84–5, 116–17, 122–3,
    128, 172
Goodwin, B. 9
Gould, P. 188
Gouldner, A. 150
Gorz, A. 84, 105, 155–60
Gray, J. 28–9, 174–8
Greco, T. 140–1
'green consumerism' 62, 78, 98, 131, 214
green movement 14, 29, 34, 125, 146,
    153, 154, 179
Green Party (Britain) 83, 125
Green Party, England and Wales 58,
    81, 110
Green Party, Germany 58, 60, 61, 126–7
Green Party, Sweden 4
Gross National Product (GNP) 75, 93
Grubb, M. 70
Grünen, die 26, 133

Habermas, J. 153
Haeckel, E. 32, 40
Hall, S. 4, 7, 12
Hamilton, M. 5–6
Hampson, N. 10
Hardin, G. 64, 71, 83
Harper, P. 137–8, 139
Harvey, D. 179, 185, 186
Hay, P. 163
Hayward, T. ix, 12, 51, 56–7, 164, 165,
    168, 169, 170, 172, 178, 202–3, 212,
    213
Haywood, B. 143–4, 204
Heilbroner, R. 71, 114, 115, 121
Heisenberg, W. 38, 39
Henderson, H. 190–1
Heywood, A. xi, 5, 31
Hildebrand, P. 209, 212

Hildyard, N. 27, 113
Himmler, H 32
Hitler, A. 32
Hoyle, F. 15
Hülsberg, W. 125–6, 127
'human chauvinism' 56–7

ideology 3–6, 12, 13, 22, 29, 30
'industrialism' 27, 29, 30, 34, 180, 181
Inglehart, R. 151
intrinsic value 18, 34, 42–3, 44, 45–6,
    49, 55, 60, 202
Irvine, S. 18, 64, 66, 67, 68, 74, 77, 78,
    79, 80, 81, 82, 85, 88–9, 94, 95–6,
    105, 110, 179

Jacobs, M. 37, 119
Johnson, L. 42, 44
justice, social ix

Kahn, H. 68, 207
Kelly, P. 127, 128
Kenny, M. xi
King, Y. 190, 191, 192, 194
Kropotkin, Prince P. 188
Kumar, K. 177–8

Lafferty, W. 114, 117, 121
Lambert, J. 125
land ethic 42
Leach, R. xi, 5
Lee, K. 188
Leland, S. 190, 191
Leopold, A. 42
LETS 140–2, 162
Lewis, M. 31, 202, 203–4, 211
liberalism ix, 1, 2, 4, 5, 6, 7, 9, 10, 12,
    23, 28, 29, 103, 105, 115, 118, 124,
    163, 164, 164–72, 173, 176, 200
liberty 10, 72, 103, 165, 166
lifestyle 130–5, 136
Light, A. 54
limits to growth 5, 15–16, 17, 20, 33,
    34, 36, 62–9, 74, 97, 113, 115, 147,
    154, 158, 169, 173, 177, 185–6, 200,
    201, 202

Locke, J. 168
Lucas, C. 125
Lutz, W. 81

McLellan, D. 12
Macridis, R. xi, 31
Malthus, T. 31, 34, 69, 82, 173
Manes, C. 52
Mao 107
Marien, M. 8–9, 10
Martell, L. 72, 73, 74, 106, 109, 110, 151, 152, 159, 163, 165, 174
Marx, K. 12, 60–1, 147–50, 155, 159, 170, 173, 180
'materialism' 154, 160–1, 197
Mathews, F. 44, 49, 114
Max-Neef, M. 80
Meadowcroft, J. 114, 117, 121
Meadows, D. 17, 20, 33, 63–7, 77, 113, 115, 147, 177
Mellor, M. 93, 190, 191, 193, 196–7, 199, 200
Merchant, C. 196
Midgley, M. 43
Miliband, R 181
Mill, J. S. 77, 120, 168, 169
Miller, A. 95
Miller, D. 164
Morgan-Grenville, F. 19, 25, 36, 45, 47, 68, 78, 79, 81, 88, 89, 106, 110, 124, 131
Morris, W. 188
Morrison, H. 188
Myers, N. 15–16, 68, 207

Naess, A. 40, 43, 44, 47, 82, 91, 103
nationalism 2, 164
'natural value' 37, 118–9
nature/natural 21–2, 25, 26, 56, 59, 72, 73, 84, 100, 104, 116, 161, 167, 168, 171, 173, 174, 175, 177, 183, 184, 186, 194, 198, 211
needs 17, 79–80, 89, 90
'new social movements' 153
Newton, I. 10, 38, 39, 214
'NIMBY' 142

North, P. 142, 144–5
Norton, B. 208, 211, 212, 213
Nozick, R. 97
nuclear energy 87–8

O'Connor, J. 179, 180
O'Neill, J. 45, 46
O'Riordan, T. 55, 67, 70–1, 99
Oelschlaeger, M. 31
Ophuls, W. 70, 77, 87, 91, 102, 114, 115, 121
organic food, 147
Ostwald, W. 69
Owen, D. 40
Owen, W. 188

Paine, T. 67
Paehlke, R. 115, 121
Pearce, D. 75
Pepper, D. 30, 137, 139, 145–6, 179, 180, 181, 182, 184, 186, 187, 188
Pirages, D. 24
Plant, J. 190, 194, 198
Plumwood, V. 57, 190, 191, 192–3, 195, 196, 198–9, 200
Poguntke, T. 128, 129
Pollok Free State 144
pollution 15, 64, 66, 77, 201, 207, 210
Ponting, C. 32
Ponton, A. 18, 64, 66, 67, 68, 74, 77, 78, 79, 80, 81, 82, 85, 88–9, 94, 95, 95–6, 105, 110, 179
population 15, 20, 70, 76, 80–3, 170, 173, 198
Porritt, J. 9, 13, 16, 17, 19, 21–2, 26–7, 30, 34, 38, 55, 57–8, 75, 76, 77, 79, 80, 81, 82, 83, 84, 86–7, 88, 90, 91, 92–3, 97, 98, 102, 113, 124, 126, 131, 132, 133, 139, 145, 150, 151, 152, 179, 180, 187, 188, 205, 206, 213–14
post-industrialism 8, 11, 12
postmodernism 149–50
precautionary principle 119, 175
proletariat 149, 157, 160
protectionism 90, 91
Pulido, L. 183

Rawls, J. 171
recycling 16–17, 85, 88, 201
Reed, C. 51, 52, 54
Regan, T. 41, 42
responsibilities 172
Reuther, R. 194
Richards, F. 187
Riechmann, J. 5
rights 169–72
Roderick, R. 153
Rodman, J. 164
Rolston, H. 45
Romanticism 11, 12, 28, 31, 175
Rousseau, J-J 111
Rubel, M. 149
Ryle, M. 71, 73, 74, 106–7, 108, 185,
    187, 189

Sagoff, M. 164, 166–7, 168
Sale, K. 99–101, 102, 108, 109
Salleh, A. 160–1, 196
Saward, M. 22, 114–15, 118, 119, 121–2,
    128
Schumacher, E.F. 106, 131
Schwarz W. and D. 112, 137
Seabrook, J. 157–8
Seel, B. 134, 137, 143
Seymour, J. 130–1
shallow ecology 40
Sierra Club 204
Simon, J. 68, 207
Simons, M. 18
Singer, P. 41
'social ecology' 52–4
social justice 72, 103
socialism ix, xii, 1, 2, 3, 4, 5, 6, 9, 10,
    12, 15, 28, 29–30, 80, 130, 163, 164,
    179–89, 200, 201
Solsbury Hill 145
Smith, M. ix
'speciesism' 56–7
Spinoza, B. 184
spirituality 17, 19
Spretnak, C. 26, 39, 55, 57, 127, 128,
    129
Stoett, P. 104

Stonehenge 135
sustainability 11, 18, 34, 37, 62, 66, 70,
    73, 75, 88, 99, 111, 119, 132, 170,
    171, 203, 212
sustainable society xii, 16–18, 23,
    62–111, 126, 130, 162, 201
Sylvan, R. 44, 48, 54–5
Szasz, A. 158

technology 15, 84–7
thermodynamics 69
Thomas, C. 194
Thompson, J. 50
Toffler, A. 84
Tokar, B. 26, 51, 81, 84, 85, 86, 99,
    101–2, 106
Toynbee, A. 145, 157
trade 89–91
travel 91
'transpersonal ecology' 48
Tudge, C. 117

unemployment 74, 75, 94, 95, 140–1,
    153, 154, 155–60
United Nations 109
utilitarianism 169

Vincent, A. xi, 14, 31–2

Wall, D. 143, 144
Wallace, A. 173
Ward, B. 70
Weale, A. 207–11
Wells, D. 173
Weston, J. 28, 29–30, 136, 156, 179,
    180, 181, 182, 183, 184, 185–6, 188
Williams, R. 130, 179, 185–7, 188
Winner, N. 9, 132, 133, 179, 180
Wissenburg, M. 164, 165, 166, 167–8,
    169, 170, 171
Witherspoon, S. 122
work 91–9
World Trade Organisation 90
Wright, T. 4, 5

Young, S. 14